THE COOK,
THE RAT
& THE HERETIC

living in the shadow of rennes-le-château

HUGO SOSKIN

THE COOK, THE RAT AND THE HERETIC

Copyright © Hugo Soskin, 2008

All rights reserved.

No part of this book may be reproduced by any means, nor transmitted, nor translated into a machine language, without the written permission of the publishers.

The right of Hugo Soskin to be identified as the author of this work has been asserted in accordance with sections 77 and 78 of the Copyright, Designs and Patents Act 1988.

Condition of Sale
This book is sold subject to the condition that it shall not, by way of trade or otherwise, be lent, re-sold, hired out or otherwise circulated in any form of binding or cover other than that in which it is published and without a similar condition including this condition being imposed on the subsequent publisher.

Summersdale Publishers Ltd
46 West Street
Chichester
West Sussex
PO19 1RP
UK

www.summersdale.com

Printed and bound in Great Britain

ISBN 13: 978-1-84024-658-2

For Trip

CONTENTS

Acknowledgements   7

If something looks too good to be true...   9

And so to France   14

A toe in the wine lake   25

Flics and fairies   42

Aliens only abduct Americans   54

Yew cannot leeve zat zere   67

Vous êtes nicked, son   86

Get out of ze buzz, you naughty monk   95

Winning friends and influencing people   112

Of Billy, Bart and bank managers too   118

The Gypo's revenge   135

Grails aren't us   152

Maybe grails are us, after all   172

Hihon hihon, you're jus' anuzzer breek een ze woll   191

Welcome to my nightmare   212

And so to Rennes   231

Poussin's hole   244

The wrath of Rennes   253

Meeting the mole and the master   269

The emperor's got no clothes   281

ACKNOWLEDGEMENTS

Jan Brown, Chris Colyer, Rat Scabies, Christopher Dawes a.k.a Push, John and Joy Millar, Kate, Kim and Gus Colyer, Stewart Ferris, Jan Ozimkowski, Sara Light, all the Rennies I have met over the years – bonkers or otherwise – and, last but not least, the Wrong Way Rounders for just being there.

IF SOMETHING LOOKS TOO GOOD TO BE TRUE...

It was whilst on a family holiday in France in 1969 that my father bought a copy of a cheap paperback by Gérard de Sède called *Le Trésor Maudit*.

Le Trésor Maudit ('the accursed treasure') tells the story of a priest named Berenger Saunière. In 1891 he supposedly discovered a couple of strange and exotic parchments whilst renovating his church in the tiny, time forgotten, mountain top village of Rennes-le-Château in the Languedoc. After a visit to Paris with the mysterious parchments, Saunière began spending money like a lottery winner on speed when previously he had made a church mouse seem positively Croesus-like. He paid for the three and a half kilometre track from Rennes to Couiza at the bottom of the mountain to be turned into a proper road. He built the Villa Bethania, a large and luxurious property compared to the others in the village, and used it as the centrepiece of a lavish social life. He had a water tower constructed so the villagers could have water piped into their homes. He had a dumpy, square, crenellated tower, the Tour Magdala, built supposedly to house his library. He paid for the church to be completely renovated and redecorated in the gaudiest of fashions. Just where had all of this money come from?

This was the not unreasonable question that was running through the Old Man's brain as he dozed under a tree on the farm where we were holidaying. *Le Trésor Maudit* had fallen open on his lap at the page illustrating one of the parchments Saunière had supposedly found. In the Old Man's semi-somnolent state, eyes not really focusing on anything, he spotted that some of the letters in the parchment's text seemed to be raised slightly higher than the majority. These letters, quite simply read in order, spelled out a message: *à Dagobert II roi et à Sion est ce trésor et il est là mort* (this treasure belongs to king Dagobert II and Sion and he is there dead). There had been no mention of hidden messages in the book. What had the Old Man stumbled onto?

Being a writer of television drama under the assumed name of Henry Lincoln, the Old Man could smell a good story when he saw one. He took the story outline to *Chronicle*, the BBC's historical and archaeological programme, which commissioned him to make a film about it.

He dutifully began his research for his first effort at writing non-fiction by toddling over to Paris to meet de Sède and to interview him. During their little chats de Sède gave the

Old Man more tantalising clues such as a photo of a roadside tomb that bore a striking resemblance to the one in Poussin's painting *Et in Arcadia Ego* on the back of which was the rubber stamp of the Priory of Sion. Who were the Priory of Sion when they were at home and what did they have to do with anything? When the Old Man finally asked de Sède why he hadn't published the parchment's hidden message he was told 'because we thought it might interest someone like you to find it'. Who the hell were 'we'? Were they the Priory of Sion? De Sède then gave the Old Man the decipherment of the coded message in the other parchment. This message was hidden behind the most ball-breakingly complex code but by using the correct key it was revealed as saying 'shepherdess no temptation that Poussin Teniers hold the key peace 681 by the cross and this sword of God I complete this daemon guardian at midday blue apples.' What on earth did that load of gibberish mean?

De Sède then introduced him to Pierre Plantard who claimed to be the current grand master of the Priory of Sion, an order that has supposedly been going for centuries and that founded the Knights Templar and, over the ages of its existence, claims such luminaries as Leonardo da Vinci, Isaac Newton, Victor Hugo and Jean Cocteau as previous grand masters.

Then, wonder of wonders, he found that five of the local mountain peaks formed an almost perfect pentagram and that the churches of the region seemed to be lying in straight lines and almost equidistantly sited from each other. That had to be worth investigating further.

From these and other questions came the Old Man's first *Chronicle* film which was transmitted in 1972. The public response was good enough that he started work on a second film. Then along came a third and then the book *The Holy Blood and the Holy Grail* which, with some clever marketing by the publishers, became a worldwide bestseller. The story had well and truly grabbed the public's imagination. The Old Man had spawned an entirely new industry.

Over the ensuing years loads of films and DVDs have been made and hundreds of books and articles have been written about the mystery of Rennes-le-Château, from small private press editions up to such mega-sellers as Dan Brown's *The Da Vinci Code*, all of the writers having first encountered the story through one of the Old Man's films or reading his book. Every writer has their own pet theory that they are sure is the correct answer to this historical whodunit. Many seem to agree that it is somehow involved with the Holy Grail, and with Jesus and Mary Magdalene having been married, and that not only did their family come to France but their descendants are still around today. Grooviest of all, however, is that these descendants are being protected by a secret society, the Priory of Sion.

I have never believed one word of this story. I had never bothered trying to work out why this was but deep down in my guts it all sounded just too damn good to be true. As far as I was concerned this just sounded like the synopsis of a pseudo-historical novel. People seem to expect me to have access to all of the Old Man's research and therefore to have wonderful insider knowledge, to know more than I let on. Why will nobody listen to me when I say I don't give a tinker's cuss about Saunière, Rennes and the Priory of Sion?

AND SO TO FRANCE

Jan was a smart, attractive woman in her early forties. Quite why she put up with and married me, a scruffy sod one year her junior, I could never fathom. When I was dressed in my normal uniform of jeans and T-shirt I looked a mess; when she wore the same clothing she managed to look immaculate. But one beautiful summer's evening, when we were sitting in the garden cuddling glasses of chilled rosé, there was something similar about us. She could see it in my eyes, and I could see it in hers. Jan's Cornish heritage had given her a fetching, fair complexion but today she was slightly off-colour. I was positively monochrome. Clearly we were not feeling overly at one with the world. There was a problem that ran all the way down to our feet.

They were itchy.

For as long as we'd known each other we'd had this vague, nebulous notion that being a pair of old hippies with a penchant for poultry, growing our own food and all things bucolic it might be nice to get on the road in search of a piece of land to buy where we could live as self-sufficiently as was possible. The idea started slowly, almost subliminally, to take shape. We spent more and more of our time talking about it. Before I met Jan I had spent several years living in southern Spain and had rather enjoyed the experience.

We decided that when our time finally came we would move to Spain.

The first positive step in that direction was the purchase of an old, left-hand drive VW campervan. It had originally been owned by the Dutch army but had since been lovingly converted into a home. The marine ply interior was spotless and the little sink and cooker seemed to be perfectly adequate for the jobs required of them. The bed – when it was created by pulling the bench seats flat – was as big as any regular double bed.

We now had a vehicle in which to chase our dream. But still, at this stage, it was little more than a dream. Our friends inevitably laughed and made unkind comments about mid-life crises while we ignored their insults and formulated a plan.

So far our plan was simple. We would potter down through France enjoying the countryside and the comestibles, taking as long as it took, eventually heading into Spain to buy our bit of land. No timetable, no pressures, no hassles: we were going to play it all by ear. *Que sera, sera* as they say.

Getting out of England, however, entailed hassles, pressures and a near-impossible timetable. We were running around like blue-arsed flies, stuffing my mother's attic with our furniture, bidding our farewells, digging up the garden, and having essential maintenance jobs done on the van – such as having a bookcase installed. Oh, and getting it serviced. We took the bus to a VW specialist in Farnborough, some 120 miles away. A long way to go, granted, but they were the nearest that we could find. The bus was pampered, exfoliated, manicured and massaged by the experts. It was returned to us purring, with a satisfied smile on its face. We now felt confident in its ability to deliver us to Spain without problems.

From a very tender age I realised that I was not like other folk. Pinocchio had Jiminy Cricket sitting up beside him, whispering helpful words of wisdom and advice into his ear; I had the Fuck-up Fairy. The FUF had taken a personal dislike to me and has been sitting on my shoulder ever since the day I was born. If ever there was a chance of a fuck-up happening then I was the man it would happen to. Whenever friends were feeling a bit glum they would think, 'Hey, let's phone Hugo, see what's happened to him now.' It never failed to make them feel better.

Halfway home, the bus started to judder and lose power. Then it stopped dead. Jan and I looked in horror at each other. If this was how reliable the campervan was immediately after a service and not far from home, what kind of horrors would the FUF let loose on us when we were deep into a foreign land? It turned out, according to the extremely helpful man who stopped and sorted us out, that the FUF had amusingly placed a kink in the fuel pipe.

Departure now required the loading into the van of our clothes, books, bedding, kitchen stuff, books, cassettes, more books, maps and a kilo of borax to help my arthritis (should be interesting trying to explain away that bag of white powder to an observant customs officer). We were also going to take our home-grown food. We had timed our departure to coincide with the optimum season for harvesting everything we could from the garden, to keep us supplied with basics whilst we were on the road. We had sacks of potatoes, onions and garlic. Why we were taking garlic to France is a mystery even greater than that of Rennes-le-Château. We also had beans, tomatoes and fruit in varying stages of ripeness. We were a bloody mobile greengrocer.

Crossing the Channel via Portsmouth, we started the long drive south. We had a merry time visiting the tourist attractions along the way that were still open this late in the season. There were mushroom museums and corset museums and cheese museums and shoe museums; there were museums for anything and everything. If there was a museum to visit we visited the bugger and bought the T-shirts to prove it. Unfortunately the Calvados museum was closed. That upset me quite a bit, but then I've learnt over the years how to cope with the little disappointments life keeps chucking my way.

A marvellous and un-thought of bonus of our autumnal departure, however, was that we were travelling through France at the height of the mushroom season. We were both becoming quite obsessive about our quest for fungi and for one in particular, Shaggy Parasol or as it's known over here, *la lepiote* – the finest-tasting mushroom I've yet eaten. Growing as many varieties of fungi as it does, France very sensibly decided that pharmacists have to study mycology as part of their degree. Gatherers of mushrooms can walk into their local chemist's shop and have their haul looked over and be told if it is safe to eat or not: extremely useful for would-be poisoners or novices like us.

On we journeyed, juddering to the occasional halt for food, loo, mushroom picking or museums. We crawled sedately in a southerly direction, reaching the heart of the Dordogne, where geese are stuffed and snails sucked, where socks sport Toulouse-Lautrec designs and spectacle frames are made of wood. A country that is closed on Mondays.

It was Jan's birthday so it seemed appropriate that we should go out for a meal to celebrate. We drove into Sarlat grinning in gustatory anticipation. We probably ought to have known better. Every bloody restaurant was closed. We stomped around the sparsely lit and silent town getting grumpier and grumpier. The tall grey buildings loomed over us as we made our way along the narrow streets. Medieval and atmospheric the town may well have been but it certainly didn't seem to be any epicure's idea of Mecca. Our stomachs protested vociferously at their emptiness.

'This is ridiculous,' Jan moaned. 'Let's go back to the bus and you can make me an omelette instead.'

'We'd better have your birthday scoff tomorrow,' I told her. 'At least some of the restaurants seem to bother opening for lunch.' Walking back towards the bus we passed a bar that appeared to be open. 'Fancy a quick noggin before we go back?' I asked her.

The bar was high-ceilinged, with dark brown wood and nicotine-stained paintwork. There were no other customers, but as we were already halfway through the door before we realised this we were rather caught. We couldn't just turn round and walk out again: that would have been too impolite for our English sensitivities.

I ordered us a beer each and we chatted to the young and impossibly healthy-looking (despite spending his life in a fog of Gitanes smoke) barman for a bit. I don't know why but strangers seemed to like discussing sport with me. Could they not tell that I detested sport in all its manifestations and that when I take over the world I shall have all sports (but especially bloody football) outlawed? I grinned politely at him wishing we could talk about some other topic. To interrupt him, I asked if he knew of a restaurant that was open. This was the only eating establishment in town that was still open, he told me. Jan and I looked at each other and shrugged.

An ancient, bearded crone appeared and guided us through to a barn with a few tables and chairs scattered around it. Her grubby black clothes swished through the air and brushed against the furniture as she walked, leaving dirt marks on all points of contact. Her ancient face looked like it was made of cracked and gnarled leather, the kind of face that instantly reminded you of nineteenth-century photographs of proud and noble Red Indians even though she certainly seemed neither particularly proud nor noble herself. Decades of disapproving expressions had seared deep crevices into her tarry skin and even her artificially black hair tumbling all around it did little to disguise the fact that she had in all probability been responsible for Custer's last food poisoning.

Ominously, there was only one other couple dining, and they looked up almost pleadingly at us. The crone placed us as far away from them as was possible. Jan and I looked at each other. It seemed as though the FUF was at it again. Fully expecting the worst we psyched ourselves up for the ordeal and settled back to wait for a menu. The crone brought us a basket of bread and a bottle of rough red wine which we hadn't ordered, then shuffled away again. We decided we might as well have a glass of the plonk whilst we were waiting for something to happen. It had a full and rich flavour, and I particularly enjoyed the feeling of the enamel of my teeth disintegrating as I sipped it.

The crone reappeared carrying two soup bowls, and banged them down in front of us. Jan and I stared at the offering. Why had she given us each a bowl of oily dishwater with a bit of old sponge floating in it? The centime dropped. This was the old 'menu of no choice whatsoever'. There's nothing like a bit of tension, wondering what you're going to be served next. It aids the digestion wonderfully.

The soup was vile but fortunately this was where the wine came into its own. The French like nothing better than saving the last spoonful or two of their soup then flinging a generous slug of plonk into their bowl, swirling it around to mix it all up then picking the bowl up and downing it in one. Fellow diners have given me some odd looks when I have tried this in restaurants in England, but on this occasion the soup became far less vile with the addition of the plonk. I wiped my mouth with the heavy linen napkin and smacked my lips, wondering what culinary curiosity would be coming next.

Back came the crone bearing a silver serving plate. On it were two pieces of skate wing, blackened butter dribbled over and around it, all set off by the chopped parsley sprinkled over the top. The fish slid obligingly onto my fork and slithered seductively down my throat. This was superb. She brought cauliflower, cooked to perfection, sprinkled with parsley, hard boiled egg and breadcrumbs. This was turning into a surprisingly passable meal. I toasted Jan and wished her happy birthday.

'I've had a thought,' she suddenly announced.

I glowered at her. I didn't trust her when she came up with mutterings like this.

'What?' I asked suspiciously.

'Why don't we go and visit Rennes-le-Château on our way through, since I've never been there?' She grinned at me.

'No bloody chance. It's a total dive,' I told her, hoping that would put an end to her bright idea before it got any further. She just raised her eyebrows but said nothing. The crone was at our side again; this time, unfortunately for Jan who is a vegetarian, it was the meat course. I rubbed my hands happily at the thought of getting a double portion while Jan sulked good humouredly. She had become used to the French attitude towards her culinary perversions.

It was pigeon. I'm very partial to pigeon, but why did the crone bring three halves of birds for two people? I couldn't be arsed to do the sums; I just ate the lot and was called a pig by my wife. Waiting until my mouth was full, Jan continued with her idea.

'I don't see why you're so against going there,' she said.

'Look, I went there years ago,' I told her, licking pigeon juices from my fingers, 'and apart from the views, which I grant you are magnificent, there's sod all there to warrant wasting any time visiting the place.'

She *looked* at me.

'Honestly,' I continued, 'it really is a seriously grotty little place.'

'Well I still want to see it and it is my birthday so you ought to be nice to me for a change.'

I was starting to get the feeling I might well lose this particular argument.

'Look love, you know how I feel about going to New Zealand. Well that's how I feel about Rennes. Just because I know it exists it doesn't mean I want to visit the damn place.'

She snorted derisorily at that excuse and continued with her argument as to why she wanted to see it. 'Well I've still never been there and I want to see how your father's supposed to have become so well known and how he's been earning his living for the last thirty years.'

I scowled at her.

Food came and was devoured; wine bottles came and were emptied. In the end I was beaten down. I knew I'd never get any peace until I agreed with her.

'I s'pose we might as well go and see where the makings of our inheritance is coming from,' I conceded. I could see there might be some vague sort of sense in paying it a fleeting visit on the way past. We wouldn't be staying long. It wasn't exactly out of our way and half an hour wandering round a manky little village was hardly going to mess up our schedules too much.

The crone reappeared, this time bearing a couple of strange-looking, pungent pustules on a plate that she seemed to expect us to eat. The urine-yellow abscesses oozed malevolently, like a miniature lava flow, across the plate towards us. Jan and I stared in horror. Was this some sort of omen? I gave one of the things a tentative poke with my knife. I don't know what I expected it to do in response to this affront to its dignity but all it did was just ooze out a little more of its rancid overflow.

Carefully, I separated a small piece of this goop from the main blob and brought it up towards my mouth. The stench was overpowering; there was no way I was eating these things. There was no alternative, we had to release them back into the wild. I prised them from their plate and wrapped them in a tatty paper hanky I had in my pocket, intending to dump them in a hedge on our way back to the van. I tucked the packet under my chair to be going on with but the obnoxious olfactory assault drifting up and around my body continued to beat the living daylights out of my sinuses. Scooping up the 'kerchief-swaddled *fromages* I passed them to Jan and told her to stash them in her handbag. She called me names as unsavoury as the aromas swirling around me, but hearing the approach of the old crone she quickly shut up and squeezed them in amongst her purse, the bus keys and papers, our passports and whatever other rubbish she kept in her bag. I hoped they didn't suppurate over everything.

When the crone saw that our cheese plate was empty she rearranged her face into something reminiscent of a smile. Some of the cracks were stretched, others compressed, as she grinned a dentally-challenged smile at me. I asked what the things we had just 'eaten' were called. *Crote du diable*, she explained. A kind of goat's cheese. Dropping the bill on our table she disappeared for a moment. On her return I held out a wad of notes, but she didn't appear interested in money. She was carrying another plate of *crote du diable*, and held it in front of us. This plate of *diable* was 'on the house', and refusing to eat it was simply not an option.

However much we cleaned our teeth we couldn't breathe on each other for days afterwards without being reminded of our brush with the Devil.

A TOE IN THE WINE LAKE

Having lost the Rennes argument, I was now driving there. I'd tried my hand at sulking but, as usual, that had gotten me nowhere.

The bus rumbled past Limoux, the closest proper town to Rennes. There were no signs to the village yet, but I knew it was only minutes away. Jan, just like everybody else, expected me to know the entire story of Rennes inside-out and was waiting for me to give her a running commentary on everything we passed. I managed to give her a thumbnail sketch of the Knights Templar, the order of knights founded in 1118, its original members supposedly going on to form a breakaway group called the Priory of Sion. I even managed a bit about the Cathars, the heretical sect that was so violently suppressed in the fourteenth century and who had made their home in this region and how they believed in a god of good who was boss of heaven and a god of evil who was boss of the earth but otherwise I just waffled vaguely. She seemed miffed that when she asked me a question I tried covering my ignorance by answering her with what I fondly imagined to be enigmatic looks and silence or withering, scornful looks and sneers to suggest that she really ought to know that particular answer herself. For reasons that I shall never fully understand my replies were treated with utter contempt, derision and not a little piss-taking.

'You're going to have to do a wee bit better than that, Hewgs,' she laughed at me.

We were on a mission, however, so the history lesson could wait for a bit. We badly needed a proper campsite so we could restore some semblance of decency and cleanliness to both ourselves and our wardrobes. Free camping is a wonderful thing, and you get to stay in some superb spots. Unfortunately, what you gain on the scenery you lose on the facilities, so tonight we were prepared to pay for the luxury of not sleeping in a sylvan grove.

As we drove deeper into the region it should have become pretty apparent to us that something quite major had recently happened here but, living in our camper van, we were totally oblivious to the things that were going on out there in the big wide world. The debris around us that hinted of a major calamity simply didn't register in our minds. Believe me, listening to The Rolling Stones, eating freshly caught mushrooms, drinking cheaply bought wine, smoking the odd exotic cheroot and playing Connect 4 tends to take one's mind off trivialities like natural disasters. Tiredness and unpleasant body odours had also stunted our otherwise normally fairly good powers of observation. Blissfully ignorant of the recent fate of the area we continued in our quest for a campsite.

October in France is not the greatest time of the year to try to find a campsite that is open: it's even more difficult than finding a restaurant that's open in the evenings. We had been searching for one since lunchtime and we were getting irritable. We were weary, hungry, smelly and had a real need to stop for the day. Suddenly, just round a bend, a badly-painted sign nailed onto a tree hove into view advertising *camping à la ferme*. It pointed us off towards a rather interesting-looking mountain road. I flung the van, as much as you can fling a combi, across the road in a manic left-hand turn and trundled onwards and upwards into the descending gloom of the evening.

'Fercryinowtloud!' Jan squawked.

'Had you been watching for the signs, omens and portents my dear, like what the co-pilot is supposed to do,' I sweetly replied, 'I wouldn't have had to take such drastic action.'

I pretended not to notice the *look* she gave me.

The road turned and twisted ever upwards. I could feel my biceps bulging from hauling the beast of a wagon round such tortuous roads. If we didn't find the bloody campsite soon I was in danger of ending up with arms larger than Charles Atlas'.

One thing I do like about driving up mountains is that there are almost never any alternative turnings to confuse me, therefore it is nigh on impossible, contrary to the usual Law of Sod, to get lost. After what seemed like hours and hours of uphill driving we finally came round the last bend and there, at the top of the rise, was the campsite nestling in the folds of the mountain, lying behind the most immaculate château that I had ever seen. Or it would have been had it been finished.

I slammed my foot on the brake and we ground to a dignified halt. This was it, we'd arrived. Being extremely hospitable people, the owners turned the water and electricity back on so we could avail ourselves of the wonderful shower block they had built slap bang in the middle of a very interesting-looking field.

The scenery around the greener parts of the region is quite alpine and the cows with bells around their necks clonging and donging away in the evening gloom helped to confirm the picture. Unfortunately there is one feature of an alpine landscape which doesn't suit campsites. If you have ever tried parking a campervan in a field that is almost vertical you'll appreciate the problem. Unless you have a large supply of tranquillisers, weed or booze to calm the nerves I would advise most strongly against it.

After several lifetimes, Jan decided the bus was level enough for us to cook and sleep, for one night.

'You can sort it out properly in the morning,' I was informed.

I know I didn't have a spirit level to hand but I don't think I did too bad a job. Jan managed to produce some perfectly acceptable scoff and there was no unnecessary physical contact with each other when we crawled into bed.

'Result,' I thought.

The following morning I was feeling pretty chuffed with this masterpiece of parking when it was pointed out to me that we needed to hit the town for supplies. Oh well, I could do with the parking practice.

Off we set, this time going down the other side of the mountain we had climbed so exhaustedly the previous evening. I discovered a new game. Just put the car into neutral and see how far it's possible to travel before you need to use the engine again. Great sport.

As Stirling Soskin was fully set to beat his own world record for downhill combi cruising he was a bit distracted when Jan started squeaking in that funny way she has when she's seen something that's excited her.

'Oooh, oooh look,' she squeaked, thumping my arm. 'Llamas.'

'I don't care if they're Whirling bloody Dervishes,' I growled at her, 'can't you see I'm in the lead? I can't waste my time admiring saffron-covered practitioners of the terpsichorean twirlings. The very safety of the universe depends on me winning this race.'

We hit the bottom of the mountain, bouncing over a narrow bridge, hurtling past a building that at that speed was nothing but a blur, the wind whistling around the bus in protest.

'Oh look, it's an auberge and the menu's got steak tartare on it,' Jan read. 'You like that.'

On we flew, and then bugger, bugger, damn and blast, we hit the bottom of the valley and the road started to climb again. So, popping the van back into gear we drove on. We passed through a minute hamlet which had its four streets all meeting at the narrowest of junctions and all slightly dog-legging onto each other. Just to make things more interesting, the way we wanted to go meant passing between two buildings which would have been fine on a donkey or with the odd ox. Even the much-loved *mobylette* could have phutted through a brace abreast. Not so a combi. I think we had just enough room to pass a single sheet of Izal between us and the walls.

The trauma of this hazard was almost immediately erased by the scenery that, on leaving the shelter of the village, hits you right between the eyes. A huge expanse of green opened in front of us, conifer-clad mountains as the backdrop, the flash of a solitary bee eater as it hurled itself from the telephone wire flying off in hot pursuit of its lunch. The trauma was fully erased when I spotted, much to my delight, some Transylvanian Naked Necks, as ludicrous looking a chicken as you'll ever see, scratting around in a garden looking as though they might have played the vultures in a scene from Disney's *Jungle Book*. How very at home they seemed.

We finally arrived at Quillan to find it was holding its market. Oh deep joy, we love markets. It's a shame that Britain doesn't really do the market thing properly. Maybe it's something to do with our climate or maybe it's just that nowadays we all rely on supermarkets far too much? We mooched along the wide main street packed full of stalls. We ambled round a small square off the far end of the market, stocking up on goodies as we went. Soon we were laden with tomatoes, olives, cheeses, salamis and still-warm bread. Memories from my childhood of silly television games played on *Crackerjack* with Peter Glaze and Leslie Crowther flitted through my mind. We munched and mooched. We were happy little bunnies. Much to my squeaking amusement I spotted a road sign.

'Ooh, ooh, look!' I squeaked excitedly, spraying baguette crumbs everywhere and prodding Jan in the ribs.

'Don't make that stupid noise. And stop poking me. What?'

'Look, that street,' I pointed at the sign, 'it's called Rue Barbe.'

'Pillock,' she lovingly riposted.

My humour having fallen on stony ground yet again, we made our way to a *café* where we sat ourselves at one of the tables on the street, ordered our coffees and Calvadosses then idled away an hour or so indulging in that wonderful pastime of drinking and people-watching.

Now we were scrubbed, pressed and recovered from the days on the road we were quite happy to play tourists for a bit. The precision parking was starting to become second nature. Our field had the most romantic of views all around it, looking as though Caspar David Friedrich in one of his lighter moods could have used them as the backdrop for one of his paintings, and our landlords were extremely hospitable. They were, quite rightly, very proud of their château, which they were building themselves. We were taken on a guided tour of their work in progress and were absolutely stunned at the incredible range of skills and the level of craftsmanship this family displayed. It was a masterpiece and I was extremely jealous.

It seemed odd to be driving up that road to Rennes-le-Château again after so many years. What was even odder was that although this was the end of October, there were other cars going up and down the mountain. This had certainly not been the case in 1975. Then it had been only me and my holiday companion on this road and that had been at the height of the tourist season, too. We climbed on, round and up. The road hadn't improved at all, as far as I recalled it. Then there, on rounding a bend, high above you that tantalising first glimpse of the village, then gone again, and on, round and up, the road still as vertiginous and serpentine as I had remembered it. Onwards, roundwards and upwards we trundled, then finally, at the entrance to the village there was the notice forbidding anybody to dig. The wording of the edict was the same, it still said *'fouilles interdit'* as it had on my first visit but it certainly seemed to have grown in size and presence since I had last seen it. As I nosed the combi along the narrow street I was struck by the enormous change to the place. There were people milling around everywhere, there was a gift shop, a bookshop, the car park was full of cars sporting their differing countries' registration plates, different languages and accents all around us.

I was staggered by it. Sure, the basic layout of the place and its totally decrepit and dilapidated condition looked unaltered but nothing else felt the same. This village was supposed to be deserted, forgotten by time, not crawling in masses of tourists. For crying out loud, there were even two bars here now. I tried explaining to Jan how things had been in 1975 but it's difficult to appreciate just how empty and bleak the place had been before, when now all around was hustle and bustle.

OK, so it was something like twenty-five years since I had last visited the region but it really hadn't entered my mind that the place could have changed quite so dramatically. The increasing fame of the village meant that tourism was now the only reason for Rennes-le-Château's existence.

Had I realised that I would be entering 'Rennie World' and all that meant I would have run, screaming, for the not-so-distant hills. But I didn't, so I didn't.

We joined the throng making its way towards the church. Tucked at the end of a narrow path was this small, scruffy-looking building. Dull ochre walls, a weather-beaten arch surrounding the heavy wooden doors. It didn't have the air of a place that was used to seeing a regular worshipping congregation of any size. It looked drab, forlorn and neglected. *'Terribilis est locus iste'* engraved above the doors didn't come anywhere near it. *'Tattyus est locus iste'* was far closer to an accurate description of this supposedly significant and historical edifice, the place that holds the key to unlocking the mystery of Rennes-le-Château. This was where I made another nasty discovery: tucked out of sight, standing just behind the door was a woman clutching a book of tickets. You now had to pay an entrance fee to get into the church, surely something God would object to if he did exist. Either way, I objected, there was no way I was paying. I'm more than happy to put a donation in a church's collection box, something we do as a matter of course when we visit such places, but to be forced to pay to go into what is after all supposed to be a place of worship was, I thought, not on. We peered through the door into the gloom of the church's interior, the tourists who were prepared to pay their entrance fee pushing irritatedly past us. I pointed out the little red devil standing just inside the door supporting the holy water stoup. As I told Jan, it was thought by some to represent Asmodeus, the guardian of King Solomon's treasure, and by many that the contortions of his body contain clues as to the whereabouts of Sauniere's missing treasure. As far as I was concerned it just looked as though he was making a rude gesture at people as they walked into the place.

Jan, fortunately in total agreement with my sentiments about the forced payment, turned and strolled back up the lane with me following a couple of paces behind muttering about usury, money lenders and temples of thieves. Then I spotted the entrance to what looked like a secret garden. Ivy was growing untidily across the gateway, and the garden was overgrown and neglected. I called Jan back and, wondering what I would find, walked through the gate. I was instantly pounced upon by yet another seller of tickets and had my wallet lightened of quite a lot of euros and was ushered towards an open door. This place, it turned out, was a museum of sorts. There didn't seem to be anything of any great interest on display so we were making our way pretty rapidly through the few rooms. Jan suddenly burst out laughing and called me over to the display case she was peering into.

'It says here,' she howled, 'your father has become a monument for having given the world this story.'

'Yeah,' I sighed, 'and you know what dogs do to monuments.' There was something really quite depressing about this place.

We finished our tour, agreeing that Rennes seemed to be nothing more than a rather amateurish attempt to make money from visitors at every conceivable opportunity and to give as little back as possible, then made our way back to our bus and down the mountain to return to normality. I doubted I'd ever go up that road again. Rennes-le-Château? I'd been apathetic enough about it before but now we'd been there and seen what it had become, we weren't impressed in the slightest. It was firmly crossed off our list of places to ever bother revisiting.

We decided that seeing as we were here now we might as well have a look around the area a bit. We did the churches, the castles and the hermitages. We gorged ourselves on gorges, grottoes and local gastronomy. We admired multicoloured lizards sprinting over rocks and tiptoed carefully around slumbering serpents soaking up the sun. As for the autumnal colours, mists and storms – well, they just took your breath away. We frolicked and played and generally decided that this was one mighty fine region in which to be wasting some time.

We were beginning to notice some of the rather unusual sights as we drove around the countryside, however. To say that it looked as though something cataclysmic had occurred would have been an understatement. Little clues started to hit home, clues that we should have picked up on when we'd first arrived had tiredness allowed our minds to register them. We really should have wondered how a car had got itself onto that side of the river where there was no road, just sheer, forested mountainside above it. How had that articulated lorry ended up lying on its side, diagonally across the warehouse? How the hell had that huge hole in the road got there? The magnificent thermal hotel of Rennes les Bains, a little town stuffed full of history, now stood with its side ripped out and the town's bridges that had stood since Roman times, no longer there.

We found out that a flash flood had hit the area just a couple of days before we turned up. The river rose and fell over thirty feet in less than half an hour. The devastation was incredible, though, miraculously, only one person had died. This was a wasteland. We reeled around the little town in shock. How would they ever be able to rebuild the place? It felt rather ghoulish walking round, looking at the remains of this town. The next ten days saw us pottering around the area doing our utmost to avoid any of the sites too closely associated with the Rennes story. We did visit the ruined remains of several Templar and Cathar castles perched high on top of incredibly steep and difficult to climb mountains, though this was more for the fantastic views than for any other reason. Finally, we agreed, it was time to move on.

As a last night treat we decided to walk down the mountain to have a meal at the auberge with the llamas. Jan is a spinner and was rather hoping that whoever owned the llamas was keeping them for their fibre so they could have a chat about wheels and wool and whatnots. As we walked into the restaurant, keeping our fingers crossed that it was open for business, we were greeted by the sight of open books spread over every available inch of space. Before we had a chance to squeak excitedly and start ferreting through them the startled face of an early middle-aged man poked round the kitchen door and instantly retreated. Jan and I shrugged at each other and hit the books. With horror we were picking up books that were soaking wet when the startled man poked his head around the door once more, perhaps hoping we had gone away. On hearing us chatting he suddenly perked up.

'You're English,' he told us in a mildly accusatory tone, which I thought somewhat hypocritical given that he clearly was also.

Jan and I looked at each other, agreed we couldn't tell a lie and admitted we were indeed of that persuasion and if it wasn't too much trouble, was there any chance of anything to eat? He beat a second hasty retreat. Eyebrows raised, we grinned at each other but the startled man returned bearing menus, a bottle of wine and three glasses. He filled the glasses, handed us one each, drank a healthy mouthful from his, topped it up again and started to move books carefully from one table to another to make space for us to dine. As he was doing this he explained that the moist literature was the result of the recent flood which had caused total chaos in his newly-acquired auberge and campsite.

We ate, we talked and we drank. We talked of books and Rennes and my apathy towards Rennes and we drank. We talked of llamas and Rennes and I repeated how I felt about Rennes and we drank. We talked of our adventures and Rennes and yet again I repeated my feelings towards Rennes and we drank. We talked of his adventures and Rennes and I was starting to get a bit cheesed off with Jan and him hammering on about the bloody place so much and we drank. By the end of the evening he couldn't be bothered to work out the bill and we were in no state to pay it so, promising to return to pay him in the morning, we waved goodnight to our new best friend and rolled our way, arm in arm, back up the mountain to the bus and drunken oblivion. I have vague recollections of Jan and I having a farting competition as we made our way uphill though I'm sure she will quickly deny that it ever happened.

The following morning the sun rose bright and full of hope for the new day. We rose full of pain and hope of an imminent death.

It had been our intention to head over the border to Spain that day but there was no way that was going to be achieved. The way we felt just then, driving was completely out of the question; far too complicated, dangerous and painful. We pathetically supported each other as we stumbled back down the mountain to settle our previous night's account.

'Can you remember his name?' I groaned.

'I can't even remember my own,' Jan whimpered helpfully.

We crossed the narrow bridge over which I had so bravely raced a lifetime before and hobbled round the bend in the road.

'Ah look,' I pointed feebly to a wooden sign in need of repainting. 'At least we know what the place is called now.'

'So, that doesn't help, does it?' she groaned. 'The place is called Moulin du Roc. He's hardly going to be called Mr Roc, is he?'

Jan always was good at picking up on those things that I had so stupidly not thought of for myself.

'Oh my God, look at the state of you two.' We were greeted by the raucous laughter of our host, seemingly none the worse for the previous night's excesses. 'You'd better come and have a medicinal hair of the proverbial *chien*.'

'You are joking, aren't you?' Jan pleaded. 'We drank the entire EU wine lake last night.'

'Not quite, I've still got a few puddles left,' he reassured us. 'Look,' our host continued, 'I don't want to seem rude but,' he broke off, scratching his pate embarrassedly, 'well, we were all a bit pissed last night.'

'I know. That's why we feel so bloody awful this morning.' I moaned self-pityingly.

'Do you?' he asked, looking surprised. 'Oh well.' He shook his head in amazement. 'Anyway, I'm Chris. Chris Colyer. I'm sorry, I really can't remember your names.'

Chris was almost as bald as me, though I guess being about eight or nine years my senior he did at least have a better excuse for his tonsorial shortcoming. He was a stocky man of about five feet nine inches, who, were it not for the permanent smile on his face, could probably manage to look quite menacing in a Bob Hoskins-y sort of way if he put his mind to it. With a dress sense, or lack thereof, identical to my own, I quickly sensed that this congenial chap was going to be on my wavelength. Introductions having been made, or re-made, we returned to the restaurant where we did our level best to finish the rest of the European wine lake.

Chris proved to be a very entertaining and generous host. Our glasses were kept full and our hangovers finally started to recede. As the wine flowed so did the conversation and we began to hear the story of the 'Moolong' as Chris so quaintly pronounced the name of his home, his own little midlife crisis. He had only recently bought Moulin du Roc and the llamas, almost on a whim, when he decided that running something like this might be rather fun, and was still finding his feet when the flood struck. The campsite had been transformed into a jumble of boulders, up-rooted trees and rubbish strewn everywhere. It could have been a World War One battlefield. The swimming pool was now filled with a muddy brown soup and the main house was a sopping wet shambles. There was a terrifying amount of work to be done before he could think of opening the following season and so much of the work could not be started until insurance companies had visited to inspect the damage and given the go ahead for repair work to begin.

Chris started to take us on a tour of the estate, and we got as far as being introduced to the four llamas: Victoria, the highly imperious matriarch of the pod; Freckles, who looked permanently bemused by life; Charlie who, with a soppy grin on his face, looked the joker of the bunch, the single brown beastie in an otherwise white herd; and little Alfie, the dressage llama. I'd never been up close and personal to a llama before. They are beautiful beasties. We left the llamas' field and returned to the auberge, Chris telling us of his plans for the place. Picking up yet another couple of bottles of wine, he led us to a picnic table under the shade of a giant walnut tree. As we sat there opposite the llamas, watching them enjoy the autumnal sunshine and drinking yet more of the European wine lake I suddenly heard myself say: 'We're not in any great hurry to go anywhere. If you need a hand, we can always hang around and help you out for a bit.'

And thus it was that we found ourselves living within a spit's throw of the dreaded Rennes-le-Château. As simple and as drunken as that. Well, it seemed like a good idea at the time.

FLIGS AND FAIRIES

Over the following winter months our friendship with Chris grew. We developed muscles where we didn't think it possible as we struggled to clear the campsite of its flood-donated detritus and return it to something resembling its *raison d'être*. We spent our time off walking, exploring the countryside around us, becoming a regular sight around the nearby hamlets and farms as, with llamas on leads, we wandered off to see what birds, flowers and fossils we could find. We were happy spending the evenings drinking and chilling with Chris.

The swimming pool was emptied of its mulligatawny, a day of much childish behaviour and merriment. We found buried in the silt and mud at the bottom of the pool what seemed to be the entire French newt population. We were standing, scratching our heads over the poser of how to return them safely to the wild, almost at the point of going for viticultural resuscitation and aid when Chris suddenly dashed off. This was not unusual behaviour for our new friend, so we sat back to see what would happen.

After about fifteen minutes he reappeared, proudly carrying the plastic buckets he and his siblings had taken to the beach when they were kids, which inexplicably he had just discovered at the bottom of a tea chest. He also held what looked suspiciously like a plastic Holy Grail which he explained had come with a King Arthur outfit that Father Christmas had given him one year. After dismissing the goblet as being far too small to be of any use, and then some minor scuffles over who was to have which colour of bucket, the intrepid hunters set off in search of their prey. To be able to play in mud and catch small, squishy animals and not get told off was bliss. We scampered about giggling, collecting bucketful after bucketful of newts which we then poured back to safety. One particularly fine specimen I proudly took to show Jan.

'Look,' I told her, 'it's just like the pet one I had when I was a kid.' She gave me a pretend one of those *looks*. 'Yeah,' I continued, grinning inanely, 'I called him Tiny.'

'Go on,' she said with a sigh, her shoulders drooping in mock-defeat. She knew when she was beaten, 'why did you call him Tiny?'

'Because he was minute,' I announced gleefully. I didn't think it was so bad a joke that it deserved a bucketful of muddy water over the bonce.

My technical French came on in leaps and bounds as I went off in search of new parts for the pool. I learnt that engines are measured by their *chevaux* and that the area around the pool is known as *la plage*, but what I liked best was that any mechanical type-thing for the pool, if I put *le* or *la* in front of the English word and used the appropriate accent I usually came away with something bizarre-looking and expensive which seemed to do the trick.

Sometimes I mixed cement and threw it liberally around as though I knew what I was doing. Chris spent days doing his impersonation of *un gnome de jardin* as he struggled under what looked like concrete mushrooms, to repair the electricity points in the campsite that the caravans and campervans would plug themselves into to power their fridges, microwaves and televisions. Jan scrubbed and cleaned. It was all coming together.

Spring neared and so some semblance of normality was returned to Moolong.

One evening, a couple of weeks before Easter, the three of us were sitting under the walnut tree, enjoying the evening sun and, needless to say, imbibing. As the sun set and the wine took hold of common sense we started to talk of jobs we'd had when we were still resident in the real world. Without thinking of the possible consequences, I let slip that I had trained as a chef.

'You kept that bloody quiet,' Chris slurred slightly. I shrugged offhandedly.

'Not done it for years,' I hiccuped. 'Don't think about it any more.'

Chris refilled my glass. I took an appreciative mouthful and stretched contentedly.

'How d'you fancy doing the kitchen over the Easter break?' Chris asked. 'I'd really appreciate it. There's still so much building work to do, I can press on with that if I don't have to worry 'bout doing the food too.' He paused and took a sip of his wine.

'Yeah, go on.' Jan grinned. 'Why not? We're not in any great hurry to go anywhere.'

And thus it was that we found ourselves *continuing* to live within a spit's throw of that dreadful village.

Up until that point, other than hangovers, our stay in the area had been relatively painless, but now we were going to meet the 'Rennies', that strange and disparate group of people who follow and believe in the fantasy of Rennes-le-Château in all its various shapes, guises and forms. These people that I had so assiduously and thus far successfully managed to avoid. Things were going to change.

The first indicator of this change happened only a couple of mornings later. I am not at my brightest nor particularly communicative and congenial at that time of the day until several gallons of black coffee have been poured down my throat and I've coughed my way through a packet of fags or two.

I was leaning against the restaurant door admiring the short-toed treecreeper going about its business, creeping quietly up the walnut tree, gathering its breakfast, when I was interrupted from my ornithological contemplations by a large and lively lady wearing the most inappropriate clothing. I suspect the reason for her liveliness was learning, at a very early age, that if she stood still for more than thirty seconds, town planners would start giving her the eye. She created a picture that will stay in my nightmares until my dying day and I am not generally considered to be the most sensitive of souls.

She was wearing a gossamer thin, one piece, Indian cotton creation of gentlest fluorescent pea-green that was, by the extra strain caused to it, probably revealing rather more than its designer had envisaged. The silver thread and sequinned stars of various sizes that adorned this creation made her look like a small galaxy that had somehow come adrift in space. The matching headscarf and stiletto sandals in electric cerise so perfectly complemented and completed this ensemble. The absolute crowning glory, though, was her dyed hair. This was not a gentle, pleasing colour such as the red of Jan's henna-dyed hair; this was RED. There is no colour in nature that could possibly match that hue. Whilst I was still reeling from this sensory assault and wondering if maybe I had smoked a few too many spliffs the previous evening, I realised, with alarm, that she was smiling a most predatory and cannibalistic smile and was heading straight towards me.

''Scuse me!' she brayed in a voice as large as her physique. 'Your wife said I should ask you.' I raised my eyes to the treecreeper, searching for rescue. He'd seen what was coming; he'd had the good sense to sling his hook.

'What?' I growled. I just knew Jan was lurking somewhere, watching this, wetting her knickers with laughter.

'You know books, don't you?' She smiled disconcertingly at me.

'What? What do you mean I know books?' Incredibly she didn't notice the tone of my voice.

'You read books,' she explained.

'What?' My voice rose in exasperation. 'Of course I read bloody books.'

'Good. Do you know "The Rime of the Ancient Mariner"?'

'Of course I do,' I snapped. '"The ice was here,"' I quoted, '"the ice was there, the ice was all around." Unfortunately I didn't put enough of it in my glass to dilute my drinks last night. Now what do you want?' It went straight over her head.

'Well can you tell me the next line to this quotation?'

'Go on then.' I knew that this was going to be my only road to freedom. She wrinkled her brow as she struggled to remember the beginning of her quote. Raising a finger to her lips, she started to recite.

'"You are old, Father William, the young man said."' It was then I spotted Jan, hiding by the dustbins, shaking with uncontrollable mirth. How I didn't throttle my dear spouse on the spot is quite beyond me. And to think, she has the cheek to question my sense of humour.

Later that morning I was beavering away in the kitchen when I heard a man's voice calling from the reception area. I ignored him; I was working. Where was Chris or Jan? I spotted Jan through the kitchen window. She was in the field opposite, doing something with the llamas. She'd hardly be likely to hear his calling over there and Chris, I remembered, had gone to town to pick up some building supplies. I had drawn the short straw. I gently put my knife down on the block, took a deep breath and walked out to see what he wanted. Now I knew that my brain had been irreparably damaged the previous night: I was looking at Mr Magoo.

'About time, too –' His voice trailed off as he looked at me. I have always been quite fastidious about my professional appearance and have a clean jacket and apron hanging on the back of the kitchen door if needed, so I can change into them when I go out of the kitchen. Unfortunately, as I didn't think I would find myself standing in a kitchen I didn't have the necessary uniform packed so was wearing a rather tatty pair of shorts and a T-shirt instead. This particular morning I had been doing some butchery in preparation for a binge we had coming up so I guess my appearance, covered with blood, may have looked just a tad disconcerting, especially if you had been expecting to be greeted by a clean, smartly dressed receptionist. He blinked, swallowed, coughed to clear his throat and blinked again. It really was Mr Magoo.

'My bill, please. I wish to settle my account with you.' He pompously demanded of me, his adenoidal voice as bizarre as his appearance. 'If it's not too much bother,' he added rather snidely. Oh I just love punters with attitude.

'Certainly, sir,' I replied, putting just enough stress on the 'sir' to show I really did give a damn. 'Your name?' I asked, reaching for the diary so I could work out what he owed.

'And I shall expect a discount as neither my wife nor I have been able to use your swimming pool,' he told me. 'I think you will find that it is considered standard practice within the hotel and catering industry to do your maintenance work outside the tourist season and not when you expect to have guests staying.'

'We don't charge our guests for that privilege,' I told him coldly. There didn't seem much point explaining about the flood. He was obviously the sort of punter that would hold us personally responsible for it, deciding we had caused it purely to inconvenience him.

'Don't be stupid,' he snapped at me. 'Of course you do.'

'I beg your pardon?' A warning tone entered my voice.

'Of course the privilege, as you so choose to describe it, is charged for. The cost of its running,' he explained to me as though I was a complete simpleton, 'has to be incorporated into the costs of the running of this establishment. All such costs are borne by the customer, therefore, you have charged me for the use of the pool and I do not wish to pay for something that I have been unable to use due to the obvious incompetence of the management.'

'Sir,' I stressed the word heavily and sarcastically, 'you have not been charged for the use of the pool.' I scribbled out his bill. 'This is what you owe,' I told him, placing it on the counter between us.

'Now just you listen here, young man.' If there's one thing guaranteed to get my goat it's being called 'young man', especially when the person doing the calling doesn't even appear to be ten years older than me.

'And it's non-negotiable, I'm afraid,' I told him, wondering what the chances were of my getting away with justifiable homicide.

'Do you always treat your guests like this?'

'Not at all, sir. Sometimes we can have quite awkward and unpleasant guests to contend with.' I pushed his bill further toward him. As he drew himself up to his full impressively diminutive height and opened his mouth to speak, a uniformed gendarme walked into reception, nodded politely at me and stood quietly to one side waiting for us to finish our business.

'My wife and I are serious historical researchers,' Mr Magoo informed me. 'I have never been as disgusted as I am by the service here. I demand to see the proprietor.'

'I am the proprietor,' I lied and looked across to the *flic*. *'Monsieur, un moment, seulement.'* Mr Magoo disgustedly pulled his money clip and purse from his plastic bum-bag and, having counted out the exact amount, slammed it down on the counter and stamped out announcing that he would never visit us again and would be telling everybody he knew how atrocious the place was. I was tempted to thank him for offering to do us such a service as it would mean I wouldn't have to suffer any more lunatics like him but, for once, common sense prevailed and I kept my mouth shut. I sighed wearily and turned to the gendarme who was laughing hysterically.

'Dear God Hewgs,' he said in faultless English, 'you don't 'arf get 'em here, don't you?'

It was my old chum from way back, Charlie the antique dealer. He made regular trips to France to buy stock which his wife then sold at grossly inflated prices back at their shop in Kensington. As soon as he heard that we had a permanent base in France he began using us as a place to flop whenever he was in the area, which was turning out to be rather more often than we'd bargained for. On this trip he had, for reasons that eluded him, bought a couple of hundred very old and long redundant police uniforms. He had come into Moolong in fancy dress to amuse me and had been quite happy to stand and watch Mr Magoo and me fighting.

Charlie and I had known each other since we were in primary school. We probably looked pretty odd standing next to each other as he stood a couple of inches over six feet, was always neatly dressed and carried himself with the deportment of a cavalry officer whilst I, at all of five-foot-six, slouched along with stooped shoulders looking a scruff. He was a born wheeler-dealer, always on the lookout for a chance to make another bob or two. His greatest fault, however, was his belief that he was God's gift to women, something his longsuffering wife was at pains to tell him was absolute rubbish (and if anybody ought to know it should be her).

'I tell you mate,' I said, leaning my elbows on the counter and rubbing my face into my hands, 'I swear, I was gonna deck the little bastard. Bloody historical researcher.' I almost wept at the lunacy of it. 'What did he have, *The boy's own book of Rennes-le-Château*? This is all my father's fault.'

'He's gone. Chill,' Charlie soothed me. 'Relax. Come on, let's have a drink. That'll calm you down.'

'For once, my old mate,' I agreed, 'you're talking sense.' I pushed myself back from the counter about to lead the way to the bar when Jan reeled in, a look of stunned amazement on her face.

'You are not going to believe what I've just heard.' From her expression we knew that this was going to be a goody. 'That large woman you were talking to this morning...'

'Yes, I want to talk to you about that, you swine,' I laughed, interrupting her.

'She's barking mad,' Jan informed me, as though I couldn't possibly have noticed that for myself. It was obvious she had received her comeuppance for the jolly jape she had played on me earlier.

'Jan, my love, you hadn't worked that out before you sent her to bother me?' I asked with just the right amount of sincerity. 'What was it in particular that gave you a hint she may be slightly unbalanced, apart from her dress sense?'

'I thought you'd appreciate that.' She laughed. It's at times like this that I can quite happily let my general misanthropy become more specific and turn it into a very deliberately aimed piece of misogyny.

'For crying out loud, are you two going to stand there bickering all day?' my fake policeman chum asked. 'Or are you going to tell us what she did?'

'You really aren't going to believe this one.' Jan told us.

'Go on,' Charlie and I impatiently chorused in unison.

'She's just told me that the reason she and her husband are here,' Jan sniggered, 'is because she and her husband are doing research,' she drew a deep breath to pull herself together, 'into which tribe of fairies it was that led the Knights Templar to King Solomon's treasure.' The three of us collapsed in helpless howling heaps of hysteria, tears streaming down our faces. 'The best bit, though,' Jan managed to splutter out, 'is her husband is the spitting image of Mr Magoo.' I hurt with laughing, my face and sides were killing me. They truly deserved each other. Serious historical researchers, *oy vey*.

ALIENS ONLY ABDUCT AMERICANS

The Easter break passed in a manic, busy blur. Once I was over my nerves and remembered what I was doing (it had been something like fifteen years since I had last donned whites and toque), I found that I really rather enjoyed being back in a kitchen. I had forgotten the adrenaline high of dealing with a restaurant full of starving mouths all demanding to be fed, making sure all the dishes are served as and when they should be, to the same people that ordered them, shouting at the staff to keep them moving, the crash of pan and yelling of oaths, muck and bullets flying. Running a kitchen is not a job for the faint-hearted. Neither is it a job for the sane.

The first evening that we had no punters (sorry, guests) staying, Chris, Jan and I were sitting at our favourite relaxation spot under the walnut tree indulging in our favourite pastimes of drinking copious amounts of the local *Vino Collapso,* watching the llamas and chatting. We were having an idle post-mortem of the Easter happenings and I was most gratified to be told that several of the locals had started to use Moolong as their watering hole of preference. Most of them had eaten here and had refused to believe the cooky-boy was English. Some had even been brave or foolhardy enough to return to our table. We felt chuffed. We'd obviously been doing something right, so when Chris asked us if we would stay on for the rest of the summer it was without a moment's hesitation that Jan and I both said 'yes'.

Before I would work in the kitchen for this extended period, I insisted on returning to England to collect my whites, cookery books various and, most importantly, my knives. It was also a friend's fortieth birthday coming up and we'd been invited to the party; now we had an excuse to be there.

So it was, a couple of days later, we were loading ourselves into the combi to head back to Blighty. When it actually came to the moment of turning the key in the ignition I suddenly had the strangest sensation: I really didn't want to leave this place. I felt so at home here. However, waving toodle-pip to Chris, I told myself to stop being stupid, it was only going to be a couple of weeks we'd be away, after all, and we started back up the mountain on the long drive back to Dorset.

It seemed strange to be 'on holiday' in England but we enjoyed our break and collected together a heap of extremely useful stuff for Jan to take back to France for the garden she intended starting up for the restaurant. So she could 'keep her hand in' with all this growing malarkey, she explained to me. How we would cram all this back into the van when we eventually came to leave Moolong wasn't a thought that ever crossed our minds. Thankful that we wouldn't have to cross any weighbridges, we bade our farewells to family and friends for a second time and, rubbing our hands in eager anticipation, set the van's nose in a southwardly direction and hit the road. Granted, George Thorogood blaring out 'Gear Jammer' whilst we travelled sedately along at 30 miles an hour probably looked a wee bit ridiculous but I didn't care. We were going home.

We set off in plenty of time to catch our ferry. For once there were no road works, accidents, detours, unnecessary temporary traffic lights nor miles of plastic cones littering the roads so we made good time to Portsmouth. We booked ourselves in at the port, were directed to a line of similar-looking mechanical wrecks, parked up and found ourselves with sufficient time left before embarkation for a last pint of Guinness.

Now, I know that ports generally don't have the most genteel boozers in the world, so I was pleasantly surprised when we walked into the first place we came across to find a shabby but apparently respectable Victorian drinking establishment. There was red velvet everywhere and, amazingly, they still had those screens across the bar that block the view of the drunken riff-raff in the public bar from the more refined customers in the snug. The men were all sitting engrossed, watching football on a not—very-Victorian mega-giant television with surround sound. The pub was remarkably quiet and well behaved, considering. Just the sort of place to take your ageing, grey-haired mother for her small sweet sherry before Sunday lunch, if she's ever granted her parole. We bought our drinks and found a table as far away as possible from that mind-numbingly idiotic game that has become the national religion when suddenly all hell broke loose. We were sitting on the sidelines of a real live Wild West saloon bar-type scrap. Glasses were flying and breaking all over the place, bar stools were smashed over heads, people were flung everywhere. It was mayhem. Everybody was covered in beer and broken glass.

And then it was over. Those still standing returned calmly to their drinks, or ordered fresh ones, as though nothing untoward had taken place. The whole fight couldn't have lasted more than a minute. Jan and I looked at each other in total astonishment, glasses raised, frozen midway to our lips. Trying to look as cool and unbothered by this sort of thing as possible we brushed ourselves clean of broken glass, supped our drinks rather more quickly than we had originally intended and scarpered back to the van and relative safety.

At some unearthly hour of the night, seemingly only five minutes after we'd been herded onto the boat and got to sleep, *das boot kommandant,* or at least one of his minions, informed us that it was time to get our butts out of bed and back into our busses. With eyelids stuck to the roof of my mouth, both legs through one knicker hole, I lurched like a deranged zombie to the van. The poor old bus being as ticked off as me about being woken up at such a heathen hour decided that its clutch wasn't going to behave properly, so we kangarooed our way off the boat and along the esplanade.

Bloody hell, I've got to remember to drive on the wrong side of the road again. The fact that we had deliberately bought a left hand drive van for the trip momentarily slipped my mind. The squawk that greeted this minor slip was, I thought, even worse than the *look*; it was certainly more painful. *Looks*, at least, don't burst your eardrums at six o'clock in the morning. Jan, having the God-given common sense that women are born with, or possibly a stronger sense of survival than I had just then, suggested we stop for a coffee and croissant before starting south.

'It'll give all the grockles a chance to get out from under our feet,' she tactfully and thoughtfully told me. There are times when it is really quite useful having someone sensible around. Several coffees later, we reckoned it was about as good a time as any to start the drive so, twitching slightly from caffeine overdose, I resumed my seat behind the steering wheel. Jan, clutching the map to her breast, pointed dramatically through the windscreen and declaimed in her best Margaret Rutherford voice, 'Go south, young man.'

I obeyed. We headed south. There is nothing more relaxing than a long drive taken in that safe, comfortable, amicable silence that a couple can build around themselves.

The bloody Calvados museum was still closed. I was starting to think that this might be something personal.

Sedately, we made our way along pollarded poplar-lined roads, through villages and hamlets showing no sign of human inhabitation, the only indicators of life being the distant barking of dogs and crowing of cockerels. On we drove.

'Have you got that Haynes manual handy?' I asked Jan nonchalantly.

'Why?' I could tell from the tone of her voice she was expecting some sort of joke.

'Well,' I wondered how best to broach the problem, 'there's a red light on here and it wasn't on before and I don't know what it is.' I knew this could be a bit of an iffy problem. I am the most useless bloke that has ever walked this planet, I make no bones about it. I don't do DIY. I don't know one end of the infernal combustion engine from the other. I hate every form of sport that has ever been invented and I don't have any tattoos. (I am very good at needlepoint, if that's any use.) Before we left England, Jan had insisted I do an evening class on basic car maintenance. Not being an entirely abnormal bloke, I had agreed. Anything for a quiet life.

'You're the one that did the course and got a certificate for it.' Shit, I knew I was in trouble. Again.

'Look, there's a Champion coming up in a few K,' I flannelled desperately. 'We need some more *essence* and you want to stop to get some scoff for tonight. I'll have a look at it there. It's probably nothing,' I said, crossing my fingers. Jan looked at me, an eyebrow slightly raised. I was winning: it was only a *demi*-look. I had her conned so far.

We pulled into the garagey bit of the supermarket. I took a deep breath and switched off the bus. Oh God, please let it start again. I got out of the cab, smiling sickly at Jan and filled us with petrol. I joked with the jolly man at the cash desk about *les rosbifs* and froggies as we waited for my card to cough up the necessary virtual dosh. I signed the scrap of paper and got back into the bus. With fingers still firmly crossed and breath held, I turned the key. Bus thought about it for a bit, long enough for me to break out in a muck sweat, then she caught. I sighed a huge sigh of relief and promptly, accidentally stuffed her into third gear. We leapt forward a pump's length and stalled.

I grinned a 'whoopsy' grin at Jan and turned the key again. I grinned a second, slightly more panic-stricken 'whoopsy' grin at her, swallowed and tried again.

Not a sausage.

I gulped and tried again. *Pas d'un saucisson,* as they say in this neck of the woods. This was when Hewgies knew he was well and truly in the *merde*. I turned to Jan who was *looking* at me.

'Well?' she said, making the word 'well' sound like a death sentence being passed. I squirmed and coughed uncomfortably.

'I think we ought to push the bus away from the pump, darling. So they can still use it,' I offered pathetically. The *look* was there in a flash. I was in deep doo-doo. Thankfully the jolly man at the cash desk had seen our predicament and came to help push us away from one of his sales points, thus averting World War Three. We tried bump-starting the damn bus for yonks, but the best the bloody thing would do was to cough half-heartedly.

We had every Frenchman in the *département* come and give us advice. I'm sure that somewhere amid the Gallic babble were words of wisdom but, as I didn't know the names of any bits of an engine in my native tongue, what chance did I have in a foreign one? I wouldn't know who was talking rubbish or not. Having kicked the tyres as though I had a vague idea of what I was doing I came up with the startling brainwave of toddling off in search of a garage that might be able to help us in our hour of need. After about fifteen minutes I stumbled across a very dubious-looking back-street outfit. By now, I really didn't care who or what they were, I just wanted to get going again. I bobbed up and down impatiently whilst I waited for the blue overall-clad mechanic to remove his head from under the bonnet of the ancient 2CV he was working on. Eventually he extracted himself from the object of his desire, looked me up and down, cleared his throat of Gauloise phlegm and uttered that great Gallic greeting,

'*Ouais?*'

I explained, to the best of my incapabilities, the problems we had with our bus and that we would be eternally grateful if he could see his way to sorting us out pretty damn quick. I was horrified when he laughed at me. Surely my French wasn't that bad? Had I made some ridiculous linguistic cock-up? I was pretty sure I hadn't told him my hovercraft's auntie wasn't full of the eels of my aardvark's uncle's bureau.

We had managed to break down at lunchtime. Lunchtime on a Friday. And this Friday was the start of the town's annual shindig. There was no way we were going to get our problem looked at before Tuesday and even then... he shrugged in that peculiarly French way, leaving the question mark hanging.

Wondering how the hell I was going to explain the FUF's latest jest to Jan, I made my way back to the bus as slowly as I dared. Neither of us fancied several days living in a supermarket car park. Kicking the bus didn't do anything, contrary to all the educational films I'd seen. Thankfully, Jan's sensible side reared its head again.

'Christ.' She suddenly shrieked. 'Bank holidays, everything'll be closed. We've got no food.' We made a mad dash to the supermarket, getting through the doors just in time to win ourselves the title of 'customers of the year'. We scurried round stocking up on useful things like wine, cheese, bread, packet soup and those yummy cream puddings that you don't seem to be able to buy anywhere else in the world, and managed to escape without being lynched by the staff who had been following our every move as we tried to make our purchases, willing us to get our *culs* into gear.

Having dined on Knorr brown onion soup with huge chunks of the world's greatest blue cheese, *fourme d'ambert*, swimming in it, followed by a yummy cream pudding, we figured we ought to phone Chris to let him know we'd be arriving back at Moolong a few days later than originally anticipated. Being the all-round good egg that he is, Chris said that, as the campsite was almost empty, he would leap into his lorry and drive up to get us sorted out.

Knowing that there was a minimum of six hours' driving between us and Moolong, Jan and I decided we'd go for a mooch around town to discover what style of bean-feastery it could be that would deprive us of our freedom and imprison us in its mighty supermarket car park for days on end. If there were any sort of shenanigans going on, they were obviously not intended for sharing with itinerant scruffs like us. At least the ghost towns we'd passed through had a dog barking somewhere but here, absolutely nothing. There was not a person on the street, no traffic, no sound of television from behind net curtains, no bunting, not even any posters giving any clue as to what, where, when and how it would all be going down. It was almost as though the entire town had been abducted by aliens. This was obviously a ridiculous notion. We were in France, after all, not America, and aliens only abduct Americans. They still haven't managed to work out the next tabloid headline yet.

'Gosh I'm knackered,' Jan quipped. 'All this excitement is killing me.'

'Know what you mean, my dear. It's almost more than a young man can take.'

'Bus?' she asked.

'Bus,' I agreed. There was food, wine and books there to keep us amused whilst we idled away the hours waiting for Chris to turn up. Hopefully we'd be safe from alien abduction back at the van. We read and drank, we dined on our runcible quince. We even chatted to each other.

The sun slowly set. We sat there for hours and not a soul did we see or hear. No cars, no *mobylettes* screaming past sounding like irate wasps driving supercharged lawnmowers, no nothing. Where had everybody gone? This was spooky. Was Stephen King lurking behind the shrubbery? I was right, it was bloody Stephen King, I just saw a bush move. I prodded Jan, squeaking at her, disturbing her reading.

'Ooh, ooh, look.'

'I've told you before about doing that,' she growled at me. 'What?'

'That bush.' I bounced up and down on my seat in my excitement.

'What about it?'

I should know by now that Jan doesn't like being interrupted from her reading by a stoned idiot squeaking at her. Fair enough I suppose, who does? It's just that I never remember in time.

'It moved.' I pointed towards the offending berberis.

'For Christ's sake,' Jan sighed, 'it was probably the wind. Now sit down, shut up, read your book, and do not,' she commanded me, 'I repeat, do not have any more to smoke, we've still got miles to drive yet.'

'But it did move, honest,' I persisted.

'Hugo,' she *looked* at me, 'just sit still and be quiet, there's a good boy. While you still have two testes.'

'Yes dear.' I sat, surreptitiously checking on my bits.

'And stop fiddling with yourself.'

Thankfully, at the very moment the combi car park castration was about to commence, an old and mangy fox emerged from the shrubbery, gave us a look of total disdain then wandered off, no doubt to check out the local vulpine bars and discos. Jan laughed.

'OK smart arse, so there was something there, but that doesn't mean you're not still on a warning. Now make yourself useful for a change and put the kettle on.'

The moon rose as lethargically as the sun had set. It was reluctantly crawling across the night sky and we were bored and restless. I was sitting there idly contemplating putting my life and bits at risk again by suggesting that Jan might like to take her clothes off when a pair of headlights suddenly came careering across the car park. As this was the first sign of life, other than our foxy friend, that we had seen since the supermarket slammed its doors closed behind our backs we figured it had to be St Chris. The lorry juddered to a halt beside us, its doors were flung open and out jumped Chris and a gangly, bespectacled man in his mid-to-late twenties who looked just like a cartoon boy scout who'd been riding shotgun.

'This is Chris,' Chris told us. 'When I told him where I was going he decided to come along, see if he could help.'

'Brilliant. You are heartily welcome St Chris the Second.' I hugged Chris the First and Jan in relief and thankfulness. 'A mechanic is just what we need.'

'No,' Chris the Second said, looking slightly perplexed. 'I'm not a mechanic. I don't know anything about cars. I don't even drive.'

'You don't fix cars? So how can you help?' I growled.

'Well, as soon as Chris said you were living here I just had to meet you. I can help you.' My arms dropped from around Jan and Chris' shoulders.

'What? How?' I asked, with more than a mere soupçon of menace in my voice.

'I wanted to meet you. I can help you. I want to talk to you about Rennes.'

'Ahah,' I said, slowly filling with rage. If there was a whistle in my ear the steam would have set it off.

'It's your father. Everything he's written is wrong and I can prove it. I know where the treasure is.'

I bit my tongue and paced in a tight circle while the frustration drained to manageable levels. Then it suddenly dawned on me, this was just the start of the season. We hadn't even got back to Moolong yet. We had at least another four or five months of having to suffer these lunatics all wanting me to tell them the deepest secrets of Rennes-le-Château and Saunière and to discuss their theories with me. If my father was a bank manager people wouldn't come to me for financial advice or be surprised that I chose not to follow him into banking so why, just because he writes about this stuff, do people presume that I should be as fascinated by it as he and they are and that I am following in his footsteps?

What had I let myself in for?

YEW CANNOT
LEEVE ZAT ZERE

There is always a lull between the madness of that first-escape-
of-the-year euphoria that comes with the Easter break, when
holidaymakers are like excited cattle let out to grass after the
long winter, and the all out, non-stop lunacy of the summer
season at its height when you just never seem to stop running
from the second you get out of bed in the morning till you
finally manage to crawl, exhausted, back into it the following
morning. This short period is a very pleasant time of the year
to be working in this industry. There were enough people
passing through to keep us occupied but not so many that they
got in the way. As Easter had been particularly early this year
it meant we'd be well and truly 'broken in' before the *merde*
hit the *ventilateur*, so we were cruising a bit. There was still
more than enough patching and mending and building and

God knows what to do, and of course there were the evenings of red wine and forgetfulness.

Charlie was becoming quite a fixture of the place. He'd managed to con a television and film wardrobe company into buying his gendarme cossies and had made a healthy profit, so now, having heard that a mega blockbuster set in France during World War Two was about to be made, he was dashing backwards and forwards between London and Moolong, buying what seemed to us to be utter garbage but to him was a very lucrative little earner. It never ceases to amaze me how one man's junk can be another man's goldmine. Charlie's van was very useful too. Chris could give Charlie shopping lists of buildingy stuff that he wanted and Charlie would pick it up whilst he was out for the day, scrounging through dustbins or however it was that he came by his treasures.

All was peace and tranquillity as we pottered around doing our daily chores. The spring burst of plant-life was magical. Without setting foot off Moolong land Jan and I had found something like forty different types of orchid. There were things popping up all over the place so we were trying to get as much llama walking in as we could whilst we still had the time.

There were a couple of retired Germans staying with us who travelled all over Europe looking for orchids. They didn't speak any English and we don't speak any German, but Jan and I wanted to talk to these guys. Undaunted, I went off in search of a translator. I wandered through the campsite looking at the various cars' and vans' registration plates until I found a

Dutch-plated bus and, knowing that Dutch seems to be the second language of Holland, I knocked on the door confident that the owner would speak English. A bare-chested young lad with dreadlocks appeared. It was obvious what he'd been up to even at this early hour of the day: his eyeballs were bloodshot and spinning. Grinning knowingly at him, I explained my needs. Yeah, of course he spoke German and would be happy to translate for us.

It was a shame he wasn't in the slightest bit interested in botany. The poor lad was stuck between two pairs of lunatics excitedly trying to explain to each other where each had seen something really, really groovy. He was confused, he tried his best but we all started getting too technical for him. He wanted to get back to his bus and safety, away from these weird country folk who wanted to talk about plants in such minute and intimate detail.

'Just schmoke dem, man,' he said as he staggered back to the safety of his own alternative reality leaving us to solve our communication difficulties by resorting to pointing to a spot on a local map and then at the appropriate page in our field guide.

The four of us, Chris, Charlie, Jan and I, were sitting under the walnut tree munching on croissants and *pains au chocolat*, pouring the requisite amounts of coffee down our beaks to kick-start us for the day and mulling over what exciting things we could get up to. Charlie was heading over the border towards Gerona to pillage some Spanish dustbins. Chris was alternately tearing his hair out trying to solve an intermittent electric fault to the campsite's concrete mushrooms or rushing about like a thing possessed trying to finish the *plage* before it well and truly became swimming pool weather. Jan and I had other plans for the day, though. We were having a day off; we were going on a picnic.

Moolong sits at the bottom of a very steep valley and facing it is Le Bec, the huge, towering, glowering mountain of grey rock that, depending on its mood and the weather, either smiled beatifically or threw oaths and imprecations down upon us. The Bec, its covering of holm oak, thyme and gorse petering out to odd splashes of colour against the stark grey of the rock the higher you went, had been calling to us ever since we had arrived at Moolong and, the weather being absolutely perfect, today was going to be the day we climbed it. I needed a quick hike to restore my equilibrium after the shock I'd been given yesterday.

Chris had been expecting an agent from the insurance company to visit, to see what stage the repair work was at and if they were going to cough up any more of the promised money yet, so he had asked me to be on hand to help with any translating that needed doing.

A smart new car pulled into the car park and a smartly-dressed gentleman climbed out carrying a briefcase. We trotted over to meet him; after all, it was obvious who he was. We shook hands and Chris took him off on a tour of the estate, showing him the work we had done and what we were doing now and what was still waiting to be done. I tagged along behind them as Chris seemed to be doing fine all by himself. It was when we got to the shower block and loos that the agent finally spoke.

'*Monsieur*, I think maybe you mistake me for someone else.' Chris and I looked at each other.

'You're not from the insurance company?' I asked him.

'*Mais non, monsieur.*' He laughed. How could we have been so silly as to have thought that? What a jolly wheeze. '*Non, monsieur*, my name is Francois Bertrand, I am a freelance journalist and I 'ave 'eard that Henry Lincoln's son is living near 'ere now. I wondered if maybe you knew where 'e was staying? I was wanting to interview 'im about Rennes-le-Château and why 'e is 'ere and if 'e is continuing 'is father's work?'

I didn't wait for Chris to open his mouth.

'*Je suis désolé, monsieur,*' I told him. 'We also have heard that. I would rather like to meet him too. Perhaps if you leave me your business card I could give it to him if ever our paths cross.'

Glaring at Chris, daring him to open his mouth, I took the card and bade the journalist au revoir.

'What the hell was that all about?' Chris asked, stunned that I had behaved so politely and calmly towards this man.

'I've told you Chris,' I explained quietly, 'I'm not in the slightest bit interested in Rennes-le-Château. If I'd told that guy to bugger off he'd know who I am and then I'd have never got him off my back. He can think what he likes but I'm not playing their games. I do not want to know about it.'

I sighed and shook my head. 'Will you tell me why it is that I am being picked on?' I was starting to feel decidedly paranoid about this. 'I've had a non-mechanical mechanic and now a non-insurance insurance agent pretending to be who they're not just so they can talk to me about bloody Rennes. What am I going to get next, a non-pontifical pontiff wanting to discuss this bloody fairy story with me?' Chris put his arm consolingly around my shoulders.

'Ah, never mind, Hewgs. We can always invite your father to move here and live with us too. That'd keep the nutters off your back.'

'Chris, shut up, there's a good fellow.'

There is something about a professional kitchen when it's quiet that I really rather enjoy. No banging and crashing of pans, no screaming of waiters as they are plunged into deep-fat fryers, no sweating your butt off, just peace and quiet and a chance to do a bit of work without being hassled. So there I was, happily humming *'ça plane pour moi'* to myself, banging together the odd Kendal mint cake and frog's-leg-flavoured Pringles baguette in readiness for our hike when Chris came bursting into the kitchen, a look of total, abject panic on his face. Something dire and dreadful beyond belief had happened to the swimming pool and my techno-Franglais was required to phone round the shops in the area to see if anyone was wonderful enough to stock whatever it was that had died so direly and dreadfully. I was starting to get that funny feeling the FUF was lurking close at hand.

Reluctantly I picked up the *Pages Jaunes,* flicked to the appropriate page and started on my telephonic hunt. Now, my techno-frog is none too sloppy. When I'm face-to-face with the unlucky shopkeeper, I can point, gesticulate, wave my arms about, jump up and down, scream *'Non, non, ce truc là. Oui, le truc pour le truc,'* and things like that. This method of communication was not awfully successful over the phone as they had no idea which particular *truc* I was attempting to mime. Add to this the fact that Chris had no idea what the name of the *truc* was in English, let alone any other language, and it made for some interesting conversations.

Eventually, a kindly lady decided she understood enough of my inane, gibberish ramblings and would be pleased to flog us one of these things we so badly needed this very day. Just so long as we got there before lunch as today she was having to close early to go to a funeral. Chris was now bouncing up and down squeaking with relief, telling me to say we'd be along as quickly as we could. She was only an hour or so's drive away, after all. I pointed out that it'd better be a royal 'we' he was talking about 'cos I had my day pretty well mapped out and it didn't include a drive over to Perpignan, so there.

An hour and a half later and I was standing in a swimming pool bits shop in Perpignan.

'Non madame,' I made frantic twiddling motions with my fingers. *'J'ai besoin d'un truc...'* She moved along the racks smiling patiently at my gesticulations. *'Non, non.'* She moved on a bit further. *'Non, non. Ah.'* I let out a yelp of triumph.

'*Oui, oui, ce truc là.*' I pointed excitedly at the *truc* she was standing by. '*Oui, le truc pour le truc.*'

Success, another mission accomplished and with much *merci*-ing from all concerned we were back out on the street again, the *truc* tucked safely under Chris' arm. I don't know why people have any trouble with foreign languages. All you need to know is what the appropriate language's versions of 'one of them', 'please' and 'thank you' are and have an ability to point. Works every time.

However, Chris and I were now stuck in Perpignan, my day's plans well and truly scuppered. The sun having crossed a yardarm somewhere in the world, Chris thought it would be a nice idea to take me to lunch, to make up for things a bit. Having lunched it then seemed a sensible idea to go for an idle stroll along the beach to go boob spotting. Having spotted a few boobs we then needed a beer or two to help us recover. Having recovered from the shock of seeing so many unclad boobies it then seemed a piece of necessary research to check them out again... and again... and again. Finally, boobed and beered out, we figured we ought to head back to Moolong, just in case anybody turned up wanting feeding and watering.

We started our descent to Moolong in a state of beery, booby bliss. The sun was lighting the valley in a warming, welcoming glow. This really was a beautiful spot. I coasted down the mountain and into the car park, coming to rest in my usual spot. We were walking back towards the front door when we heard Jan's none-too-pleased voice. Chris and I looked at each other. The feeling of euphoria that was happily hugging me began to fade as I heard who it was that she was snapping at.

'Charlie, just get out of the bloody kitchen will you.' I wondered what my idiot chum was up to now.

'Oh come on Jan, it won't take long,' I heard him schmooze her. Chris and I looked at each other again trying not to giggle. *What was my idiot chum up to?*

Charlie was the first of my friends that I had introduced to Jan when we started going out together. That meant he'd known her a fair few years now so he really ought to have learnt to read the warning signs and not to start winding her up. If in doubt, shut up; it saves all sorts of unnecessary unpleasantness. That works in any situation too, from domestic to workplace. It doesn't work for Charlie, though, 'cos he never has any doubts to suffer from.

'Go on, you know you want to,' Charlie continued with full-on salaciousness. 'I'll pay you,' he added as an inducing afterthought. This was getting interesting. Chris and I stood with bated breath, waiting for the next exchange. We didn't have long to wait as Charlie came backing out of the kitchen, hands held palm out towards Jan, trying to calm her down, his usual inane grin on his face. I could tell he'd just been given the *look*.

'And just what d'you think you're trying to get my wife to do?' I asked, making Charlie jump out of his skin as he'd not noticed us lurking in the doorway.

'Bloody hell mate, d'you always go round creeping up on people?'

'Only when they're trying to pull my wife.' I laughed at Charlie's expression of mock hurt and innocence.

'Hewgs, you know me, mate.' His little-boy-lost look came into play. It may work on some of the women he's tried to pull but it didn't work on me. 'And anyway, doesn't matter now, you'll do instead.'

'If you think I'm gonna indulge in any of your sexual perversions...'

'Why do you always accuse me of being a perv?' Charlie interrupted, sounding most miffed by this slur to his otherwise not-very-good name.

'Charlie, I went to school with you. We've known each other since we were in single figures,' I explained patiently, 'I know you're a perv. Now what are you trying to scam from Jan?'

'I only want her to drive my van for me.' As far as explanations went, even by Charlie's standard, this one was pretty thin.

'So now you're trying to turn my wife into a getaway driver? I think I preferred it when you were trying to pull her.'

Chris, having got bored with this banter, had quite sensibly toddled off to the bar. I turned to follow, hoping Charlie would find someone else to go and pester. With Charlie hard on my heels, I walked into the bar and stopped dead. Charlie hadn't noticed my brake lights go on so just ploughed straight into the back of me.

An extremely petite and attractive young blonde lady was perched on a barstool, legs crossed and sipping on a spritzer.

Chris was doing his impersonation of a lounge lizard. Chris in lounge-lizard mode when he is at his sartorially most elegant is really not a pretty sight. Chris in lounge-lizard mode when still in work gear, covered in cement dust and sporting the biggest builder's gap yet created is really, really, really not a pretty sight.

'There you are, darlin',' Charlie squealed and ran to hug the young blonde lady that Chris was trying so hard to impress. She simpered most coquettishly, just like French women are supposed to. My knees went weak. Chris looked miffed. Charlie looked smug.

Several hours and several wine lakes later we finally got to the bottom of it all, after a fashion. The combination of Charlie, Rennes and the FUF is a daunting trinity, so really we shouldn't have been surprised. Chantal, for that was her name, turned out not to be French at all but a Belgian hitchhiker Charlie had picked up earlier in the day. That she was attractive was in no doubt and that she was blonde was in no doubt. I wondered if Belgian blondes were as intellectually gifted as their Essex counterparts.

Charlie had found her standing by the side of the road, and, as he stores his brain in a slightly different place to most other people, couldn't resist stopping to offer her a lift in his van. She wanted to spend some time in the region doing her own research into the Rennes mystery and had decided to look for a job to support this when she arrived. Good old Charlie, helpful as ever, knowing that Chris, Jan and I had been having half-hearted chats about needing another pair of hands about the place, took it upon himself to offer her the job of waitress at Moolong. Chantal assured us this was a doddle as she had done her fair share of waitressing whilst she had been at college. I didn't care who she was or where she came from, just so long as she didn't spend her time singing 'Dominique, nique, nique', drinking fruit-flavoured beer and trying to discuss Rennes-le-Château with me. What we needed was someone who could do the job. Chris didn't give a stuff where she came from either: he was in lust. Chantal passed the interview and became the newest member of our jolly little team. Jan and I gave each other sly, knowing, drunken glances. Neither of us was overly convinced of her work skills and hoped she would be able to do slightly more than just look attractive and simper.

'Now then Hewgs,' Charlie spun round drunkenly to face me, slapping me heartily on the back, 'I promise, on my honour,' Charlie slurred, attempting to give me a wolf cub salute, 'to have you back in time for lunch,' and staggered off to his room. Apart from questioning his sanity and the fact that Charlie's parents had actually been married to each other on the day of his birth, I didn't bother with what he had just said. We were used to his meaningless, valedictory mutterings.

The following morning we had fed the llamas and Jan had gone to do some work in her nice new veg garden. I was pottering around in the kitchen doing cheffy type-things when Charlie wandered in looking as though he'd been dragged through several hedges backwards and clutching an American army helmet.

'Come on then Hewgs, let's get going.'

I looked blankly at him. 'Charlie, just go away, there's a good chap,' I told him.

'Stop messin' about mate,' he chivvied me. 'We're going to have to get a wiggle on if we're gonna get to Perpignan and back again before lunch.'

'A, for a start,' I began, 'I have no idea what you're talking about and B, I am not going to Perpignan two days on the trot. Now go away.'

An hour and a half later and I was completely disorientated. We had driven through parts of Perpignan I never knew existed. Through industrial estates that Hitchcock and Tarantino would have been well chuffed to have found. I was now standing in the yard of a highly disreputable-looking purveyor of highly dubious-looking commercial vehicles. Charlie had handed over a huge wedge of euros to the highly disreputable-looking chappy and had been given a key and some papers in return which were thrown with great ceremony into his army helmet. Finalising the contract with much spitting on palms and shaking of hands the deal was done. The two of them then disappeared behind a huge earth-moving machine leaving me standing there intrigued, wondering what the hell Charlie had bought now?

The sound of a constipated, consumptive elephant suddenly erupted from the bowels of hell which made me squeal and jump with shock. When I saw what was creating this noise I fell about laughing. A constipated, consumptive elephant would probably be more use than Charlie's latest purchase.

The huge, drab green and rust, ex-army lorry that juddered and shuddered and kangarooed its way towards me had clearly been obsolete long before World War Two. With a grin bigger than the Cheshire Cat's, Charlie was hanging onto the steering wheel of the beast. He stalled, pitching forward, his helmet slipping most jauntily over his eyes. He sat back, repositioned his headwear, checked it in the rear-view mirror and, satisfied it was as it ought to be, turned to lean out of the window. Knocking his helmet skew again he shouted down at me from his lofty position.

'Well don't just stand there you lazy get.' I moved forward to get into the lorry. 'What are you doing?' Charlie yelled at me, 'You're driving my van back, you pillock.'

He got the lorry restarted and farted off, leaving me to leg it back to the van so I could follow the lunatic out of this maze of streets. By the time I'd coaxed Charlie's van into life, performed a ninety-seven-point turn to extract it from the spot he'd chosen to park it in, then made it to the yard gate the bastard had disappeared, totally, completely and utterly from sight. Calling my dear friend all the names under the sun and a few more besides, I turned right, desperately hoping, fingers crossed, I'd manage to get myself out of this bloody warren. I'm famous for getting lost. I even managed it driving to work once. Well, I had only been using the route for two years.

Two and a half hours later I was finally back at Moolong. I was not in a good mood. Thankfully the lunchtime session had been particularly quiet and Jan had managed without any problems. Much to her surprise Chantal had turned out to be pretty competent. I 'humphed' my reservations at Jan and stomped off to have a shower so I could then get back to doing some proper work.

Freshly showered and changed, I was feeling in much better humour. I was strolling from our apartment back to the restaurant when Chris and Charlie chundered past in the lorry. Leaning out of the window, making obscene gestures at me and shouting strange, male hunter-gatherer type noises, they disappeared round the bend, heading off towards Quillan. Maybe the rest of the day wouldn't be totally wasted. With Chris out of the way my techno-frog telephoning technique wouldn't be needed and with Charlie gone, well, that was just good news in itself. With a smile on my face, a spring in my step and singing a quick snatch of 'Dominique, nique, nique' I strolled into the kitchen.

I was having a nice relaxed time in the kitchen, pottering around, making sure all was ready for the imminent opening of the restaurant for the evening's service. I had just clambered down from the chair on which I had been standing so I could write the specials on the blackboard when I heard the distinctive sound of Charlie's lorry returning. I heaved a sigh of relief that I had managed to get as much work done as I had, knowing from bitter experience how difficult it is trying to work with a pair of idiots getting under your feet and rambling at you. The lorry slowed as it passed the front of Moolong, and Chris leaped from the cabin yelling something to Charlie as he came hurtling into the kitchen.

'Come on, come on,' Chris ordered me, 'it's urgent. Come on.' The lorry was being turned round in the car park, looking as though they were going straight back out again.

'What the hell have you two done now?' I asked with a feeling of resigned dread. Charlie was looking an interesting shade of grey. Chris grabbed my arm and started dragging me to the lorry. I started to resist: 'I cannot go out anywhere you idiot. Service is starting in half an hour.'

'Please,' Chris begged me. 'This really is urgent.' From the expressions on their faces I could tell this was slightly more than the usual run of the mill cock-up. Shaking my head, I yelled through to Jan in the dining room that I was having to pop out for a few minutes. The terms of endearment that greeted this announcement were lost as I was dragged into the lorry. Charlie slammed the beast into gear and we roared off.

From what I could make out from their gibbering, it seemed that the two of them had been playing with Charlie's new toy when they discovered it was a tipper lorry. 'Oh deep joy' and things like that, they thought. Chris then had the brainwave of collecting the ready-mixed cement he had on order direct from the cement shop, rather than having it delivered, thus saving himself vast numbers of euros. A sound idea normally, but not round here, not when there's an FUF lurking in the shrubbery.

The lorry had been greeted with much amused interest when they pulled into the cement works and soon all the men were gathered around admiring it, grunting the strange, male-bonding type grunts that seem so obligatory in such situations.

All the lorry's levers were pulled and pushed, the tyres kicked and muttered over and finally the cement was poured, with great ceremony, onto the bed of the lorry. With much waving and *bon chance*-ing the return trip began. Heartily cheered by the success of their mission they were singing lustily, warriors home with the kill.

'Have you noticed how many cars keep on honking at us as they go past?' Chris asked Charlie.

'It's appreciation of a fine historic vehicle, mate, that's what that is,' Charlie replied smugly. Another car overtook them, honking frantically, the driver gesticulating wildly. Charlie returned the gesture, yelling non-cordial Anglo-French sentiments.

'Jesus fucking H. Christ!' Chris had turned in his seat to look behind them. Thumping Charlie on the arm he screamed 'Stop, fer fuck's sake, stop! The bloody tipper's going!'

Charlie stamped on the brakes, the sudden slowing causing the cement to flow even more smoothly over the end of the lorry and onto President Chirac's highway. Applying the brakes also seemed to give the tipping mechanism an extra bit of oomph, and it promptly went as high as it could and dumped the rest of their load onto the road.

'What we gonna do?' Chris asked faintly.

'Run?' Charlie suggested.

The lorry grumbled to a halt at the site of their disaster. I peered through the windscreen and stared blankly at this unwanted *flic qui dort*, its tail spreading up the road and into the distance. I didn't know whether to laugh or cry. More by luck than judgement, stashed in the lorry's cab were two very long handled spades, which looked as though they would be of far more use for stuffing pizzas into ovens. I got Chris and Charlie frantically shovelling the cement onto the verge. As I was in my whites, there was no way I was even considering getting filthy with them, so I took on the duty of traffic controller and tried to direct the cars round our ever hardening pile.

The lump had barely seemed to decrease in size despite their best efforts when the almost inevitable happened and a police car pulled up beside us. With a rictus grin and stomach churning, I walked up to the car trying to look as innocent as possible so I could explain things to the two intimidating-looking gendarmes sitting inside it. I gave a hurried account of what had happened and what two raggedy-arsed chaps and a chef were trying to do to remedy the situation. They muttered strange intimidating Gallic mutterings to each other and looked even more intimidating. The boss *flic* demanded to see the paperwork for the lorry. I turned shouting to Charlie to get his licence and insurance and stuff. More strange Gallic mutterings came from the police car.

'*Vous êtes anglais?*' the driver snapped at me.

'*Oui,*' I apologised

'*Merde,*' he said, slipping the car into gear. 'Clean zat away, yew cannot leeve zat 'ere,' he barked in his best Franglais, roaring off up the road leaving us standing, thanking the heavens that we weren't being carted off to the local nick for a quick kicking. The thought of the paperwork this trio of deranged foreigners could engender was obviously far too much for them. Thank God, there are times when it's quite useful being a foreign idiot.

VOUS ÊTES NICKED, SON

One Friday morning, Jan and I were heading off to Limoux market to see what exciting produce was on offer that day when Chris asked us to pop into the swimming pool shop and pick up a long awaited *truc* that had finally arrived. I pointed out that we didn't have enough loose cash lying around to buy *trucs* as well as the stock that we needed. It would have to wait until either Chris went to Quillan to draw the cash out of the bank, a few punters left and paid their bills in cash or, last but not least, Chris could go get it himself when he had time and could pay for it by cheque.

'Just take the chequebook yourself,' Chris suggested in his usual rather blasé manner.

'Oh yeah,' I jeered back sarcastically, 'I'm sure the bank won't be able to tell the difference between your scrawl and mine.'

Five minutes and a couple of sheets of A4 later I was tucking the company chequebook in my back pocket, confident in the knowledge that I could forge Chris's signature perfectly.

I went out every morning to buy fresh the things that I needed for the day's menu so Chris would now ask me to pop into wherever to pick up whatever and if necessary pay by cheque. It wasn't long before the chequebook was living in the glove box of the campervan as I was the only person using the thing.

I was quietly fiddling with food in the kitchen when Chris came in clutching a letter and looking more than a tad concerned about things. His *billet doux* was from the bank manager, asking him to make an appointment for as soon as possible as the bank would rather like a chance to indulge in a spot of the third degree and fingernail removal whilst discussing various irregularities in Moolong's account. Chris passed me the letter so I could read it and check he'd understood the summons. We looked at each other, and acid burns of worry started to bubble in the pit of my stomach. Were we about to be busted for forgery?

Chris's French is creative rather than accurate so it had rather become the custom for me to be dragged along in the capacity of translator when he wanted to be sure that he was understood. It hadn't been that long since we'd been to see this bank manager and he hadn't struck me as the friendliest of life forms then. The huge and unexpected expenses incurred after the flood had put quite a dent in Moolong's reserves and the insurance money was as slow coming in as the insurance agents had been in coming to asses the damage in the first place. Chris thought that it would be a good idea to arrange an overdraft facility as a safety net should anything else untoward rear its ugly head, at least until the season got properly going and the euros started flowing in. The palaver the man we called B.M. caused Chris was unbelievable. You'd have thought Chris was being asked to underwrite personally France's national debt. Finally, having discovered the colour of his bathroom furniture, the name of his first girlfriend and sent him to a proctologist, the B.M. agreed to his request. Reluctantly. Having seen this guy in action I was not looking forward to renewing our acquaintanceship. From the expression on Chris's face, neither was he.

I nervously telephoned the bank to arrange the appointment. I was put on hold. Five minutes of silence ensued, then the receptionist returned and told me that there was a convenient gap in the manager's diary in one hour. Chris prodded me in the kidney asking me to find out why they wanted to see him. I was politely told that it would be discussed when he presented himself. Hell's teeth, we were busted, for sure. I had visions of burly gendarmes waiting to clap us in chains and then hauling us off to a life of imprisonment, torture and deprivation in the French Foreign Leg-iron. Hang on, hadn't Papillon being banged up on Devil's Island for forgery? I dunno, maybe it was Dustin Hoffman. It didn't seem too inviting a prospect.

Jan tried calming us down, pointing out that even though what we'd done wasn't strictly legal, it wasn't as though we'd really committed any crime. The company cheques had been used to pay for company purchases, it was just that it hadn't been the company director's autograph on the cheques.

Nobody had been ripped off and if we really thought we were going to get slammed up for something like that then we were bigger fools than she had ever taken us for in the first place. Chris and I weren't entirely convinced by her argument but as that seemed all the reassurance, comfort and support we were going to get we decided we'd best smarten ourselves up a bit for the ordeal.

The bank was housed in a beautiful old building that wouldn't have looked out of place as an antebellum Mississippi riverfront mansion. It did look slightly odd on the main street of a little French country town, however. The soft ochre tones of its stonework made it look warm and welcoming. The deceiving swine. As you entered the building the air conditioning made the temperature plummet and the shift from bright sunlight into electric lighting left you stumbling in a blind and shivering mess of nerves and discoordination. The open plan, smoked glass and stainless steel of this modern bank interior gave off an aura of cold, reptilian threat.

I nervously walked to the reception counter and announced our arrival. The lip of the immaculately dressed and coiffed receptionist curled in contempt as she reluctantly placed her nail-file on her desk. In silence she stood and indicated that we should follow her. She led us across the floor and up a spiral staircase to a mezzanine floor that housed the private offices of the bank's senior staff. Having performed this arduous task she turned her back on us and, as though we didn't exist, returned to her desk from where she could continue her important manicure work. We were left standing in the middle of the floor of this fish tank, on full display to all of the other people in the bank, wondering what the hell to do next.

I was on the point of holding hands with Chris for a bit of security when the middle of the three office doors opened. The bank manager was a tall, blond, rapier-thin, ferrety-faced gentleman wearing gold, wire-rimmed spectacles. He looked like the archetypal evil German officer, lacking only a schlager scar to complete the picture. He smiled thinly and stood to one side of the door, allowing us to enter his office, then closed the door with an unsettling firmness, came round from behind us and sat at his desk.

Lying on it, in full view, were a pile of cheques with my signature on them. He picked up some account sheets from beside the cheques and started to look through them, pausing every so often to study a particular entry more closely. Chris and I stood there waiting to be told what to do. It wasn't going to be long before we'd be hugging each other for security, since holding hands wasn't going to be enough. B.M. looked up from the papers and indicated we should sit. We scuttled round to the front of the chairs he had pointed at and perched on the edges.

'Monsieur Colyer...' he began wearily.

'*Pardon.*' Chris interrupted him. '*Vous expliquez* to Hugo, *s'il vous plaît.*'

I hurriedly tried to refresh his memory, how I had been here with Chris several times before to translate for him. The gimlet eyes bored into my head as he started to relay the full horror and seriousness of the situation. I could feel the sweat pouring off me. As B.M. got into the swing of it, it became apparent that we were not about to be banged up for writing dodgy cheques but that Chris was in deep financial doo-doo. He was in a state of acute pecuniary embarrassment. I translated for Chris, trying not to sound too relieved. His reaction was explosive. I'd not seen Chris like this before. He thumped the table demanding to know how the hell he could be overdrawn. The bank manager told him coldly to sit his arse back down. Neither of them seemed to understand a word the other was shouting so I was stuck in the middle trying to calm them both down.

We sank back into our seats, red in the face and breathing heavily. I tried desperately to take control of the situation. I told Chris, who was still spluttering his protestations, to shut up for a minute and turned to the manager and asked him to explain, as clearly and concisely as possible, the full problem with Monsieur Colyer's account. Please.

I listened to B.M.'s diatribe then turned to Chris to explain it to him. It seemed that our friend on the other side of the desk was threatening to start bouncing Moolong's cheques left, right and centre. The company was far too overdrawn for the bank even to consider allowing this parlous state of affairs to continue any longer. This time Chris' explosion could probably have been heard in Paris. What was this idiot talking about? Moolong was nowhere near the overdraft limit which he himself had agreed to. I translated back for B.M. Even though I didn't bother with the expletives, I think he got the drift. As I got to the bit about 'agreed overdraft limit' he blenched slightly. He glanced down at the papers he was holding, put them back on his desk and went through each page item by item. He looked blankly first at Chris, then at me and excused himself from the room. Chris sat and fumed whilst I sat and sympathised.

M. le B.M. returned, looking embarrassed and ashamed. Obsequiousness oozed from his every pore.

'Monsieur Hugo,' he said, treating me no longer as something unmentionable he'd scraped from the bottom of his shoe. I was now the valued colleague of a valued customer of the bank. I had become someone he couldn't do enough for – even though he had, as so many of his countrymen do, mistaken my forename for my surname, which usually included some sort of feeble joke about me being related to Victor Hugo. As he explained what had happened I could barely stop myself from laughing. Chris was prodding me, wanting me to translate. I kept knocking his hand away: I was enjoying B.M.'s discomfort too much. Well, it's not every day you get a bank manager grovelling and apologising to you. It's only ever been the other way round for me before. I wanted to hear this one right through to the end. At last, apologised out, he stopped speaking. I turned to Chris, shaking my head with stunned amazement at the stupidity of what I had just been told.

'Oh man,' I grinned, 'you ain't gonna believe what this dickhead has done.'

'What?' Chris growled threateningly at B.M.

'Well,' I put my hand on his arm, gently keeping him in his chair, 'all those forms you signed the last time we were here, the overdraft ones? Guess what twat forgot to action his own decision?'

The speed with which Chris sat forward and the threat he exuded took me totally by surprise and caused B.M. to flinch visibly. I grabbed hold of his arm.

'Chris!' I warned him sternly.

He glowered at B.M. then sat, slowly, back into his chair, holding the manager's stare, daring him to drop his eyes. I gave Chris a quick rundown on what the now rather sick looking manager had said. The basic gist of it being that if B.M. had been Japanese he would have happily committed *seppuku,* here in front of us, to atone for his sins. However, failing that, the bank cannot apologise enough for the harm, pain, anguish, distress, grief and so on and so on that they've caused you. So whatever you want in the future, they'll be only too happy to offer their help, if it's at all humanly possible.

'Now, just shake the nice gentleman's hand,' I told Chris, 'and let's get the hell out of here.'

We were soon sitting at the bar next door to the bank, nursing our beers. Chris took a long pull from his glass and looked at me with the normal good-humoured twinkle back in his eyes.

'Ooh,' he twittered camply, flopping a limp wrist at me, 'I tell you, Heart, I'd forgotten just how tiring acting is. It's nice to know that all those years at drama college weren't wasted.'

'Yeah, but what if you had been overdrawn?' I laughed at Chris. 'That would hardly have made him your best buddy.'

'Strange as it may seem,' he informed me, huffily, 'I do know pretty well how much money we have or haven't got at any one time and I also know that we ain't overdrawn at the moment either, so it had to be a bank cock-up.' He shrugged and grinned at me. 'I just thought I might as well have a bit of fun while we were there.'

GET OUT OF ZE BUZZ, YOU NAUGHTY MONK

Jan and I were sitting in the llamas' field, quietly watching the world go by when Chris came bursting out of Moolong, yelling excitedly and waving his arms at us. Trying to work out what possible disaster could have struck now, we picked ourselves up and started to stroll, none too hurriedly, back towards the explanation. Chris came running towards us.

'We've got a "shock" party to do,' he announced proudly and breathlessly.

'Do what?' Jan and I chorused.

Chris had just received a phone call from his younger brother Gus who was working in Norway. It was coming up to his fortieth birthday and he wanted to celebrate in style. He was taking over the whole place for a long weekend and bringing twenty of his chums along to help him boogie on down. The one slight snag was that Gus was telling them nothing about where they were going and so wanted us to pull some sort of jolly jape on said chums when they arrived. We had to come up with something. And we had just a fortnight to get it organised.

Giving Chris, Jan and me a silly idea to play with is, by and large, not the smartest of things to do. Over the following few days the three of us put our heads together. I smoked exotic cheroots and we drank another wine lake or two and giggled like overgrown schoolkids. Eventually we had our little scenario worked out. We had added one little extra though. If the guests didn't know what was about to happen then neither would Gus. It just didn't seem to be fair.

'Can't we say we've got beri beri or ebola or something like that and have to cancel?' asked Jan, a touch too wisely.

'Right troops,' Chris started his rallying speech, 'we can do it, no probs. Peeps of our calibre, easy peasy.' We did have ten days left, after all. Why did I feel so nervy? How do I get myself into these situations? Will I ever learn?

What should have been a fairly simple task almost put an end to the plans before we'd even properly got going. I spent the best part of a week working my way through the *Pages Jaunes,* phoning all the fancy dress suppliers in the region, as well as anybody else that looked in the slightest bit useful. We had automatically assumed that every nationality likes to play naughty monks and nuns. I eventually tracked down a shop near Montpellier that said they could help. The three of us piled into the campervan and set off to be ordained.

Some three and a half hours after leaving Moolong, after way too many unwanted scenic detours, we finally found our shop. It was closed for lunch. After we had cussed and sworn and stamped our little feet in annoyance, Jan came up with what, to her at least, was a startlingly simple solution.

'When in Rome, or in our case somewhere near Montpellier, do as the Romans do, or in this case the somewhere-near-Montpellians do.'

If Chris and I had understood what she was rabbitting on about I'm sure we would have agreed with her. As it was, we went and had lunch instead.

We wined, we dined and wined some more. We mooched and wasted time. Surely the shop would be open by now. Wrong again. We mooched and wasted yet more time, by doing the circuit the other way around. An hour later than the time advertised on the sign hanging in the shop door, *M. le gardien du magasin* finally returned.

We stood there like prize lemons as he swayed back and forth, trying to align the key and lock. He dropped the key, bent and fumbled around on the doorstep, hiccuped wetly, stood upright and tried again. This man was taking drunkenness to a whole new level and this in a country that considers drunkenness an art form. Had we not already wasted so much of the day his sozzled incompetence might have been amusing but by the time the idiot had dropped the keys for the nine millionth occasion I'd had enough. I stepped forward, picked the key up and unlocked the door. I pulled the key from the lock, pushed open the door, returned the key to its rightful owner with a polite '*monsieur*' then stood to one side so he could lead us into his emporium. This seemed to cause more than a little confusion for the shopkeeper's poor marinated brain cells but, after the most painful of pauses, he somehow worked out where his forward gear was hiding and rolled gently into the shop. Breathing heartfelt sighs of gratitude and relief we trooped in after him.

Bizarrely, the shop had exactly the same smell as a real, old-fashioned, English hardware shop: musty, dusty and paraffin wax. Peering through the gloom we could make out racks of clothes. Unfortunately we couldn't see *monsieur*. He had disappeared. This was turning into an episode of *Mr Benn* on acid. We stood there squinting at each other, wondering what the hell to do when fluorescent strips began flickering weakly into light. We could finally see some of this place.

It was vast. The building wasn't very wide but it went on forever, with rack upon rack of weird and wonderful cossies filling just about every inch of the hangar. If we couldn't find what we wanted here, then short of mugging an ecclesiastical tourist party on a trip to Rennes and pinching their dirty habits, we were well and truly buggered, so to speak. Jan was making a bee-line for some rather beautiful medieval type dresses when *monsieur* reappeared, *Gitane sans filtre* firmly glued to his lower lip and huge glass of the ubiquitous *vino collapso reddo* in hand.

I explained what it was that we needed, feeling more and more foolish with each word that crawled from my mouth as he looked goggle-eyed at us. Why should three foreigners wanting to rent some habits, monks and nuns for the use of, cause such a problem? Was it my French, the apparent strangeness of my request or just the fact that *monsieur* was as *soul* as a newt that was causing this confusion? He offered every other type of costume. No, we didn't want to be star troopers. *Non merci,* neither did we want to be a pantomime cow and milkmaid nor any of the other multitudinous choices offered. All we wanted was, quite simply, to be monks and nuns. *Enfin,* some vile polyester habits were produced. As we had almost lost the will to live by this time, we pounced on them. Size and price did not matter. Well, it did when we worked out the drunken git had charged us the equivalent of the cost of a small car for the hire of the damn cossies.

'Shan't be using him again,' said Chris. We all agreed.

'Chris,' I begged, 'don't say we'll do anything like this again. I can't cope with the pain.'

'You helped think it up,' he pointed out with unnecessary accuracy.

'Since when has that had anything to do with it?' I snorted.

'Just shut up and drive,' Jan ordered. 'I wanna get home and try my cossy on properly.'

'I wonder what Chantal'll look like in hers?' Chris mused, dribbling quietly.

I was eyeing Jan up in her habit. Do nuns normally wear exotic lingerie? She'd known me long enough to read me like a book.

'You can get that idea right out of your head,' she told me. 'You're supposed to be a monk. Go play with Chris or find an altar boy if you really want to do things properly'

'Sister, you are a spoilsport,' I told her.

'And Father,' she bobbed a slight curtsey, 'you are nothing but a quaint, old-fashioned pervert.'

'Nay Sister,' I corrected her, 'a quaint, old-fashioned, Franciscan pervert.'

'And up yours too, darling,' Sister Jan laughed, crossing herself.

Chris having sweet-talked Chantal into trying her habit on, the four of us were sitting under the walnut tree at what we had designated our table of safety in full ecumenical fig. Chris had ritually and with full solemnity blessed the wine lake we were in the process of consuming when a pack of cyclists roared past. Quite what they made of four raucous members of the cloth yelling drunken cheers of encouragement at them we neither knew nor cared. We were having fun.

The following morning with not very many days left to get everything sorted we had decided a quick panic attack would be in order. A meeting of the battle committee was convened. Chris, Jan and I stared blankly at each other. It never ceases to amaze me how the mind is capable of reaching such depths of uselessness at the most inconvenient of times. My notepad was getting covered in doodles but we weren't managing to come up with anything of any use. There had to be more to this than just being monks for ten minutes at the airport when we went to collect Gus and his little chums. After the pain, anguish and expense of getting the outfits, we wanted to gain the maximum possible usage out of them. They'd cost e-bloody-nough, and we wanted our euros' worth. We scratched our heads and thought.

'Ha!' Chris yelled, getting up and dashing off. I used the break as an excuse to refill our wine glasses. Chris came back clutching his plastic Holy Grail. 'We can bury this somewhere and organise a treasure hunt.'

'Great idea Chris,' I moaned, 'but we haven't got enough time left to work out loads of clues and stuff like that.'

'Yeah,' he reluctantly agreed. 'Tell you what, I'll bury it somewhere anyway, just in case we do get time to do something with it. If we don't we can always leave it buried and work out clues when we've got time, then we can have a treasure hunt later in the season.' Chris chewed the side of his face as he thought some more, and went misty eyed: 'I know, stripping nuns.' He sighed. I choked on my mouthful of wine, laughing my appreciation of the suggestion. Jan gave him one of her *looks*.

'If you want stripping nuns you'd better have a word with Chantal. Either that or change your habit to a nun's one 'cos if you think I'm getting my kit off for a load of drunken letches then you are even more insane than I'd ever taken you for.' That was that idea dealt with then.

The morning of the day of the party and even Chantal was hopping around like a headless chicken on tenterhooks. The way the four of us were jumping you'd have thought we were all suffering from an infestation of fleas. Everything was checked and rechecked then checked again, just to make sure that it had been checked properly the last time it had been checked. We had worked our little butts off, performing the odd makeover miracle along the way. Moolong had become a tranquil house of retreat.

We had transformed the place into something magical and monkish. The refectory tables and tatty chairs were found mouldering in an old barn that Chris hadn't even got round to exploring properly yet, along with a huge pile of hessian sacks that looked as though they would come in useful for something. Authentic wooden bowls and spoons had been found at nearby Esperaza market the previous Sunday. Jan ran up some fine quality table napkins made from the sacks. Plain white candles, held upright in pots filled with sand, was all the lighting we were allowing. The wine bottles, sitting so invitingly on the table, held nothing but tap water and small terracotta pots that originally contained a supermarket dessert of which I was particularly fond were being used as drinking vessels. A giant Bible, bought in a local flea market, had been placed at the head of the table.

High noon and we were ready. Any script-tweaking that was needed would have to be worked out on the hoof. With Chantal left in charge of Moolong, Chris, Jan and I, in all our glory, piled into the little coach that had been hired for the occasion and, with stomachs full of butterflies, set off for Carcassonne and the airport.

Chris parked as close as possible to the airport entrance and after a last-minute panic pray, leaving Chris in the coach,

Jan and I crossed ourselves, took a deep breath, stuck our shoulders back and our chests out and set off to meet our doom.

Our confidence grew as we made our way to the arrivals area. People were looking down, muttering greetings at us and crossing themselves as we walked by. It looked as though we might just get away with this. After all, people do usually believe what they see.

God was on our side, the plane was on time and being a small airport it only took a couple of minutes for the luggage handlers to fling the bags from the plane onto the collection carrousel. Fortunately, no mass of monks got off the plane to cause confusion so it was fairly easy to spot our bundle of brethren. They were the only group, all male or not, who got off the plane. The fact that they were all half-ripped, noisy and excited sort of helped us to pick them out, too.

We watched as they lurched about collecting their luggage and Gus tried to gather them all together. He was scanning the entry hall to see if Chris was there when I stepped forward and said in my best *'Allo 'Allo!* accent, 'Good afternoon bruzzer Colyer. We are 'ere to take you to ze retreat. Please to follow me.'

I turned and, with Jan beside me, led the way to the car park, trying not to laugh at the worried mutterings going on behind our backs. Gus wasn't exactly sure what was going on either. He knew that an English couple were helping at the place but he hadn't met us yet. He also knew that his brother had a questionable sense of humour and was the sort of person who could con a perfectly respectable member of the cloth into collecting his brother and chums from the airport for him, as a favour, just to see what the reactions might be.

We reached the coach and stood either side of the door, smiling and nodding politely at the bewildered multitude as they clambered aboard. Chris, sitting at the steering wheel, cowl over his head, totally ignored them but continued mumbling and fiddling with a set of rosary beads. With everybody safely loaded, Jan and I climbed in and sat ourselves down. Chris continued with his prayers. We sat and waited, and then we waited a little bit more. The mumblings behind us were getting more and more unsure about things. Gus was looking somewhat embarrassed. I was sure he was having difficulty explaining this to his chums.

'Eet eez all right,' I reassured them. ''Ee is just praying to Saint Christopher for a safe journey 'ome.'

'And to Saint Anthony, I hope,' Jan sniggered quietly, sitting at my right hand.

Having recited as many verses of *Eskimo Nell* in Latin as he could remember, Chris finally turned the key in the ignition. As we crawled into motion a cheer came up from the party-goers which rapidly descended into shamed coughs and splutters as they remembered who we were.

There had been some discussion before we set off about whether Chris should come along for the collection so we could maintain the charade for as long as possible. The blindingly simple solution was for Chris to keep his cowl up, thereby covering his face, so Gus wouldn't be able to see him.

The simplicity may have been blinding; unfortunately, so too was the cowl. Thankfully, the road back from Carcassonne is pretty straight. It's just a shame that there are several roundabouts. With Chris's peripheral vision cut to almost zero, he was relying on Saint Christopher's help rather more than he ought to have been. The terrifying screech of brakes and honk of horn that came from the car approaching us was extremely loud and dramatic. Watching the driver hurriedly trying to change the rather obvious gesture of giving us the finger into a fumbled crossing of himself would have been more amusing to see had I not been so in agreement with his original sentiment.

'Saint Christopher, 'ee is wiz us,' I reassured the now quiet, trembling passengers, for once hoping that it was true.

Nerves having stopped jangling, it was time to put phase two of the operation into action. Reaching into my priestly purse I pulled out a spliff I had rolled. I sparked up, toked a deep, deep toke and settled back into my seat. Our pre-planned lay-by came into sight, Chris drove in and stopped the coach. Silently, he reached under his seat and brought out the toy cat o' nine tails that Jan and I had bought him at Quillan market as a Christmas pressie. Clasping his whip, he sat back upright and, staring straight ahead through the windscreen, hissed at me with all due menace and wrath,

'Get out of ze buzz you naughty monk!'

A stunned silence filled the bus as I got down, head bowed and stood beside the coach. Slowly, very slowly, Chris got up from behind the steering wheel and climbed down behind me. As though he could barely bring himself to do it, he walked around me until we were face to face with each other. We were trying desperately not to make eye contact. He looked me up and down then continued walking the circuit until he was behind me once again. He turned and climbed back into the coach, picked up his rosary, kissed it, got back out of the coach and started to pray loudly at my shaking back. Standing behind me he made final adjustments to my position then, after crossing himself, he began to flagellate me, with slightly more gusto than I thought was really necessary. Jan was breaking her teeth as she clamped them together tightly in an almost vain attempt to stop her laughter.

The birthday party said not a word. They sat there trying to pretend nothing untoward in the slightest was happening out there. This was even worse than the Christmas that granny got drunk and broke wind when she was standing in front of the open fire. Some several dozen lashes later Chris stopped and tucked his whip into his belt.

'Now zen, you naughty monk,' he ordered me, 'get back on ze buzz. I never want to see you do zat again and I do not eggspect to 'ave to repeat myself.'

I turned, my head hanging contritely, and got back on board. Chris followed. We continued our journey, the sound of embarrassed silence deafening us.

Not wishing to upset, dismay and alarm our guests too much before we got them back to Abbaye du Roc, we took them on a slightly circuitous route back home so that they could see something of the astounding countryside of the region. It did the trick. They started to relax and the hum of conversation started to pick up. They were ready for phase three.

Chris pulled to a halt a couple of bends in the road above Moolong. Jan climbed down and stood in the gateway to a field, waiting for me to chuck our novitiates out after her. I smiled at them, a smile of beatific gentleness and peace and asked them please to follow Sister Jan. Warily, suspiciously, they disembarked and gathered around her. She smiled her guileless smile and indicated a dilapidated barn in the field.

'Zat, my friends, is where you will be sleepings but now pleeze first to follow me, pleeze'. Jan led them through the gate, her little flock following silently. Behind the hedge we had piled various spades, shovels, hoes, a wheelbarrow and assorted other horticultural implements of destruction. She distributed these amongst the party, and they reluctantly took what she gave them.

'Now pleeze be to following me,' she told them and set off down the mountain, her victims following. 'I will be showing you the fields for you.' She smiled innocently at them. 'We have many diggings to do while you are here.' The nervous mutterings were building up again. It was very obvious that Gus had us well and truly sussed by now but was happily playing along with the game, letting his friends suffer. Well, it was his birthday.

Leaving Jan to take Gus, his friends and their tools for a little walk around the Moolong estate, Chris drove us back down to the car park. We legged it into the restaurant for a last-minute check. It was perfect. Monks and nuns in a rustic setting like this, all we needed was a screaming brat, a donkey and a few sheep and we'd have been fit to grace any Christmas card.

Moolong's restaurant and bar were one long room with a couple of pillars separating and defining the areas. Today there was a wall doing the job. With all the ineptitude and enthusiasm of *Blue Peter* presenters we had created a temporary wall from a framework of lumps of old lumber, stapling loads of the hessian sacks to it. Jan solemnly led our victims in, their conversation grinding abruptly to a halt when they saw the dining room. It was fascinating watching human nature in action. From the loud and excited holiday makers of a couple of hours or so back they were now silent and starting to gather together for comfort and protection, rather like children on their first day at primary school.

Chris made his way to the head of the table, cowl still pulled over his face. Doing his best messianic impersonation he spread his arms, hands palm uppermost and indicated that places should be taken. With much clattering and banging of wood on wood or shin, a seating order was worked out. On the wooden plates in front of each person, on top of their hessian napkins, was a piece of A4 paper lying face down. A couple of the guys were nervously fingering theirs, wishing that somebody else would turn theirs over first to see what it was that was written on them.

'Pleeze bend your heads in praying,' Chris beseeched the congregation. This time, I think, it was *The Good Ship Venus* in Latin. Prayers having been said, Jan brought in the meal. This caused great consternation amongst the gathered throng. They had been rounded up at the airport and now, with no time to draw breath, they were expected to eat and it was only half past four. Ignoring their worries we proceeded to serve the finest, ecclesiastically authentic repast. (The recipe is simplicity itself: take one gallon of best quality tap-drawn corporation stock, one carrot, one onion, one potato and a handful or two of dog rice. Boil for as long as you feel like it or until all the water's evaporated.) Jan picked up the first bowl, passing it to me to fill, and turned over the piece of paper so it could now be read.

Hours of the slightly silent order of St Aloysius of Aqaba:

04.00–06.00 morning prays singing for the goodness of being a life
06.00–06.15 brekfasting
06.15–08.00 prays to thanking for brekfast
08.00–10.00 workings in feilds planting and cutting our foods
10.00–10.25 prays to thanking for workings
10.25–10.30 self wartering
10.30–12.00 workings more in feilds
12.00–12.30 prays to thanking for working in feilds
12.30–13.00 lunchs

13.00–14.15 prays to thanking for lunchs
14.15–15.45 workings in biuldings
15.45–16.25 prays to thanking for working in biuldings
16.25–16.30 self wartering
16.30–18.30 workings in biuldings more
18.30–19.45 prays to thanking for working in biuldings
19.45–20.15 suppings
20.15–21.00 prays to thanking for suppings
21.00–21.15 self wartering
21.15–22.15 prays to thanking for doings of this day
22.15–23.00 prays to thanking for sleepings
23.00–04.00 sleepings

The mutterings rising from the table were showing a mix of reactions. Some had realised that this might not be awfully for real but, pleasingly, there were still several that hadn't twigged and thought this was a really, really bad nightmare holiday. Even more enjoyable for us, though, was the fact that nobody had the bottle to call our bluff.

I was starting to wonder how much longer we could drag this out when the unmistakable bang of a champagne cork leaving a bottle – sounding as though Dirty Harry had opened fire with his large and fearsome handgun – caused the entire birthday party to jump. Chantal had read her script and kicked our wall down. It crashed to the floor revealing a not awfully sober-looking nun clutching a bottle of bubbly, standing in front of a huge buffet spread out with lashings of proper food and booze. It took several seconds for the partygoers to realise what had happened and for them to dive in and make total, riotous pigs of themselves.

The following morning Jan, Chris and I were sitting under our tree chuckling over the success of the previous evening. The sight of a rather dishevelled Chantal, still in habit, scurrying back to her room caused some ribald comment about the standards of some nuns nowadays not being like what they was.

Not long after, the first stirrings of the mob coughed and spluttered their hungover way into life. We promised that we wouldn't pull any more jolly japes on them and they should just get on and have as degenerate a time as they felt like (but they could always do some digging if they wanted). I was about to sneak off to the kitchen to start work, as feeding this little lot was going to keep us all busy, when one of the slightly more serious guys came up to me and said he'd been told who I was and could I possibly take him on a tour of Rennes and the area if I had time. The man was clearly a complete and utter fool. He had just suffered being made to look a prat by us and yet he trusted me to give him a sensible tour. It's just as well I genuinely was too busy. He promised he'd come back later in the year when we weren't so busy. I could barely wait.

WINNING FRIENDS AND
INFLUENCING PEOPLE

Life was good. Somehow or other we had found ourselves living and working in France even though that had never been part of the game-plan. I was back in a kitchen, something I had sworn I would never do again, and much to my surprise was enjoying it enormously. Jan seemed to be enjoying things as much as me, too. We had the llamas and the countryside to keep us amused and we had Chris. This was what the adventure was supposed to be all about.

As the weeks passed we fell into a natural and comfortable work regime. Jan and I were quite happy in the kitchen and Chris was far happier front of house, entertaining the punters, something he was remarkably good at doing. Chantal waitressed and cleaned and Charlie kept popping up, getting in the way.

Through our locals and with being regular customers at various shops and market stalls we were becoming known around the area and had developed an array of people we could stop and have a quick natter with if we bumped into them on the streets. It was a wonderful boost to the self-confidence when we were invited to join a group of French chums for a dinner party. We'd been accepted, this was what it was all about. Blimey, I was cooking in France and not being laughed out of the country, and now we were about to sit at a dinner party, the only foreigners present .

Bruno and Nadine had an organic smallholding near St Ferriol where they grew vegetables which they sold at Quillan market on Wednesdays and Saturdays. Their produce was consistently of superb quality so I bought just about everything we needed in the greenery line from them. Nadine's English was infinitely superior to my French so she became a very useful friend to have around. Bruno, on the other hand, spoke French and that was it. He was also one of the driest, most dead-pan people I had ever met. I was never really 100 per cent sure whether he was taking the piss out of me or not, but what the hell, he made me laugh. Whenever we met up in town we would waste a few minutes in a bar over a glass of Suze. Thinking about it, he must have been taking the piss, why else would he keep buying me Suze? Could have been worse though; it could have been Fernet-Branca.

Their house, however, was definitely taking the piss. Well, the house itself was a rather fine place that Bruno had built with his own fair hands; the problem was the track leading to and from it. It was perfectly serviceable if there was no rain but the moment any moisture hit it, it became a mud bath, passable only with the use of water buffalo, tractor or four-wheel-drive car. There had been no rain for weeks so, the house being accessible, the gang were gathering for a Gallic get-together. They were a rum bunch. There was a chap who did the lighting at rock concerts, a teacher, a civil servant (almost obligatory in France) and a boss-eyed builder that we had already met. There was also a strange-looking cove with very short, peroxide blonde hair and unfortunately green teeth who, we were told, never seemed to do any work but was never short of a bob or two, and an extremely skeletal female who, it transpired, could out-eat and drink anybody. One thing was certain, with this eclectic collection of peeps there would be no chance of running out of subjects to talk about.

The evening was starting off well enough. Jan and the other women were in one corner of the room talking lady things whilst I, in the opposite corner, was being lectured on cookery techniques and business stratagems. I was just thinking that I'd been the dupe of a rather vulgar play on words judging by the reaction to my last utterance when a very scruffy, drunken idiot lurched into the room. The heartfelt groan that went up at his entrance was well deserved. The gang had been trying to shake him off for years but with no luck. He would occasionally disappear for a month or so during which time everyone would keep their fingers crossed that this time he really had gone but then, like the proverbial bad penny, he'd turn back up again, roaring drunk, stoned and as obnoxious as ever. Probably having been locked away in the nick.

Nobody had ever bothered introducing him to us so Jan and I had no idea what his name really was. We had therefore christened him 'the Gypo'. This was not entirely due to his swarthy Romany looks but more to do with his incredibly annoying habit of snatching up a guitar the second he saw one and thrashing away on it like a three year old, howling in pseudo Hispanic agony his rendition of Gypsy Kings classics. That he was tone deaf and couldn't play a note on the guitar did not deter him in the slightest but made it all the more excruciatingly painful for anybody within earshot. Thankfully, Nadine called us to table and Bruno managed to grab his guitar and hurry it out of the room to hide it before any harm could be inflicted upon our collective eardrums.

We had had a little falling out a month or so previously and it looked as though he hadn't forgotten about it. He had staggered into Moolong at almost midnight demanding a meal. I had told him *'Pas d'un* hope *dans* Hades, *mon petit chou-fleur'* as everything in the kitchen had been turned off a long time since. He leant back in the sofa, spread his arms along the back of the cushions, crossed his legs and proceeded to lecture me with all the arrogance and aggression of the truly ignorant. He told me that this was France and that no restaurant closed until the diners gave permission for it to do so and, as a bloody foreigner, it would behove me to mind my 'p's and 'q's and remove myself to the kitchen pretty damn quick and to do as I was told.

A supercilious expression on my face, I nodded my agreement with everything he had said, then, thanking him for his wise words of advice, told him that when I had absolutely nothing left to do in the whole wide world, I might have a little think about what he had said, but I doubted it. I returned to my conversations with the sensible people at the bar thinking nothing more about this confrontation. It had obviously been festering away in Gypo ever since though.

These parties apparently followed a set pattern: the host supplied the main course; the guests the other courses; and everyone brought along something to drink or smoke. As each course was finished we would wipe our plates clean with a chunk of bread or two taken from the mountains of it sitting in baskets along the table in readiness for the next round. With ninety-seven different, very loud and animated conversations going on, everybody was having a fine old time, apart from Gypo, who was sitting three seats away from me on the opposite side of the table. He sat there glowering venomously at me.

Nadine brought in the main course, *Cassoulet*. This is one of the world's all time greatest dishes. There is something about the combination of ingredients that enables *Cassoulet* to be not only the almost perfect comfort food but also one of the gastronomic highlights of your life, with all points in between. Nadine's was perfection. The golden brown crust crunched as the large wooden serving spoon broke through, releasing aromas that wafted out, filling the room, swirling all around us, tendrils of savoury flavoured steam snaking up our nostrils and wrapping down around our tonsils, all mouths filling with eager, anticipatory saliva. The duck, the sausages, the beans, the bliss. Tasting it at last I realised that this was, without a doubt, the finest *Cassoulet* I had ever eaten. Doing my utmost not to make a total pig of myself by demolishing the entire bowlful I was asking Nadine if she could let me have a copy of her recipe. I had barely got the words out of my mouth before Gypo was off. He started banging on the table with his fists, calling me all the names under the sun and a thieving bastard, to boot. It was obvious, he had decided, that this meant I would be putting *Cassoulet* on the menu at Moolong to make loads of money from it which should be Nadine's and of which, you could bet your bottom dollar, I'd be giving her diddly squat. I had a funny feeling that he really didn't like me very much.

Gradually, Gypo got bored being ignored by everybody and glowering at me so, muttering words that nobody understood, he bounced off the wall and disappeared into the darkness outside, leaving us to enjoy the rest of the evening. Which we most certainly did. When it was time for dessert we simply turned our plates over and ate from their bottoms. It was a shame we couldn't get away with this practice in the restaurant, it would have saved a fortune on washing up.

OF BILLY, BART AND
BANK MANAGERS TOO

I was staring blankly out of the window, watching the world go by, when I spotted Jan scurrying towards the restaurant. It occurred to me that whenever she walked into the kitchen I was usually either buried in a fridge or standing with my hand in a dead animal. This particular visit, I had my hand in a chicken and was ripping its innards out. God, I love cooking. Jan pushed open the door to the kitchen and walked in, her nose wrinkling in disgust as she saw what I was doing.

'Jesus, Hewgs, that is revolting.' The gentle shade of green her face turned complemented the henna red of her hair quite, quite perfectly. I extracted my fist from the expired *poule*, examined its entrails like a demented haruspex seeking the answer to the meaning of life, then offered them to Jan for her to inspect. She looked at me pityingly and shook her head.

'There are times when I really do wonder why I married you,' she told me. I blew her a kiss.

'You love me really,' I winked suggestively at her.

'Don't push yer luck,' she smirked.

'Come on then, what was it you were after? It didn't look as though you were coming here for a crash course in butchery.' I could tell from the amused expression on her face that whatever was coming she had a goody. I'd never seen her flapping her hands around or doing a soft shoe shuffle like this before. Feminine she may be, a girlie she ain't. 'For God's sake woman, pull yourself together before I hit you over the head with my dead chicken.'

'Try it, pal,' she warned me through her splutterings of laughter. 'Can you please explain to me what it is about this place that attracts such weirdoes?' She wiped her eyes with the rather grubby tea-towel I'd been using to wipe my bloody hands on.

'You've only just noticed?' I asked in mock amazement.

'I've been living with you too long.' A fair explanation.

'Thank you, dear,' I answered smugly. 'Now are you gonna tell me, or what?' I waved the chicken threateningly.

'You had better take note of this. Let this be a warning or it could end up happening to you.' She waggled a cautionary finger at me.

'Will you get on with it?' I interrupted.

'I've just heard a fascinating conversation between a Dutchman and an Englishman,' she began.

'The *entente cordiale* is alive and strong then,' I laughed. 'Was the English guy trying to buy a bit of herbage from our Dutch campist?'

'Much better than that.'

'Viagra?' I tried again.

'Closer, but you'll never guess. Not even you could come up with this one,' she told me. 'They were discussing prostate problems.' My eyebrows shot up and a huge grin crossed my face. 'I heard them mention having a problem with golden showers and I thought they were talking about roses.' She sniggered, rolling her eyes at her own folly.

'As you would,' I laughed.

'Oh it gets better, just you wait,' she continued. 'It would seem that men of a certain age develop a wee problem, if you'll pardon the pun, with their plumbing.'

'Hmmm?' I hmmm'd warily.

'Yeah, you get to have a problem peeing,' Jan told me, slightly maliciously I thought.

'Hmmm?' I hmmm'd warily and uncomfortably.

'Umm,' she continued, 'it seems it takes time for it all to start flowing, as it were.'

'Yeees?' I asked, squirming quietly.

'Well, if you cough it can cut you off in mid-flow…'

The kitchen door was unexpectedly, violently flung open cutting Jan off in the midst of hers as Chris made a grand theatrical entrance. The pained expression on my face brought him up short.

'What's up with you?' he asked me. 'What're you two chatting about then?'

'Prostate problems,' Jan told him, grinning happily. I grimaced pathetically at Chris.

'Masturbation,' he announced emphatically, thumping his fist on the work surface, making my chicken jump.

'What?' Jan and I squawked.

'Yup, it's the exercise,' he informed us, 'it's good for it. It's a bit like jogging or circuit training only far more fun.'

My mouth fell open to answer but before I could utter a word Jan had turned and, pointing at me, informed me in no uncertain manner to not even think about going down that particular conversational avenue. I smiled a smile of cherubic innocence and virtue at Jan. I opted for the safe route and asked Chris what he wanted instead. He was, unfortunately, warming to his theme.

'It's like this Tantric sex malarkey,' he continued, 'it's nothing more than a cunning excuse thought up by middle-aged men so they can take a breather whenever they need one without it looking as though they're past it.'

I was starting to feel we could be standing here for quite some time.

'Chris,' I interrupted, 'much as I would love to waste some time talking dirty with you, I am rather busy just now. What did you want?'

Looking slightly flummoxed for a second he brought himself back to reality and asked me if I was busy. I held up the chicken in one hand, its innards in the other and raised a questioning eyebrow.

'Ah,' he acknowledged. 'What're you making?'

'A halibut and artichoke soufflé,' I lied. 'Now, do either of you actually want anything or can I please get on with some work?'

As neither he nor Jan could now remember why they were in the kitchen I managed to usher them out and return to the more gentle pursuit of ripping dead animals to pieces. Apart from anything else wrestling was on the television this evening and I was damned if I was gonna miss another gripping instalment in the lives of Hulk Hogan, Randy Savage et al, so really wanted to get as much prep done as possible in readiness for tonight's service.

It had become a running joke amongst the locals that we didn't open the restaurant until eight on a Friday as the entire Moolong staff were all glued to their seats in front of the television watching large sweaty men with shaven armpits throwing each other around a squared circle. It hadn't taken many weeks for the excitement of the thrills and spills to spread. On Friday evenings our sitting room was now full of locals drinking beer and joining us in the intellectual stimulation, discussion and debate this fascinating sport had to offer.

Wrestling was also useful in that it supplied us with idiot codenames by which to refer to punters. Useful when the population around you is changing constantly and a trait, mannerism or way of dressing can be fixed upon to identify who you are talking about. Far more useful is being able to talk about people under their noses without them realising it and, as none of us was really sure how much English any of the locals understood, we had already re-christened several of them to this end.

One couple had taken to using us for their intimate weekends away together. They were a very quiet pair who kept themselves to themselves, so why we decided to name this man and woman after a pair of not awfully good wrestlers that pretended to be cowboy sharpshooters I have no idea. Anyway, Billy and Bart they became and each Friday evening they would arrive and each Sunday afternoon, having barely set foot outside their room all weekend, other than to eat, they would toddle off again having settled their bill in cash. One day I was determined to find out something about our mysterious guests, like what their names really were. Until then, I would just have to content myself with making up my own stories about them. I figured they were international art thieves. I wasn't sure what they would be next week, maybe spies. I would have to wait and see.

The Bartmobile had only just pulled into the car park that Friday evening when it was followed in by an English-plated VW camper. Jan and I had become very fond of our bus and to see what these people had done to theirs was rather depressing. It was obviously a DIY job; nobody could have paid money for this artwork. The poor bus was covered in Templar crosses and someone had pithily stencilled along the side of it the legend copied from above the door of the church at Rennes, *terribilis est locus iste*. I had a sudden, dreadful feeling this *locus* was about to become pretty *terribilis* too. Chris had wandered into the kitchen to make himself a coffee and to point out it was only half an hour to wrestling when he spotted the van through the window. The groan that rumbled up from the very pit of his soul was, I thought, a bit over the top but I was touched to see that he too felt the artwork was rather insulting to the vehicle.

'Oh no,' he moaned, 'not them. Please, not them.'

'Chris,' I yelped, more than a little alarmed at his reaction. I have only ever known him welcome people with open arms and a friendly smile. This abnormal behaviour did not bode well. 'Chris,' I repeated, 'what about them?'

He laughed feebly as though that would be sufficient explanation. I glowered at him over the top of my glasses. Even I can do the *look* when I think it's needed. My look turned to one of complete and utter disbelief when I saw what clambered out of the van. I know my eyesight is useless and I'm as blind as a bat without my glasses on, and I know the car park was a reasonable distance from the kitchen, but that sure as hell looked like a naked, dumpy, middle-aged woman standing there. I turned towards Chris, pointing dumbly at the sight, seeking some sort of reassurance that I was hallucinating. As if by magic Chris had transformed into a swinging door. All I was left with was the sound of footsteps hurrying up stairs and a feeling that I had possibly plucked some not very lucky entrails for the day.

I dashed out of the kitchen in hot pursuit of Chris. I wanted to know what the hell was going on. If there was going to be any sort of trouble I wanted to be forewarned. As I stumbled through the kitchen door I fell over Chantal who was looking totally perplexed.

''Ave you seen…?' she wheezed huskily at me.

'Yes!' I yelled back at her as I disappeared rapidly up the stairs. I burst into Chris' apartment yelling his name. His silence was deafening. I checked each of the rooms. I couldn't find the swine anywhere. Then I noticed the open window. He'd gone straight through the apartment and out of the window. He was probably half way to Quillan by now. What the hell was this all about? Were these people debt collectors? About to serve a paternity notice? Maybe it was somebody's wife he'd had a bit of drunken rumpety-tumpety with and her husband was coming to sort him out? It had to be something pretty severe to have caused Chris to run away like that.

'Hewgs?' Jan's shout up the stairs let me know that she'd seen the newest arrival too. I sped back down. We needed a quick conference of war. Actually, I needed to get my breath back first, not being used to such exercise. It's bad for you. As I panted and wheezed Jan asked me if I knew we had a naked woman in the car park. I'm not at my bitingly sarcastic best whilst fighting for oxygen so made do with nodding weakly and grunting. The ping of the reception desk bell gave me a few seconds' respite as Jan went to see what was wanted.

I made it back to the kitchen and as I couldn't find an oxygen tent to climb into I poured myself a medicinal glass of plonk. I was staring out of the window trying to work out what was going on when Jan came hurrying in demanding to know what was happening.

'Nothing,' I told her. 'Who was that?'

She helped herself to my glass of wine.

'The man from that awful camper booking in,' she replied.

'What?' I howled doing a very passable imitation of a banshee with terminal haemorrhoids. 'That's the bloody car that woman's in.'

'What?' Jan echoed, 'Why didn't you tell me? I thought she got out of that other car.'

'That's the Bartmobile. Dear God, woman, you've seen it often enough.'

We could have stood there bickering pointlessly but yet another car carrying a family with a couple of teenage kids in the back pulled into the car park. When I saw the driver I almost wet myself in panic: it was the bloody bank manager. What the hell was he doing here? I could see all our goodwill with him fast disappearing. Why did he have to turn up now? What sort of place would he think we were running? Oh it really did look as though the FUF had something special lined up for us tonight: the bank manager, a naked woman and us. I hoped to God she'd keep hidden on the campsite for as long as the B.M. was with us. I was going to bloody massacre Chris when I caught him, that was a certainty.

I cringed behind Jan whimpering as the bank manager *et famille* passed the window. Telling me to pull myself together she went off to investigate further. I saw Chantal greet the family, blissfully ignorant of who she was serving, guide them to a table and take their order for drinks. With any luck they'd just stay for the one then go home again and leave us in peace.

The bar started filling with customers and soon the hum of conversation and clink of glasses had restored a feeling of normalcy to the evening. Restaurant orders began trickling in and as the pace of work built up I forgot all about the panic of earlier. We had a very pleasant service, all the orders were nicely spaced apart so we never had any mad rushes and Chantal was able to cope without Chris who had not reappeared.

Everybody had been served their desserts when Jan and I decided to have a quick drink in the bar before we hit the clearing up. Walking through the restaurant I glanced across to the terrace where most of the diners were seated. I couldn't believe my eyes: Billy and Bart were sitting with the bank manager and his family and judging from the number of dessert bowls on the table, they had dined together. Curiouser and curiouser.

Jan hopped up onto a barstool. I went behind the bar to pour us a couple of glasses of wine. Chantal came into the bar to collect a round of drinks for someone, so we started to interrogate her. Fortunately there had been no reported sightings of any naked women but she knew nothing about Billy and Bart's chums and had been kept too busy to overhear any of their conversation. I threatened her with the sack if she didn't start doing something useful, whereupon she collected her order together, told me very prettily to do something anatomically impossible to myself and went back to work.

'That'll teach you,' Jan laughed. 'It's amazing how her English has come on since she's been knocking around with you and Chris.'

My snigger froze in my throat as the bank manager walked into the bar and smiled a greeting at me. I returned it as best I could.

'I would like to convey my thanks to ze chef,' he told me in barely accented English, offering his hand. 'It really was a most enjoyable meal, thank you.' I looked at him dumbfounded, remembering all the translating I'd done last time. Goggle-eyed I bleated, '*Mais…mais…mais*,' as though I was an orphaned lamb and weakly took his proffered palm. He shrugged a shrug which only the French are capable of shrugging and gave me a wry, good-humoured smile.

'Zere is, I am sure you understand, a difference between business and pleasure, *monsieur*. Though I do think you miss some of Mr Colyer's more colourful phrases and expressions from your translations.'

I burst out into huge guffaws of laughter at his explanation. It was priceless. I had just taken an immense liking to him. At least it seemed he hadn't taken any offence at the names we'd called him in his office. Even more did he become my new best friend when he invited Jan and me to join his family for a drink. As we drank he told us that he had heard favourable reports of the food we served so thought, another shrug, that he would bring his family out for a meal. He told us how pleasantly surprised he had been to bump into his old school friend: not Billy and Bart at all, but Claude with his secretary,

Marie. All in all he'd had such a jolly evening that he would be bringing his family here again. We all raised our glasses and toasted each other's health. Conversation was the usual mix of French, English, Franglais and gibberish that seemed to have become the lingua franca of Moolong.

Billy and Bart made their excuses and went back to their room saying they were tired after their drive here but as Georges and Sophie, the bank manager and his wife, were proving to be good company, Jan and I stayed to have another drink with them. Who'd have thought it could be so much fun talking to a bank manager?

Jan and I were lying in bed later, mulling over the oddities that today had chucked our way. We were going to get some mileage out of Chris' ignorance of our new best friend, if either of them ever deigned to return. Sniggering malevolently, I pecked Jan goodnight on the cheek and turned my light off. I had just snuggled down comfortably when she poked me in the ribs and hissed at me to listen. I grunted unkindly words at her then I heard it too, the unmistakable drunken stumble of someone attempting to tiptoe silently past our apartment. I leapt out of bed, grabbed a pair of trousers to preserve my modesty and hopped into them as I began to give chase.

I flung the door open, startling Chris who spun round in an alcoholic pirouette of some grace and beauty then promptly fell flat on his backside. Leaning back on his elbows he stared, goggle-eyed, up at me. He hiccupped wetly, opened his mouth to utter God-knew-what garbage and tried to wave an arm around to illustrate his point. Now, all sober people can remember Newton's Third Law of Drunkenness that states 'the inverse ratio between booze and balance equals lashings of bashes and bruises', but drunks always forget about it. Chris was drunk so he'd forgotten about it. He followed the arc of his arm and rolled gently onto his side, his face thumping onto the ground. Settling down comfortably he lay there. He grunted, farted a fart that would forever change the way he walked, smiled with quiet self-satisfaction and closed his eyes. As far as he was concerned the day was over.

Tempting though it was to leave him there, I knew as we weren't married to each other it wouldn't really be the decent thing to do. Groaning, I bent over and grabbed hold of him. Newton's Fifth Law of Drunkenness, which has got something to do with the inverse ratio of size and weight between the drunken unconscionable bum on the floor and the poor eejit left to cope with him, was proving to be correct yet again. Promising that the following morning I would perform an act on him very similar to the one he had seen me perform on that chicken earlier, I rolled Chris onto his back and tried to sit him upright. Five minutes later and Chris was still supine and snoring; I, however, was dripping in sweat, getting thoroughly bad tempered and wondering if our insurance was going to cover my injured back. Eventually, by kneeling behind him and with judicious use of a knee as a support, I had Chris sitting. With my left leg firmly wedged against his back I had managed to haul myself to my feet and was wondering what to do next when a voice came from behind me. Startled, I jumped back. Unfortunately, in doing that I lost hold of

Chris who crashed back onto the floor. I spun around to vent my spleen to be confronted by the sight of the naked woman, now not totally naked but sporting a very natty camper's head-torch.

'Oh, is that Chris?' she trilled.

I winced.

'We've been so looking forward to seeing him again.'

'Bully for you,' I replied, none too charitably, thankful that I hadn't put my glasses on. I turned and knelt to begin the next round of my battle with the beached whale formally known as Chris. I could see why some murderers cut up their victims: it's so much easier to move something that uncooperative a small piece at a time.

'Is he sick?' she asked.

'As a bloody newt,' I snapped. 'Now either go away or give me a hand. Please,' I added as an afterthought. Fortunately, Jan had seen fit to come and find out what was going on, fearing I may have injured Chris. Somehow, between the three of us, we managed to drag him to his boudoir and hauled him onto his bed. This left us all so exhausted that we ignored any social niceties and departed for our beds without any further words between us. At the moment I couldn't cope with naked women, they could wait till the morning. I was sure all would be revealed then, as they say.

One thing I hated, loathed and detested about Chris was that he never ever seemed to suffer from hangovers. I know that if I had been as hammered as he had I would have been incapable of doing anything other than whimpering weakly and lying in a darkened room for several days, wondering why I wasn't getting any sympathy for my plight. Apart from a few bruises that he couldn't explain, Chris was remarkably chipper as we sat under the walnut tree having our coffee and croissants and not in the slightest bit apologetic.

'Don't blame me,' Chris declared, full of righteous indignation. 'It was Charlie that found them. They're lunatics.'

I thought this was a bit rich coming from him seeing as I wouldn't have classed any of us residents of Moolong as that tightly wrapped ourselves.

It turned out that Chris and Charlie had met this couple in a bar when they were out on a shopping jaunt somewhere near Clermont-Ferrand. The two 'C's were happily ensconced outside a bar drinking beer and had been more than happy to chat to the odd couple of English peeps sitting beside them, even if the woman was naked. Except she wasn't really naked. She was, it seems, a thwarted nudist. They owned a pub in Essex where it had been pointed out to her that not only would the Health and Safety bods have a word or two to say about it but people entering her establishment might be put off staying by the sight of a naked woman working behind the bar. Let's face it, who wants pubes in their pints or their ploughman's? Her answer to the problem was to have skin-tight body-stockings specially made for her, each one depicting a naked body. Bizarrely, this solution to her dilemma had turned into a bit of a hit. Once word started to get around people were travelling from miles away to witness her wardrobe.

The two of them were complete Rennes nuts, had recently sold their pub back in England and were now looking around for a bar to buy in this area. Charlie had pointed out that Moolong was a campsite awfully close to the place so they ought to use it as a base whilst on their property hunt and that the great Henry Lincoln's son was chef in residence, to boot. Groaning at Charlie's absolute, thoughtless stupidity at telling them this and wondering where I ought to run away to before I got caught up in their idiocy I realised, by the expression on Chris' face, that it was too late. Bugger, bottom, damn and blast. All I wanted to do was cook a bit of scoff here, not be a fan club secretary and tour guide to a couple that were evidently more than a couple of burgers short of a barbecue. Their over-effusive greeting of Chris totally belied the fact they had spent no more than sixty minutes in each other's company, ever. Without waiting for an invitation they plonked themselves down beside us at the table. I found myself introduced to Rosy and Al: she, as Chris later so poetically and sarcastically described her, a naked nylon nymph; he a perfect example of medallion man. Screaming inwardly, I smiled and shook hands with them. A couple of minutes of listening to them and I made my excuses, I had to get back to the kitchen, it was lovely meeting them and all that.

'Ooh,' Rosy trilled. I winced. Could she only speak like this? 'I love cooking. Where did you learn?'

'In prison,' I told her flatly. Al nodded sagely. Rosy was struck with a bad case of embarrassed spluttering. I shrugged offhandedly.

'What were you down for?' Al asked, sounding like a man who had knocked around a bit and understood such things.

'Attempted murder,' I said, staring at Rosy while Chris collapsed in a coughing, sniggling heap beside her. 'I tried to kill my parents,' I explained. 'Cooked them a meal with a little extra special added ingredient.' I laughed fondly at the memory. 'The prison authorities, in their wisdom, deemed it fit and proper for my rehabilitation that I learn to cook properly. So now,' I leant forward into Rosy's face and smiled coldly at her, 'here I am.' I laughed a short, manic laugh. 'You will be dining with us, I trust.'

You want mad? I'll give you bloody mad.

THE GYPO'S REVENGE

I was mooching around the bar one morning, not in search of anything to drink but in the vain hope that we had some strawberry liqueur I could steep some fruit in before dumping it in a pud I wanted to make, when Jean-Paul strolled in. Jean-Paul was a lorry driver for a local builders' merchant who, when not busy with that, headed the local hunt. He had spent all his life working outdoors and so looked rather weather-beaten. This, combined with his Mediterranean complexion, his permanent five o'clock stubble and the fact that his work clothes, which he almost invariably wore, were torn and oil stained, meant he could almost be any age from thirty to sixty-plus.

Apart from the early hour there was nothing particularly untoward in this visit. He quite often dropped in during the day for a chat and a beer when he was supposed to be out working in his lorry. I popped the cap on a bottle of beer and passed it to him and, having accepted the futility of my search,

I returned to the kitchen with Jean-Paul following me. It was only a flying visit, he told me, but he wanted to book the restaurant for a hunt do. There was some special anniversary or event they wanted to celebrate. I hadn't the faintest idea what he was talking about but took the booking anyway. I was getting used to working things out on the hoof when needs be and I couldn't see the hunt being any problem. We already knew pretty well all of the members as they were using the bar as their local watering hole most of the time now. The locals enjoyed Chris' fun in the bar and they seemed to be enjoying the food Jan and I were throwing at them from the kitchen and they definitely enjoyed leering at Chantal.

Jean-Paul started popping in and out of Moolong rather more than normal, making sure that all the preparations for the hunt party were going well. Whatever reassurance he was given that nothing untoward would happen, he still seemed worried. We promised faithfully that there would be no monks or nuns in attendance and that I would do my level best not to poison anyone. What more did he want? I couldn't work out why he was getting himself in such a tizzy. After all, there shouldn't be much that would faze such a hairy-arsed hunter. As far as I was concerned this was as straightforward as it comes. We knew how many people we were expecting, we knew what they were eating and we knew what time they were due to eat. We could do this one blindfolded, whilst riding a bicycle, backwards.

Saturday morning and today was the day. The sun was shining as it ought and there was just the merest hint of the gentlest breeze taking the edge from the baking early summer heat. We had everything organised, we knew exactly what we were doing. We were in control. However easy you know these sorts of party ought to be there is still a nervous buzz to the day which slowly builds until the service starts and by then it's too late to do anything about it. You learn how to contain the nerves and use them constructively, not to let them take over and screw everything up.

Jan's garden was by now producing useful quantities and varieties of herbs and salad stuff and she had just delivered her first wheelbarrow load of the day. We were running through what else was ready for harvesting when a very battered Renault 5 hauled into the car park. Four men got out of the car carrying what looked worryingly like rifles. The driver opened the boot of the car and half a dozen assorted hounds bounced out, leaping and yapping, wagging their tails, bouncing and barking. They were all so happy to be dogs. They were running round and round the four men, trying to trip them up, while the men made ineffectual grabs at them when any came within grasping distance. I stared through the kitchen window at this picture, in disbelief.

'What the f....?' my voice tailed off. I had a nasty feeling about this.

'D'you want me to find out?' Jan asked, already half way through the door. I watched her walking over to the thrashing, yowling throng. There were arms, boots, rifles and dogs going everywhere. The dogs spotted Jan and charged towards her. This was going to be far more fun, saying hello to a stranger and sticking their noses into its crotch. The dogs were like a cauldron of worms. One of the beasts, deciding it wasn't fair that the rest of the pack wouldn't let it in to sniff Jan's bum, took a flying leap at her instead: it caught her square in the chest and with dogs all around her legs she didn't stand a chance. She was flat on her back in the dirt with the now deliriously happy hounds stamping all over her as they fought to lick her face to show how ecstatic they were to meet her. The more she fought to get up again the more the dogs thought it was a brilliant game. I could tell from the not-very-ladylike language that was wafting across that Jan was not exactly reciprocating their sentiments.

The huntsmen finally came to their senses and worked out that Jan needed their help so they waded into the mêlée, kicking and flinging the dogs away from her. The dogs were going bananas, rushing round and round in circles. This was one of the bestest games ever. Poor old Jan was getting knocked down again as fast as she managed to raise any part of herself from the ground. Five irate humans versus six over-excited, tail-wagging, barking, bouncing dogs isn't really an even match but I was enjoying the slapstick. All it needed was the roll of the drums, the crash of a cymbal and a clown with a water-squirting flower in his buttonhole and the picture would have been complete.

I froze to the spot and my blood ran cold as I saw one of the huntsmen kick a dog out of his way, break open his rifle and load it. I was through the door yelling at him to put the rifle down when he pointed it in the air and pulled the trigger. The crack of the shot echoed around the valley leaving a chill, still silence in its wake. The world stopped moving for a second. The dogs were the first to recover and took off. Using Jan as a springboard they disappeared into the undergrowth leaving her lying on the ground, a winded, dusty, doggy-footprint-covered nervous wreck.

Chris appeared on the balcony in a total panic, convinced a murder had just been committed at Moolong. One of the hunters gallantly offered Jan his hand and then, rather over-enthusiastically, yanked her back up onto her feet. They all began trying to brush the dust from her clothes. She was smacking their hands away, she could take care of that herself, thank you very much. Copping a quick grope was not included in the cost of the day's entertainment. I was about to grab Jan to safety and say a few words when the honking of a horn announced the arrival of a second car. It parked beside the Renault and a further two be-rifled men clambered out followed by yet another brace of dogs.

'*Mais… mais… mais…*' I burbled pathetically and ineffectually. A hunter patted me comfortingly on the shoulder.

'No problems,' he reassured me in English. Why is it that every bugger in the world knows that phrase and every time I hear it I know it is a blatant lie? I was getting the distinct feeling that the old FUF was about to come riding into town again with all guns blazing.

They were here for the party, they told us. I informed them I was over the moon to hear it but that they were a just a wee bit early, almost ten hours early, in fact. They were not in the slightest bit put out by this. They knew they were early, they happily told me. Calling their dogs to heel, a command universally and unsurprisingly ignored, the hunters strolled off together in the direction of the bar leaving Jan and me standing there open-mouthed and shell-shocked. I saw Chris standing on the balcony. He shrugged questioningly at me. All I could do was shake my head weakly back at him. I had no idea what was going on. We walked back to Moolong, small fists of nerves starting to punch painfully in the pit of my stomach.

Chris, Jan and I were having a quick, panicky, hissed, 'What's going on?' conversation when Jean-Paul arrived with another three cars following him in convoy, horns all blaring. I dashed across to the car park and grabbed him as he was hauling himself out of his car and demanded to know what the hell was going on. They weren't supposed to be here until this evening. From the grin on his face I could tell he'd already had a noggin or two; from his breath I could tell it had been anis. Oh brilliant, he's supposed to be in charge of this bunch of gun-toting throwbacks and already he's as drunk as a skunk. There were dogs and scarily-armed men all over the place. This was bedlam. Didn't I know, he slurred at me, this was what they did every year? Spend the day pouring as much booze down their necks as possible, having a bloody good scoff in the evening then rounding the day off by drinking more until they fell over.

'Why didn't you tell us about the rest of it then?' I snapped at him.

'But everybody knows,' he smiled at me as though that was explanation enough, his eyes already having difficulties focusing, 'we do this every year.'

With Chris and Chantal opening bottles of beer as fast as they could, Jan dashed back to her garden to finish picking whatever was ready and I hurried back to the kitchen to check supplies. We were expecting forty people for the binge this evening and already half of them were here and it still was not even noon. I was buried deep in the fridge when the claxon announcing the arrival of more merrymakers made me jump and crack my head on a cupboard; bottles jumped and chinked together on its shelves. Today was fast developing all the components of a first-class disaster. It wasn't a pretty picture. For the home team there were Chris, Chantal, Jan and me (why did Charlie have to be back in England when we could do with another pair of hands?). On the other *équipe* there were forty heavily-armed men intent on getting as drunk as possible, and they had all brought at least one dog. How the hell we were going to keep them out from under our feet so we could get the work done for tonight was an interesting problem. Granted, some of this was slightly of my own making as, when the restaurant wasn't actually open, I didn't discourage people from popping into the kitchen to say 'hi' and to see what I was up to. Already I'd had a couple of bodies come round the door with greetings, their dogs trying to sneak in behind them.

Chris realised that at the speed the hunt was getting through the booze our careful stock calculations were going to be several lakes short and we were in danger of running dry before the entire party had even turned up. He was going to make a mad dash to the supermarket for as much booze as he could carry. I gave him a hurriedly scrawled shopping list of my own, wished him *bonne chance*, and begged him to be as quick as possible. Once the first hunter decided he wanted some food to mop up the beer slopping around in his guts they'd all decide they wanted feeding.

Whilst they were still concentrating on the serious business of laying the initial alcoholic stomach lining down, I sneakily removed the lunchtime menus and pared them down to as few options as I dared. There was no way I was giving a bunch of drunks, and even worse, a bunch of armed drunks, any sort of leeway. Once the booze properly took hold there would be all these testosterone-pumped, macho, swaggering huntsmen trying to prove how incredibly butch they were. Primeval didn't come close to it. I've seen the sort of chaos that can happen when things get out of hand. I once stopped at an hotel which, unfortunately, had a stag party in the restaurant. By the end of the night the restaurant looked as though a bomb had hit it. I suspect it needed completely redecorating – and that had been without guns and dogs present. What chance did a pair of girlies and a pair of dilettantes have if it all kicked off here tonight? I caught sight of the llamas through the kitchen window: they were standing in a line watching the goings-on from the other side of the river, wearing condescending, imperious grins. If things did go pear-shaped they could well find themselves at the bottom of the list for feeding today. That should wipe the smug smirks off their faces.

Chantal came dashing into the kitchen in a panic to tell me that she only had twelve bottles of beer left. I was reluctantly handing her my emergency stash of six when a huge volley of shots and cheers shattered what little was left of our frazzled nerves. Chris pulled up outside and we dashed out to unload him. As I was being buried under boxes of eggs, bags of baguettes and carriers of assorted goodies Chris had bought 'just in case', I couldn't help hoping that no unsuspecting, ordinary punters turned up today.

The alcohol was flowing freely and the hunters, thankfully all playing outside, were doing exactly what they had set out to do. The conversation level was rising and men were weaving from group to group, punctuating their chats with salvos of vertically-aimed and wasted buckshot. None of them was bothering in the slightest about their dogs which had also split into groups. There were dogs paddling in the river, there were dogs bounding in and out of the trout pond, there were dogs haring up and down the mountainside disappearing into the undergrowth: they were on a 'staff outing' and were making damn sure they enjoyed themselves too.

Despite the utter chaos, the huntsmen somehow managed to keep themselves just the right side of sober to have lunch without causing us too much grief and we started to relax. We even managed the odd, mildly malicious laugh of schadenfreude. One of the huntsmen was in the middle of a particularly demonstrative arm-waving, chest-slapping, pinching, poking and punching chinwag with his chums when a group of dogs hurtled past him playing chase. The lead dog clipped the hunter's legs which made him spin drunkenly. The pack following hard on the heels of the first dog charged through to finish the job. To a barrage of shots and jeers from his chums the hunter lay flat on his back in the dust, his shirt front soaked in beer.

By mid-afternoon we had been forced to close all the doors to the restaurant and kitchen as the dogs were continually wandering in and out, checking what was going on and if there was anything to eat. One particularly acrobatic, mangy dog had the cheek to try to climb in through a half-window so we even had to close them to the narrowest of gaps. We were sweating as much as our porcine pals currently sitting in the ovens. We had become inured to the rifle blasts outside so goops of liquid were no longer being splattered across the kitchen, over ourselves or each other as we jumped at the unexpected cracks coming from the rifles of this pissed-up progeny of Herm that were littering the front of the place. Two men, we could see, were sitting at a picnic bench, leaning against each other snoring, oblivious to the maelstrom that was raging all around them. Everybody and everything was fully occupied. I couldn't have asked for better; we were able to get on with our work without disturbance and we also had amusement outside the window when we needed it. It was Jan who managed to put a damper on the proceedings by pointing out a particularly scruffy specimen of humanity that we hadn't spotted earlier.

'That's bloody Gypo over there!' she squawked indignantly.

We knew exactly what that sod was up to. If there was a way of conning free food and drink you could be sure that he was going to be found somewhere near the centre of things. I warned Chris and Chantal to keep an eye on him and to make sure he wasn't ripping off too many people. Hairy-arsed hunters they may be but they were all smashed hairy-arsed hunters and they definitely needed a responsible adult to look after them. Not that I consider myself a responsible adult, far from it, but I do have a particular abhorrence of people scrounging drinks from drunks.

By the time the diners took their seats for the meal there wasn't a sober guest in the house. Even the normally most abstemious of the group was almost incapable of standing. I had a quick peek round the kitchen door and got the feeling that knives and forks were not likely to be the most used of tools this evening.

Gypo had managed to get his feet firmly under the table. He was sitting there as though he really was a member of the party. I went through to the bar to find Chris to have a word with him about this. I sure as hell didn't want to see him getting a free meal. We agreed that we would give him the option of eating from the menu at whatever the cost worked out to be or to pay the same as the hunters and eat what they would be having. Next came the minor irritant of who was going to give him the news. I told Chris that as it was his establishment the honour should fall to him. Chris told me that as the chef I was in charge of anything to do with the kitchen and restaurant so I could tell him.

Not having time to argue over this we opted for a round of paper-scissors-stone.

I lost.

Gypo's enraged roars that greeted the information I delivered to him were, I thought, a wee bit over-dramatic. He went back into his usual rant about me being a bloody foreigner. By now I could almost recite it word for word along with him and it was boring me rigid. I can be remarkably stiff-necked at times and this was one of them. There was no way that I was backing down to this scrounging oxygen thief. Eventually, things were taken out of my hands when Chris had the common sense to avert a punch-up between Gypo and me by dragging me by the collar of my jacket back into the kitchen. I was seething. Tonight, Chris told me to chill as we really didn't need any bother when there were so many weapons lying around being tended by inebriates. Gypo would be barred the next time he came in but tonight, for the sake of peace, he would be allowed to get away with it. Reluctantly I agreed. As I couldn't be sure which plate was going to end up in front of him I couldn't even spit in his food. Some things can really ruin a service.

The orchestrated, concentrated chaos of the supper passed in a steamy, sweaty symphony of succulent smells, sounds esurient and ecstatic, all melding together, wafting, rolling back and forth twixt restaurant and kitchen. Whatever potential there had been for disaster hadn't come to fruition and the whole meal passed, thankfully, like sweaty clockwork.

Knackered, Jan and I decided to have a quick break before starting on the mountain of cleaning and clearing up that needed our attention so we toddled through to the bar to join the merrymakers for a few minutes and a restorative noggin. Our entrance was greeted with raucous cheers, applause and back slapping. Then, like magic, glasses of wine miraculously appeared and were passed to us through the murky, smoky haze that filled the room.

So we drank and chatted. Arms were being flung around in full Gallic fashion, cigarette ash and drink flying through the air. Realising that if I stayed with the party I would end up somewhat the worse for wear and the clearing up wouldn't get done, I started to make my excuses to leave. I was looking around for Jan to tell her what I was doing when Gypo appeared at my elbow, prodded me and with a great show of his reluctance to have anything to do with me, handed me a glass of wine gesticulating vaguely in the direction of the bar and told me it was from 'him'. I raised my glass at the 'him' I thought it was that Gypo had indicated. The 'him' returned the greeting and so I figured I'd got the right guy and drank the wine he had so kindly purchased for me. Five minutes later I had extricated myself from the throng and was back in the kitchen trying to return some semblance of order to it.

I had been gone for about twenty minutes when Jan finally managed to escape from an amorous and persistent hunter to get back to the kitchen. The first thing she noticed as she walked through the door was me lying unconscious on the floor. She dashed back into the bar calling for Chris to come and help. The urgency of her yells cut through the party noises. The entire bar, alerted by the tone of her voice, tried to press themselves into the kitchen to see what the hell all the fuss was about. Jan and Chris forced their way through the circle of drunks, peering at me, offering their advice and opinion. At the front of them was a smirking Gypo.

'*Il est bourré,*' he sneered.

Shoving him out of the way, Jan told Chris to get a couple of the more sensible hunters to help get me up to bed, away from this lot, then they could try to work out what had happened to me. Back in our apartment I was dropped onto the bed. Neither Jan nor Chris could see any sign of injury and I seemed to be breathing normally. To all intents and purposes it just looked as though I was fast asleep. Figuring that if I wasn't back to normal in the morning they'd call a doctor, but probably a good night's sleep would sort out whatever the problem was, Jan undressed me and rolled me under the duvet, then went back down to finish cleaning the kitchen. After all, there wasn't anything else she could do.

By the time she had finished all the cleaning and clearing up she was shattered. It had been a bloody long day and the last thing she needed was me to worry about. A quick glass of something before she came to bed should help her to relax a little.

The bar was still heaving when she walked in but space was made so she could get through. A stool was gallantly vacated for her and she gratefully hopped up onto it, settled herself comfortably, and took a long restorative glug from the glass of wine which Chantal had poured her. She was starting to unwind. She was managing to ignore the sarcastic comments about my 'accident' that drifted over from Gypo and was chatting quietly to Chantal as she served customers. A couple of the hunters had strolled over to join in their conversation and they were all nattering amicably together. Chantal was pouring the four of them fresh glasses of wine when a sight, most horrid to behold, appeared.

I burst into the bar, stark bollock naked, ranting and raving like the madman I probably am.

'Which one of you bastards has stolen the fucking loo?' I screamed at my stunned audience. The exultant howl of '*ouais*' and a footballer-style celebratory punch of the air from Gypo resulted in, as there wasn't room in the bar to swing the proverbial cat let alone a punch, him being hit repeatedly, double-handed on the chest by the hunter who was standing next to him and shoved ignominiously out of the bar and onto the street where there was more room for the hunter to administer chastisement. Jan's shock at my entrance was replaced with relief at realising that there was nothing drastically wrong with me. The relief was rapidly replaced by extreme hilarity. Trying to suppress her laughing she took me by the arm and steered me back towards modesty, dignity and the privacy of our chambers. She tried to quieten my rantings and convince me that nobody had really stolen the loo at all. It was where it always lived and no Hugo, that's a chest of drawers.

The following morning, apart from feeling as though my brain had been replaced with a soggy flannel, I remembered not a thing that had happened the previous evening after I had gone back to the kitchen. I couldn't criticise Jan, Chris or Chantal for seeing humour in my mishap. Underneath the laughter, however, was the extremely unpleasant suspicion that Gypo had had more than a little to do with it.

Our suspicions were confirmed not much later when a very hungover Jean-Paul walked into the kitchen.

'*Salut chef. Ça va?*' He looked worriedly at me. He had just been told what had actually happened and come straight round to let us know that everything had been taken care of.

Sebastian, the hunter who had taken offence at Gypo's laughter last night and pushed him outside the bar intending to give him a good thumping for his rudeness, noticed something odd. When extracting his hand from his pocket Gypo had managed to pull a small twist of paper out of it. Sebastian had snatched it up and opened it to find it contained a couple of tablets. Sebastian may not have known exactly what these tablets were but he had a pretty shrewd idea. It looked as though we were right and Gypo had been responsible. The scumbag had slipped something in my drink. Luckily for Gypo he managed to make his escape whilst Sebastian had his hands full with the evidence. Unluckily for Gypo he was awoken at about six that morning by several extremely hungover and very irate members of the hunt who explained to him the folly of his ways. We could rest assured Gypo wouldn't be showing his face around here again for a very long time, if he knew what was good for him.

As Chris so succinctly summed up the whole episode, 'Well Hewgs, that's your reputation in the same state as your liver now. Both shot to shit.'

GRAILS AREN'T US

Summer was well and truly upon us. We didn't stop running and sweating from the second we crawled out of our pits in the morning until we finally crawled, exhausted, back into them again at the end of the day. Life was just a blur, each day merging into the next, our lives accompanied by the daylight chorus of screams, laughter and splashes from around the swimming pool or the evening chink of glass and crockery and the hum of conversation around the bar and restaurant. The campsite was heaving with holiday makers. Tents of different sizes, shapes and colours polka-dotted the fields, and some of the caravans and campervans were so large that we wondered how the drivers had managed to get the things here. The lanes round here were frightening enough in an ordinary car, let alone trying to drive along them in a giant lorry. However the visitors got here we didn't care; we were just happy to see them. The majority of them were Belgian or Dutch, closely followed by Brits and Froggies and fortunately, as far as I was concerned, none seemed to have any interest in Rennes whatsoever, or if they did I was far too busy to find out about it. This was just a lovely country campsite where they could recharge their batteries and have a generally good time, and the Dutch could see what hills looked like. Mostly, everybody got on with each other. As in all large gatherings, there was the odd clash of personality or misunderstanding, but matters were usually resolved pretty quickly. People were on holiday.

It was the poor old llamas that drew the really short straw. Jan and I simply didn't have the time to take them out walkies like we had been doing. The rotten animals refused to accept this and were behaving very snottily towards us, refusing even to say 'hello' when we went to feed them. Victoria seemed the most irritated by this turn of events and we learnt very quickly to keep out of her way whilst she was eating. One morning, Jan was filling the llamas' buckets with nuts when Victoria, who being the biggest of the bunch always muscled in to get to the food first, took a mouthful from her bucket of nuts and then quite deliberately sprayed them straight into Jan's face. Being pebbledashed with llama nuts is apparently rather painful, so ever after, if any of them flicked their ears back and laid them flat, a sure sign that a llama is not in the very best of humours, then we knew to get the hell away from them.

Chris seemed to have drawn the human short straw. He was up before anyone else in the morning so he could clean the swimming pool. He was rushing around like a fiend possessed during the day doing any maintenance that was required plus keeping the place clean and tidy, and then running the bar in the evenings, which meant he was the last one to get to bed at night. I'm sure there were some nights when he didn't make it back to his bed at all as he'd had people partying on so late in the bar. He also continued to struggle with the arbitrary and sporadic fault in the electrics that fed the concrete mushrooms the caravans and campervans would plug themselves into to power their portable showers, microwaves and televisions. This glitch had now been going on all season and, short of ripping the entire electrical system out and replacing it with a new one, there didn't seem to be any obvious, instant solution to the problem. The muttered oaths and obscenities that wafted around the valley as Chris tried, yet again, to make the system work properly became just another part of the general background noise of daily life at Moolong.

Chantal worked her surprisingly efficient little socks off then, after work, seemed to play fairly hard at having them taken off her by whichever Adonis she had selected from the young gods that had been strutting their stuff around the swimming pool earlier in the day. Charlie continued to appear and disappear as he saw fit and, more often than not, when he was here, only managed to get under all our feet rather than be of any actual help – but then that's Charlie for you. The only real fly in the ointment was the continued presence of Rosy and Al who seemed to be in no great hurry to start their search for a bar.

Al was tolerable, mainly because he never said anything. He would just sit about drinking bottles of beer looking mean, moody and macho, trying to give the impression he was an 'ard man, 'ard but fair. Rosy was a totally different *marmite* of *poissons,* as they don't really say in this neck of the woods. We all now fully understood and sympathised with Chris' reaction to her arrival. Her voice. Her complete and utter lack of ownership of even one brain cell. Her exquisite sartorial taste. To be fair to them, though, they were good at leaping in to give a hand, clearing tables and washing up when we got really busy. I know Rosy would rather have been out the front, clearing the tables and chatting to the punters and scaring them but we managed to convince her that as the washing up area was so small, Al couldn't possibly fit in there without breaking every piece of crockery we had, so she would have to take care of that side of the operation for us.

So far, they had been tormenting us for what seemed like a lifetime even though it was actually only about six weeks. Miraculously, somehow, she had still not crossed Georges the bank manager's sight. Keeping her away from him had become almost an obsession. Unwarranted surprises such as Rosy in all her lycra-clad glory looming up to serve you were, we felt, not too good a way of making sure our more respectable customers stayed around. Much to Jan's and my chagrin, we hadn't been able to play any nasty jokes on Chris as he had walked out onto the terrace one evening, just in time to see Chantal, Georges and family all greeting each other. It was obvious that B.M. had been here before. I had been looking forward to a bit of naughtiness there and my guileless 'who?' did nothing to convince Chris that I hadn't had something up my sleeve. Billy and Bart had never been back after running into Georges and his family here so we needed to keep taking Georges' money to make up for losing our best, most regular and reliable guests. I'm sure he'd have appreciated the difference between business and pleasure.

Jan and I were driving back from Quillan market one day, muttering general inanities at each other when, on driving round a bend, I was forced to slam the brakes on to avoid a pannier-laden bicycle being pushed along by a man bowed double under the weight of his backpack. As he turned around to see what was coming up behind him we spotted who it was. Jan, very uncharitably, burst into peals of laughter.

'Looks like you're going to have a little chum to play with again.' She sniggered at me. It was the madman Saint Chris II, the non-mechanic.

'Please, just keep him away from me,' I growled back at Jan as I drove round him, ignoring his waves and cries for assistance. We trundled back to Moolong with me grumbling about lunatics. Jan gave me one of those 'pot-calling-kettle-black' looks, which I thought was slightly unfair of her.

Today being Saturday meant it was barbie night. As the tourist season had progressed we had noticed just how many of the campers were having barbecues so, ever on the look-out for ways to make an extra euro or two, we decided that we would have a weekly one. Saturday was the day that the majority of new guests booked in and we figured that as they had only just arrived they would be too exhausted after their journey to be in any sort of mood to cook for themselves and that the sight and smell of burgers burning on an open fire would persuade them to come over and give us some of their hard-earned dosh. Our astuteness in matters of sooty meat ensured that it soon became the busiest evening of our week.

We had been back for about an hour, unloaded the bus, changed and started work when Saint Chris II eventually staggered into Moolong's reception area to book himself in. Chantal popped her head round the kitchen door, a huge grin on her face.

'Monsieur Lincoln,' she sniggered at me, 'zere is someone in reception who would like to see you.' I didn't bother looking up from the pieces of meat I was threading onto skewers in readiness for tonight.

'Chantal,' I sighed heavily, 'will you please tell whoever it is there is no Monsieur Lincoln here and even if there was that he is far too busy to come out and chat about anything at the moment and will continue to be too busy to chat to anybody at all for the foreseeable future.'

She grinned somewhat sarcastically at me and retreated to convey my message to Saint Chris.

This was Chris II's third visit to Moolong and even when we hadn't been as frantically busy as we were at the moment I had had problems avoiding him. Now, being almost permanently trapped in the kitchen, I knew I was going to be a sitting duck for his attempts at trying to talk with me about Rennes. There was nowhere I could run and hide to get away from him.

I had been moderately civil to him on his previous visits. In some ways I actually felt rather sorry for him. He was not the brightest of souls and did take everything so seriously. He seemed to have read every single word ever written about Rennes-le-Château and its mystery and, unfortunately, he believed every word that he had read and appeared to be incapable of separating any chaff from whatever wheat there might be, not that I thought that there was any wheat to separate in the first place. Now, with the pressures we were working under I doubted I'd manage to remain polite; I really didn't have time to indulge him and his fairy stories.

The Saturday barbies, whilst not the hardest evening's work of the week, were among the longest. As so many of the happy campers had small children in tow we always tried to start cooking by six so parents could get their munchkins fed and watered and still have them in bed at a reasonable hour. This ploy proved to be pretty effective as it meant almost all of the wee brats were locked away by about half past eight so they weren't getting under the feet of the drunken revellers who were starting, by then, to descend on us.

The initial kiddy rush of the evening was over so Chris had wandered across from the bar to grab a quick bite to eat and have a chat with Jan and me before the full adult onslaught got under way a bit later.

'I see your little chum is here again,' he laughed at me.

I gave him a *look*.

'Well I'm sorry mush,' I told him, 'but I think it's gonna be your turn to get stuck with him this time. You know I'm never out of the kitchen at the moment.'

'I'd say you were out of the kitchen and into the barbecue, *mon brave*,' he grinned at me. 'Here he comes now.' He waved a cheery greeting to Chris II. 'Think I'll leave you to it,' he said, scurrying rapidly back to the safety of his bar.

'Ah, Mr Lincoln,' Chris II smiled at me, 'I'm so glad to see you again. I've got so much I need to tell you.'

'Chris, please,' I groaned at him, 'how many times do I have to tell you my name isn't Lincoln? That's just a made-up name that my father uses. If I want to use a different name, I'll make my own one up. I tell you what, if you have difficulty with Hugo why don't you call me Roach Highwalker instead?'

'But Mr Lincoln,' he persisted.

'Dear God,' I sighed wearily. 'Look Chris, please, I really am very busy at the moment so can this all wait until another time?'

'But it's important,' he whined.

'And so is me feeding our customers,' I told him firmly, 'so please can you just let me get on with my work?'

'Well, will you let me order something to eat then?' he asked, miserably.

'Of course.' I tried to keep the tone of my voice civil. 'What would you like?'

'I've become a vegan,' he announced proudly. 'Have you got any vegan cheeseburgers?'

Fortunately, before I could strangle him, Jan pulled him to one side. Being a vegetarian she does at least understand and have time for some of the more peculiar dietary fads that are knocking around these days.

The following morning Jan was coming back from her garden with some of the veg that we would need for the day's meals when Chris II came running up to her.

'Mrs Lincoln!' he called.

Jan shot him a *look*.

'What?' she snapped at him. She was getting as peeved with him as I was about being continually called by an incorrect name.

'Is Mr Lincoln around? I need to talk to him urgently,' he panted.

'As far as I know,' she told him, 'Mr Lincoln is still in Gloucestershire.' That seemed to confuse him.

'But he was here last night. I don't understand. When did he go there?'

'Oh, about thirty years ago, I think,' Jan told him over her shoulder as she tried to make good her escape to the sanctuary of the kitchen. Chris II stood there, a very confused expression on his face.

'But Mrs Lincoln,' he trotted to catch her up. 'I don't understand,' he repeated, coming alongside her. 'How can he be there, he was here last night?'

'My father-in-law wasn't here yesterday, was he?' Jan asked sarcastically. 'I didn't see him.' This seemed to throw Chris II into even deeper confusion.

'Well, when can I talk to him?' Chris persisted.

'The next time he's down at Rennes,' Jan suggested helpfully, running to the safety of the kitchen.

'Don't blame me,' I told her as she stomped through the door. I had been watching the goings-on through the window. I was starting to get the feeling that the only way any of us were going to get any peace was to bite the bullet and go and talk to the madman who was now squinting myopically through the windows at us. Noting that we really ought to get round to cleaning them, I took a deep breath and walked out to have a word with him.

'Chris,' I began.

'Ah, you are here,' he interrupted me. 'Mrs Lincoln said you were in England.'

'What?' I squawked. Now I was confused.

'She said you were in England and not coming back here for thirty years.'

Trying to deal with people whose IQs don't even reach room temperature can be very trying at times.

'You must have misunderstood her,' I snapped at him. 'As you can see, I am here but I really don't have the time to stand and chat about Rennes with you now.' He opened his mouth to talk, but I held up a calming hand to quieten him. 'Listen, if you really think that whatever you have to tell me is that important then come and talk to me when I've finished work tonight. OK?'

'But what time will that be?' he whined.

'I don't know.' I really was having difficulty remaining polite. 'Eleven, twelve, I dunno. It depends on how busy we are and how many interruptions I keep getting.'

'But I'm in bed by ten.'

I wasn't sure whether to bang my head or his head against a brick wall.

'So either stay up late,' I told him, then muttering the next few words under my breath, 'I'm sure your mummy won't mind. Or, set your alarm clock but that, I'm afraid, is the best I can do for you. Now if you'll excuse me I do have rather a lot of work to do.' He was almost crying in his frustration by this point. I turned, leaving him to it and went back into the kitchen.

Chantal had joined Jan in the kitchen and the two of them were peering out through the rather grubby windows, watching our conversation.

'What does zat silly man want zis time?' she asked me.

'The usual,' I replied. 'What else?'

'Oh dear,' she sympathised. ''E is not very...' she stopped, struggling to find quite the right word in English, but settled instead on the perfectly adequate French words. '*Il est fou. Non?*'

'*Oui,* Chantal,' Jan and I agreed with her, '*il est vachement fou.*'

Before we could get any further discussing the mental shortcomings of some of our guests the day descended a bit deeper into the cesspit as Charlie's van rumbled past and into the car park. I had hoped he wouldn't be showing up for the next few weeks trying to chat to us when we were all far too busy to stop working just to play with him. Then again, a thought popped into my head; maybe I could get Charlie and Chris II together? They could play with each other to their hearts' content. After all, when Charlie had a few drinks inside him he could be as irritating and brainless as Chris II. They ought to suit each other perfectly and there might even be a bit of malicious amusement to be gained from it.

Rosy waddled into the kitchen to see if there was anything she could do to help. By this point, I knew the day was never going to get any better than lousy.

We had almost finished the cleaning and clearing up after lunch when I spotted a rather smartly-dressed gentleman who I thought looked vaguely familiar walking across from the car park. I knew I wasn't expecting any frozen food or kitchenware reps today so figured it had to be someone for Chris. The man sat himself at a table on the terrace and quietly looked around him at the campers at play as he waited to be served. Chantal went across to take his order. She brought him the beer he ordered and stood chatting to him. I saw her shake her head categorically at him several times.

The man gave Chantal something: she shrugged, turned and walked towards the kitchen. I figured it was probably a punter who wouldn't take no for an answer about the kitchen being closed for a couple of hours.

'Oogo,' Chantal came into the kitchen looking none too pleased, 'zere eez a man outside.'

'I know,' I told her, 'I was watching through the window. What does he want?'

'You,' she replied, passing me a business card. The penny dropped. I now realised why he looked familiar. It was the journalist that Chris and I had mistaken for the insurance agent a few months back. "E knows 'oo you are and zat you are working 'ere.' She shrugged. 'I told 'im you would not want to see 'im.'

Chris wandered into the kitchen.

'Who's that bloke you were talking to?' he asked Chantal. 'He looks familiar.'

'That's 'cos he is,' I told him. 'It's that journalist that turned up here earlier in the year.' Chris's laughter did not cheer me up one bit.

'You'd better go talk to him, mate,' he grinned at me. 'You can explain why you lied to him like you did.'

'Go on, Hewgs,' Jan chipped in. 'You know he'll just sit there until he does catch you.'

I did my usual ineffectual cussing, swearing and foot stamping. Chris, Jan and Chantal were unimpressed by my tantrum.

'Just tell him the truth,' Jan told me, 'that you know nothing about Rennes and you're not interested in it. All he can do then is make things up.'

'He'll doubtless do that anyway,' I snapped back at her.

'Yeah, but think,' Chris butted in, 'if he writes rubbish about you you'll be able to sue the shirt off his back.'

'Good idea, oh wise one,' said Jan. 'That ought to make us enough in damages to buy something decent in Spain and not just a shack.'

'Not to mention,' Chris added, 'it'll probably get us more customers if they know you're here.' My apathy towards Rennes was fast turning into antipathy. Why can't people just accept that I have absolutely no interest whatsoever in Rennes and leave it at that?

'Go on, my little Grail hunter,' Jan patted me comfortingly on the back, 'go get it over with.'

''E is very insisting,' Chantal added. Normally her little mistake would have made me grin, but not today.

I poured myself a huge glass of wine and threw most of it down my neck in one gulp; coughed, spluttered, topped my glass up and, knowing that for once the others were unfortunately talking sense, stamped out to tell this nuisance to go away and to leave us in peace. Was it not bad enough that I had Chris II following me around trying to talk to me about his fantasies without a damn journalist coming to join the party?

'Ah, Monsieur Lincoln,' he extended his hand and smiled to show how clever he thought he was at finding me, 'so we meet again.' I ignored the proffered palm and looked at his business card.

'Monsieur Bertrand,' I told him, 'had you done your research properly you would know that I have never, do not and will never use the name Lincoln. If you wish to speak to me will you do me the common decency of using my correct family name and not call me by somebody else's *nom de plume*?'

'So, you admit zen zat you are Monsieur Lincoln?' What is it with some of these people? Why don't they ever listen to what I say? 'Do you mind if I ask you some questions?' he continued, regardless.

'Before you do,' I replied, 'make sure you take this into account. I know nothing about Rennes-le-Château, I know nothing about my father's work and what he is doing and what is more I care about it all even less. I am here to cook, that is what I do for a living, that is what I am interested in and care about. Now, if you wish to interview me, to see how I feel about being an English chef cooking in France then I will be more than happy to accommodate you.'

'Come, come Monsieur Lincoln.' His snort of derision and disbelief turning to a sneer of utter contempt. 'Zen tell me what you are doing here in zis region, living so close to Rennes-le-Château if, as you say, you 'ave no interest in ze story?'

I felt like screaming.

'It may have escaped your notice,' I returned his sneer, 'that, not so long ago, there was a slight flood in this area. My friend's establishment was seriously damaged in it. I am doing the sort of thing that friends do for each other if they are able. I am doing my best to help him recover from it.'

'*Et alors*, so why eez your friend here zen? You are going to have to do better zan zat, *Monsieur* Lincoln, if you wish to convince me zat you are not 'ere treasure 'unting.' He thought he had me there.

'Mr Lincoln! Mr Lincoln!' Chris II came running excitedly up to me. 'I'm sorry I didn't get to talk to you last night,' he panted, 'but I was asleep.'

This was too good an opportunity to miss.

'Chris, let me introduce you to,' I checked the name on the business card again, 'Francois Bertrand. He is a journalist who is interested in Rennes.' I turned to Bertrand. 'Monsieur Bertrand, allow me to introduce you to Chris. I'm sure he'll love to talk to you about Rennes and he can also tell you that I really do know nothing about it all.'

They deserved each other. Hopefully, they'd keep each other amused and leave me in peace. I could see that I really would have to introduce Charlie to them. Jan stuck her head out of the kitchen window.

'Hewgs, telephone call for you!' she shouted across at me. I grabbed the lifeline.

'Gentlemen,' I told them, 'if you'll please excuse me, I am needed inside,' and hurried off, leaving them to discuss whatever fantasies these fantasists find to discuss. Jan, Chris and Chantal were still in the kitchen, all laughing at me.

'It's OK, Hewgs,' Jan said, 'I thought I'd better try to save you when I saw Chris turn up too.'

'Thank you, dear,' I told her with heartfelt appreciation of her mendacity.

The evening's service passed smoothly and we were all scrubbed down and cleaned up by eleven o'clock. Figuring it ought to be safe to be seen out in the world as Chris II should be zipped up in his sleeping bag and Bertrand would have driven back to whichever stone he lived under, Jan and I wandered through to the bar for a drink. Charlie was sitting there talking to Chris as he served the drinks and Chantal was scurrying around with trays of glasses, delivering them to the appropriate punters.

'What's all this that Chris has been telling me about you having a fan club?' Charlie greeted me.

'Not now, please, Charlie. I'm far too tired. How 'bout being useful for once and buying me and Jan a drink instead?'

We'd been sitting there drinking and chatting for about half an hour when Rosy and Al walked into the bar. Rosy had an even stranger expression on her face than normal. She sidled up to me and whispered furtively in my ear.

'Hugo, I've been waiting for you to finish work but I need to tell you something.'

I groaned.

'What's that, Rosy?' I asked, reluctantly.

'Somewhere quiet,' she added. I could feel Jan sniggering beside me. This was all I needed to round the day off, Rosy trying to indecently proposition me. She dragged me back into the kitchen, hitting the light switch as she walked through the door. 'I think you need to know something important,' she trilled *sotto voce*. I winced *sotto voce*.

'Rosy, it's been a long day,' I reminded her. 'What is it?'

'Well,' she started, 'you know that funny man with the bicycle that's always hanging around?'

'I had noticed him,' I replied, sarcastically.

'Well,' she continued trilling as quietly as she was able, 'he was talking to a man today.'

I rolled my eyes and raised my eyebrows heavenwards. 'Rosy, I introduced them.'

'But I bet you don't know what they were talking about.'

I put a fingertip to my lips as I pretended to consider things.

'Could it possibly have been something to do with me and Rennes?'

She looked somewhat miffed that I had managed to work that much out.

'Yes,' she persisted, 'but they think you know all about it.'

'I know, Rosy, but thanks for warning me.' I did my best to sound appreciative of her concern.

'But that's not all.' She looked worried about whatever it was she was going to have to tell me next. 'They were going round the campsite all this afternoon asking people what they knew about you.'

'Oh, fer crying out loud,' I groaned.

'And,' she continued, 'they think that when you were taking the llamas out for walks you were using them as cover while you were really looking for the Holy Grail.'

I nearly wet myself laughing when she told me that.

'Oh Rosy, you're priceless.' I gave her a peck on the cheek; she blushed slightly. 'Thank you, you have just brightened up an otherwise thoroughly mediocre day. That is one of the most ridiculous things I've heard in ages. You keep up your spying on them for me please, let me know what the pair of lunatics get up to.'

Her face lit up with a huge smile as she thought how important she could be to me.

'And,' she added proudly as she delivered her *coup de grâce*, 'there's more. It turns out that they think the Grail is actually buried here and that you're keeping it to yourself.'

'I think they may just be in for a wee disappointment there, Rosy.' I shook my head in amazement at their stupidity. 'Anyway, never mind my little Mata Hari, you just keep an eye on them for me and keep me posted with whatever they get up to.' I put my arm round her shoulder and, grinning broadly, steered her back to the bar. As we walked in Jan, Chris and Charlie all gave me knowing looks and winks.

'Well that was certainly a quickie, even by your standards,' Jan quipped.

'Thank you, dear.' I laughed, 'Just wait till you hear what Rosy's got to tell you.'

She tried to shut me up but I told her to explain to the others what it was that she had just told me. Chris' laugh was ear-splittingly explosive.

'Yeah, so. The Grail *is* buried here,' he howled. 'I buried it myself.'

I'd forgotten all about the plastic Grail Chris had buried for the treasure hunt we had never had the time to get around to organising. Charlie, Chris, Jan and I all looked at each other. We were all obviously thinking along the same lines. Chris poured Rosy a drink and passed it to her.

'Brilliant, Rosy,' he told her. 'Thank you.'

Chris, Charlie, Jan and I spent the rest of the evening trying to work out how we could turn Chris II and Bertrand's lunacy to our own amusement. We knew there had to be some way of steering them towards our Grail. We were dying to see what their reactions would be on discovering it. The one minor flaw was that Chris could only vaguely remember where he had buried the thing as he had been drunk when he had interred it. He tried telling me that I had helped him plant it but, if that was the case, then I must have been even drunker than he had been 'cos I had no memory of having done it at all. But with the benefit of Rosy's spying we figured we still ought to be able to get some sort of naughtiness going.

MAYBE GRAILS ARE
US, AFTER ALL

Over the following couple of days Rosy was in her element. She was skulking around in the undergrowth following everything Chris II and Bertrand were doing then hurrying back to report to me. The way I looked at it, whatever the two of them were up to it was keeping them and Rosy out of my hair, which meant I could get on with my work without being hassled by lunatics.

We had finished our breakfasts and toddled off to start on our day's labours. I was slightly surprised to see Charlie's van still in the car park at ten o'clock: he was usually well on the road by this time. I guessed that he must have ended up hammered last night and had awarded himself a day off to recuperate. I shrugged my shoulders, dismissed him from my thoughts and returned to my travails.

I had become quite adept at keeping half an eye on the car park, checking if new campers were arriving and booking in.

Bertrand's silver Renault pulled up and, again, Chris II was there to greet him. Charlie strolled across towards his van: maybe he was going out, after all? He greeted Bertrand and Chris II, stopped and had a quick chat with them and seemed to pass Chris II something. After a couple of minutes chatting he shook Bertrand by the hand, patted Chris II amicably on the back then clambered aboard his van and trundled off. Chris II and Bertrand watched him drive away then, grabbing Bertrand's briefcase and some papers from his car, they hurried excitedly over to the restaurant terrace, spread themselves across a table and spent the rest of the morning poring over a map, drawing lines and squiggles and who knew what all over it. Rosy, as nonchalantly and inconspicuously as she was able, kept walking past them, trying to keep an eye on their goings-on.

She came into the kitchen to give me her latest update. 'You'll never guess what they're doing,' she trilled at me.

I winced. She was probably right.

'What's that then, Rosy?' I asked, slightly reluctantly.

'They're talking about making a film of themselves finding the Holy Grail. I heard them.'

'I tell you what, Rosy,' I laughed, 'in the immortal words of Mrs Mia Wallace, that would be "an exercise in futility".' She didn't understand what I was talking about but there was nothing new there. I ushered her out of the kitchen telling her to keep up the good work and returned to my lumps of dead animal.

'So, my little spy-master,' Chris laughed as he walked into the kitchen, 'what wonderful information did the naked secret agent have to impart this time?'

I relayed the information.

'Well that should be the world's most boring, pointless and useless film,' he guffawed. 'D'you think they'll have the common decency to ask my permission to film here?'

I grinned at him. 'I wouldn't hold your breath, mate.'

'Morning M,' Jan sniggered at me as she came in with her veg of the day. 'Any news to report from Jane Bond?'

'Piss off, hairy legs,' I told her, good-naturedly.

After work that evening Jan and I wandered through to the bar for our ritual after-work noggins. Charlie was sitting at the bar looking even smugger than usual and Chris had a rather more than normal idiot grin on his face. I thought they must have been swapping smutty jokes with each other and, not being averse to such childishness, I stupidly asked what they were up to.

'Oh, just putting a cat amongst a couple of pigeons,' Charlie informed me cryptically.

'Please, try talking English for a change, Charlie,' I groaned.

'I think Charlie has rather excelled himself this time,' Chris chipped in.

'I doubt it,' I snorted.

'Come on then, Charlie,' Jan prodded him in the ribs, 'what you bought this time? A chieftain tank?'

'Nope.' Charlie's smugness can be extremely irritating at times.

'For crying out loud,' I snapped at him, 'are you going to make us play guessing games all night or are you going to tell us what you've been up to?'

He grinned at me. Jan gave him one of her *looks*. He decided it was probably safer to tell us.

'I've written a poem for Chris.'

Jan and I looked at Chris.

'What?' we chorused.

'Are you two turning funny?' I asked.

'No, not him,' Charlie grinned. 'Idiot Chris, your Grail-hunting buddy.'

I was confused.

'So, you're trying to pull him then?'

It looked as though this nonsense could go on forever and we weren't even drunk yet.

'It's all very simple,' Charlie started to explain.

'No surprise there, then,' Jan interrupted.

Charlie tried giving her a *look*. It didn't work.

'I wrote him a little verse to help him on his quest. Told him I discovered it when I was in the Bibliothèque Nationale the last time I was in Paris.'

Charlie wasn't the most literate of people, even on a good day and with a following wind. I didn't see how he could manage to pen anything to convince a Grail hunter, however mentally deficient that hunter might be.

'I have vague memories,' I reminded him, 'that Chunky Chesterton was never too kind to you when he came to marking your English homework and as you failed your French O-level I can't see anything good coming out of your fraudulent literary exercise.'

Charlie ignored my jibe, sat upright on his stool, drew a breath then recited in his best cod poet voice: 'The Grail doth rest 'neath tiny hills that lie 'longside the river flowing black, all under the watchful eye of the beaked eyrie.'

Jan and I nearly wet ourselves laughing when we heard his rubbish.

'Charlie,' I stammered out between giggles, 'that is absolute garbage.'

'Just you wait and see,' he told us pompously. 'Just you wait and see.'

'Wasn't that what Chunky used to say to you as he flung the blackboard duster at your head?'

The following morning, for want of anything better to do, I was back in the kitchen, a steaming mug of coffee in front of me, contemplating a mountain of duck legs that had been on special offer at the market and which I had been unable to resist.

'Monsieur Lincoln!' Bertrand's voice calling from reception brought me back from my ducky dreams. 'Monsieur Lincoln!' he called again. Knowing full well that I had to get this over and done with as quickly as possible so I could get on with my work I stomped out to see what he wanted. 'Ah, Monsieur Lincoln, *bonjour*.' He extended his hand, I ignored it. '*Ça va?*' His fake smile did not amuse me.

'Monsieur Bertrand,' I began wearily, 'I am sick of telling you my name is not Lincoln. There is no such person as Hugo Lincoln. He does not exist: the family name is Soskin.

If you are incapable of calling me by my own name then, as I told your colleague, try calling me Roach Highwalker.'

'But zat is stupid,' he sneered at me. 'Zat is a made-up name.'

Hooray. He was finally getting the message.

'And so is Lincoln. Now what do you want today?'

'At least your frien' Charlie iz more amicable and willing to 'elp us.' Bertrand's sneering was really getting up my nose. I'm sure that if this had been happening to someone else I would have found it all highly amusing; as it was, it wasn't happening to someone else and he was irritating the hell out of me. 'We 'ave proof,' he continued, 'zat ze 'Oly Grail iz 'ere on your property and we shall be discovering it. Zen you will be eating your words.'

'Bully for you,' I sneered back at him sarcastically, 'you just keep on thinking that. Now, if you'll excuse me I am going back to work.'

I started back towards my lair where I could at least talk some sense to my duck legs.

'I need to talk wiz your frien' Charlie,' he called to my retreating back. 'Where iz 'e zis morning?'

'If his van's still here then I guess he's still in his pit, sleeping off the excesses of last night,' I snapped over my shoulder. 'If his van's not here, then neither is he.'

'Zis is important,' Bertrand continued. 'Surely even you,' his sneer becoming more pronounced, 'should be able to understand 'ow important zis is for ze 'ole world.'

I couldn't even be bothered to respond to this last totally preposterous utterance. I could feel a large glass of medicinal plonk being called for.

Chris was lurking in the kitchen clutching a cup of coffee when I stormed back in, waiting to find out what it was that Bertrand had wanted this time. I groaned and told him. His sympathy was genuine.

'Those two are starting to get beyond a joke,' he said, a tinge of annoyance creeping into his voice. 'I think I'm gonna have to tell them to sling their hooks.' Good idea as that sounded, I knew that it would be a serious mistake to make. They would be even more convinced that we were up to something and trying to keep it hidden from them, and then we'd never be able to get rid of them.

Jan and Chantal wandered in together whilst Chris and I were still trying to work out what to do about our resident *über*-lunatics. They were still finding Bertrand and Chris's conviction that Moolong was the final resting place of the Holy Grail mildly amusing but then, they weren't the ones being hassled all the time. Thankfully, Jan's sensible side kicked in once more and supplied us with some sort of answer to our problem.

'Look, Charlie's not really doing anything useful,' she explained. 'He's the one that's got them wound up with his silly verse, so get him to sort them out. That ought to keep all three of them occupied for a bit.' She grinned.

Chris, Chantal and I couldn't have agreed with her more. Charlie was unanimously voted the whipping boy. If necessary we'd steal his van keys and hide them so he couldn't escape. It was about time he paid for his board and lodging. It was agreed: we would let him know his fate tonight, as soon as he got back here.

Charlie was late getting back that evening. We hoped he hadn't suddenly developed psychic powers and knew what was lying in store for him. Fortunately, albeit not as far as he was concerned, the reason for his tardy arrival was far more mundane: his van had broken down. He had managed to cobble back together whatever it was that had broken but until he could get the requisite spare part he wouldn't risk driving anywhere. We poured a few gallons of consolatory wine down his neck, then broke the news to him.

It was pointed out to him in no uncertain manner that, as he'd given Bertrand and Chris the poem which had got them so worked up, it was now up to him to help them solve the riddle he had posed and to keep them as far away from us as was humanly possible. He tried telling us that he needed to work on his van, he tried all manner of excuses, none of which worked, and finally he just settled on the drunken-sulking technique. We weren't buying any of these ploys; as far as we were concerned he was now, finally, gainfully employed as chief nuisance remover. I asked him what he'd actually told the two lunatics about the poem and which book he'd supposedly found it in. He stopped sulking immediately and instead looked hugely proud of himself.

'I told 'em I found it in a book called *La Colline Fa-ni*.'

'Do what?' He had me flummoxed on that one.

'*La Colline Fa-ni*,' he repeated. 'Do I have to explain everything?' We told him he did. 'So, what does *colline* mean in English?' he asked.

'Hill,' I replied.

'Correct. And what English word does *fa-ni* sound like?'

I looked at him blankly for a moment then the penny dropped.

'*Fanny Hill*,' he translated, just to make sure that all us ignoramuses had followed his genius. 'And,' he continued, 'I do believe you will find that there is a village called "Fa" not a million miles from here.'

Oh God, did he look pleased with himself. When we'd all finished laughing we agreed that for Charlie this was an absolute masterpiece. We just hoped he could follow it through. He explained his doggerel to us.

'It's all very simple,' he said. 'The black river is the road. The little hills are the verges and the beaked eyrie is none other than,' he pointed dramatically through the door towards the mountain opposite, Le Bec. This was definitely not the Charlie I knew. It all made a perverse sort of sense that Bertrand and Chris, we were sure, could only be taken in by.

The following couple of days saw Chris II and Bertrand slowly, painstakingly, inch by inch scouring a couple of Moolong's fields. Charlie did try tagging along, offering helpful words of wisdom and advice but apparently his laughter at their excitement at unearthing a length of barbed wire was too much for the intrepid archaeologists and they told him to go away.

'What had they thought they'd discovered?' I asked Charlie when he ambled, hands in pockets, into the kitchen.

'I dunno,' he shrugged, 'the Crown of Thorns?'

'Yeah, that wouldn't surprise me,' I agreed. 'So, other than the Crown of Thorns, what else have Carter and Carnarvon discovered?' I asked him.

'A few old washers, odd bits of wire and some rusty nails.'

I opened my mouth to comment on their haul, but Charlie didn't let me get a word in.

'Don't worry,' he reassured me, 'they've worked out that the nails weren't long enough to have been used in the crucifixion.' He laughed at the expression of stunned amazement on my face. I had only been going to offer that as a sarcastic suggestion. Bertrand and Chris II were truly doing their utmost to give nincompoops a bad name. What was it about the Rennies that made them so convinced the Holy Grail was buried round here and that they would be the one to find it?

Jan and I were sprawled out in our apartment enjoying our afternoon break when Chris strolled in with a huge grin on his face. It turned out that Bertrand had come to the conclusion that he really ought to ask Chris' permission to conduct their excavations. Putting all his acting training to good use, Chris managed not to laugh at him but pointed out that whatever was found on his land belonged to him so Bertrand and Chris II could forget any ideas they had about running away with any treasures they unearthed.

Bertrand had tried blustering but rapidly gave up, realising that, for once, it might be a good idea for him to shut up. If he antagonised Chris too much his hopes of discovering the Holy Grail and who knew what other manner of wonders that might lie hidden on Moolong territory would rapidly fly out of the *fenêtre*. Chris was feeling quite pleased with himself, as it looked as though his little bout of thespianism was going to keep Bertrand and Chris II on their best behaviour, at least for a short while. He had suggested that they tried digging in one particular field which was right opposite Moolong, where he knew nobody had touched that particular piece of land for a long, long time. Bertrand believed this and almost courteously thanked Chris for his advice but, as Chris pointed out to us, he was pretty sure that was the field he'd buried his Grail in, plus it also meant that we could keep an eye on what the two madmen were up to without having to bother moving our backsides too much. There were times when Chris really did excel himself. If we were lucky, this could end up having even more amusement value than the wrestling.

A couple of afternoons later Chris and I were leaning against Moolong's wall having a crafty fag break, idly watching Bertrand and Chris II hard at work trying to discover their very own Valley of the Kings.

'Has anybody suggested dowsing to them yet?' I asked Chris.

'Don't think so.' We looked at each other and grinned. 'Not so far, anyway.'

'Pendulums or hazel wands?' I mused.

'Oh, one of each, I think,' Chris answered after a couple of moments' contemplation.

'I don't think one hazel wand will be much use,' I sniggered childishly.

'And you really think a full complement of wands will help those two?' Chris stubbed his cigarette out ready to go back to work.

'Hang on a mo, mush.' I grabbed his arm to stop him moving. We watched as Bertrand stooped then started to scrabble around on the ground for a few minutes. He leapt into the air and we could hear his howl of triumph down here where we were standing. 'What on earth have they found now?' I was staggered by the reaction to whatever it was.

'Don't worry,' Chris reassured me, 'it's probably just some bits of old flowerpot, or something. I found a load of rubbish like that piled up by the swimming pool when I moved in so I dumped it all up there out of the way.'

Whatever it was that they had found was certainly giving them cause for excitement. They stood, heads almost touching, as Bertrand cleaned the soil from their new artefact. It must have been something pretty spectacular. Seconds later, the two of them were on their knees, not offering up prayers of thanks as I first thought but sifting carefully through the pay-dirt. Chris and I looked wide eyed at each other, shook our heads in wonder at their sheer, blind stupidity and, leaving them to it, returned to our respective work stations.

As I walked into the kitchen Jan was staring through the window, watching Chris II and Bertrand hard at it.

'What have they found?' she asked. I snorted.

'Broken flower pots,' I told her.

'Well, that certainly is cause for celebration.'

Rosy poked her head out from the washing-up room.

'What are you two laughing at?' she trilled. I winced.

'The usual, Rosy. The usual,' I replied. 'Tell you what, why don't you go for a little wander and see what our mad archaeologists have succeeded in unearthing this time?'

She didn't need to be told twice. She had been given a mission and waddled off happily to investigate. Jan and I kept an eye on her through the window. At first, Bertrand and Chris II looked as though they were being incredibly secretive about things and wouldn't show her what it was that they had discovered but Rosy is nothing if not persistent. Eventually, the combination of her hassling and their excitement was too much and they granted her a glimpse of their treasure. She scurried back to base to deliver her report.

'You'll never guess what they've found,' she trilled. I winced. 'It's real this time.'

'What's real, Rosy?' Jan asked.

'They've found some Roman pottery, they have.' Rosy looked quite taken aback at the thought that there might actually be genuine artefacts lying buried here, at Moolong.

'Don't worry, Rosy,' I comforted her, 'it's not Roman, it's just broken flower pots.'

'How do you know?' she wailed painfully. 'It might be Roman.'

'Well I grant you the terracotta may indeed have come from Italy,' I tried explaining, 'it may even have been made in Rome but if you think about where it is that we live then it's far more likely to have come just the few short miles up the road from Spain. Either way, antique the stuff ain't.' Her face fell. 'Go ask Chris, he'll tell you how it really got there.' Looking slightly downcast she went to go and check with Chris what I had just told her.

'Ah, poor Rosy,' Jan lamented. 'I think you upset the poor woman, Hewgs.'

'*Moi?*' I asked, a picture of innocence.

'Hugo! Hugo!' Chris II called from reception, almost hysterical with excitement. He'd even remembered to call me by my proper name.

'Coming!' I shouted back. 'Just a mo.'

With Jan smirking at me I went to see this momentous discovery. He could barely contain himself, he was bouncing up and down like a space hopper on a pogo stick.

'See,' he held his hand out to show me several small, grubby shards of terracotta, 'I told you we'd find something.'

I laughed, probably slightly more uncharitably than was called for.

'Yes, Chris.' I tried controlling my mirth. 'It certainly looks as though you have indeed found something. What, pray tell, do you think it is?'

'It's Roman pottery, Bertrand says so.' He was going to be banging his head on the ceiling if his bouncing got any worse. 'It proves they were here.' His eyes were glistening with tears of joy at their discovery of so-called proof. 'It's not going to be much longer,' he went on, 'till we do find the Grail. Charlie's poem was right.'

It would have been churlish of me to burst his balloon.

The screams and howls that rang around the valley late the following morning could probably have been heard in the Garden of Gethsemane. Chris, Jan and I were standing in the kitchen, discussing the day's menu. Convinced some sort of horrible accident must have befallen a guest, we dashed outside to find out what the hell was going on. My heart was thumping like a steam hammer as I tried to remember what the French emergency telephone number was. How were we going to handle this catastrophe? Would my French be up to explaining the disaster over the phone and would I understand any instructions I was given? Would we be able to cope with blood all over the place? I realised that nobody else seemed to be panicking. Why not? Jan and Chris were spinning round, still trying to see where the ambulance or rescue helicopter would be needed when Chantal pointed out to us that the racket was coming from the two madmen, Bertrand and Chris II, who were bounding and leaping around the field, howling in triumph.

'I'm gonna throttle those two,' Jan panted, trying desperately to restore her breathing and pulse rate to normal.

'Not until I've done it first,' Chris barely managed to croak.

'I need wine,' I managed to say, and staggered pathetically in the direction of the bar. Jan and Chris followed me weakly.

It was difficult enough pouring the wine without spilling any of it. My hands were shaking from the shock and all three of us needed to use both hands to steady our glasses sufficiently to get them to our mouths without pouring their contents all down our fronts.

Our equilibrium had just about been restored when the two idiots came charging into the bar.

'We've done it! We've done it!' Chris II crowed exultantly, bouncing around the room. Bertrand was looking nauseatingly pleased with himself as he stood there, his hands behind his back.

'Az I knew we would do,' he said quietly and with cold pride. 'We 'ave ze Grail. We 'ave beaten you to it.' I thought it was only bad actors in B-feature horror films who laughed like he did then. 'All ze time you thought you were being so clever,' he spat the words venomously, 'but I knew what you were up to and now, it will be me, Francois Bertrand, 'oo will go down in 'istory as ze man 'oo discovered ze 'Oly Grail.' He brought his hands out from behind his back to show what he had been hiding from us and held aloft the Holy Grail. Even Chris II stopped his leaping around and looked startled at Bertrand's behaviour and tone of voice. Were it not for Bertrand's aggression this might have been mildly amusing; as it was this mad Frenchman had become strangely intimidating, not to mention slightly frightening. It was Chris who first came to his senses.

'Er, yes,' he coughed, clearing his throat, 'well, congratulations.' Bertrand smiled thinly at him. Chris held his hand out. 'May we see it? After all, you did discover it on my property.'

'Let them see it, Francois,' Chris II begged him. Reluctantly, Bertrand passed it to Chris who made a great show of admiring this wonderful object, then he passed it to me. I took it from Chris and examined it. Finally, Jan took her turn. She passed it back to Bertrand who snatched it from her hands.

'So,' again that malicious sneer in his voice, 'what do you 'ave to say for yourselves now?'

'I think, Monsieur Bertrand,' Chris started, 'that there is one major flaw to your discovery.'

'Hah,' he snorted, 'and what iz zat?'

'Well, it seems to have escaped your notice,' Chris pointed out, 'that the thing is actually made of plastic.'

'You people are so stupid,' Bertrand spat at us. ''Ow can it be made of plastic? Plastic 'ad not been invented at ze time of our Saviour.'

I was trying desperately to keep a straight face. I could feel Jan shaking beside me as she grabbed hold of my wrist, trying hard to keep herself under control too. Chris wasn't bothering with any self restraint.

'I'm sorry to piss on your parade, Francois, but I can assure you it really is made of plastic. I should know: it's mine, I've owned it since I was a child and I buried the thing only a few months ago.'

Chris II was looking worried by our attitude towards this most wonderful of Christian relics. He didn't seem to be able to work out how we hadn't thrown ourselves at their feet in awe and admiration.

'Give it to me,' Chris ordered Bertrand. 'I'll prove it to you.'

'All you will prove,' Bertrand told him, handing the Grail back, 'iz zat you are just like ze Apostle Thomas 'oo could not believe ze evidence of 'is own eyes wizout first putting 'is fingers into ze wound of our Lord. If zat iz what iz needed, zen so be it.'

Chris took the cup from Bertrand then put his hand in his pocket and brought out his cigarette lighter. He held the flame to the side of the chalice. Chris II yelped in alarm.

'You sink zat will 'arm it?' Bertrand sneered.

Chris just shrugged at him. The heat of the flame made the Grail start to melt. It bubbled slightly, then a small hole appeared in its side. Chris II snatched it from Chris' hands.

'Look what you've done to it!' he cried. 'That's sacrilege.'

Bertrand snatched the Grail from Chris II and flounced out of the bar with Chris II scurrying in hot pursuit after him.

'Well hopefully,' Chris finally managed, 'that should be the last we see of them.'

The following evening, having finished work, Jan and I went through to the bar to join Georges who had popped up for a drink.

'You will never believe what we 'ad 'appen at ze bank today,' Georges told us with a huge grin.

'Well, from the expression on your face,' I replied, 'I doubt it was a robbery.'

'Zat depends on 'ow you look at things,' he chuckled. 'No, I rented out a safety deposit box.'

'Congratulations, Georges,' Jan applauded.

'I rented a safety deposit box,' he continued, ignoring Jan's sarcasm, 'to an Englishman and a Frenchman,' he grinned at Jan, ''oo needed a secure place to store ze 'Oly Grail which zey unearthed 'ere at *Moulin du Roc*, until zey can get an expert to come and see it.' He paused. We looked at him with our eyebrows raised questioningly, waiting for him to continue. 'Strangely, it seemed to be made of plastic and 'ad a 'ole burned in its side.'

We all howled with laughter

'Didn't you try pointing their idiocy out to them?' I asked him. Georges shrugged his Gallic shrug.

'Ah, 'Oogo, you should know better zan zat. It iz not my place to comment on what my clients wish me to store securely for zem, and, I believe you do understand ze difference between business and pleasure.'

HIHON HIHON, YOU'RE JUS' ANUZZER BREEK EEN ZE WOLL

Chris and I were driving back from Lesquerde, the little town where we went to buy our wines *en vrac*. This entailed filling the large plastic barrels that we took with us, then decanting the wine into our own bottles back at Moolong. We were happily chatting about the way the business was progressing, and Chris mused on future plans for the place.

'We ought to see if we can get a band to play, some time,' he announced.

'What? A French version of The Wurzels?' I asked. Chris gave me the *look*. I shrugged and smiled innocently at him.

He had tried this once before, earlier on in the season. It had almost been a runaway disaster. Not through anything to do with us, or anything that we had done, nor the throng that was

191

waiting to hear the band and anything they did, but because of the useless band themselves. Two of the four members arrived an hour late for the kick-off, arguing heatedly with each other. The other two members didn't even bother turning up. Fortunately, we had decided to do a pretty straightforward barbecue to go with the event so whilst Jan and I frantically fed people burgers, chicken legs and kebabs, Chantal scurried about with trays of drinks and Chris dragged the speakers from his own sound system out onto the terrace and cranked the volume up to eleven. The situation saved, we all boogied the night away, in true Moolong manner. I did feel a sort of strange, sneaking admiration for the cheek of one member of the band who tried demanding payment as he had at least turned up. He was told to '*va te faire foutre*'. He very sensibly took the proffered advice.

I presumed that once Chris had thought about it, he would consign the idea of a band to the dustbin. Unfortunately not; he expanded on it. He decided that as the main season was coming to its end, we ought to have a bit of a party to celebrate. We would lay on a barbecue, invite any punters that were staying, friends we had made from the local community, maybe anybody of note we felt it might be useful to ingratiate ourselves with, and we would have a band playing for everybody to dance to. Damn, drat, bum and blast, this looked too good an opportunity for the FUF not to come crashing in and mess things up. Jan and I tried to talk some sense into him but he wouldn't hear it. We were having an end of season party and that was that.

It was whilst Jan and I were lying in bed that night, chatting about the party, that the awful, dread realisation settled on us that this was it for us, too. It was all coming to an end. It dawned on us that, as we'd been enjoying ourselves so much, we had scarcely given a thought to Spain or even to a life beyond Moolong. Once the season was over there would be no need for us to stay. No more llamas, no more wine lakes, no more Chris. No more Moolong. I didn't think it possible to feel quite so upset about having to leave somewhere and someone.

'You know we gotta do it,' Jan said forlornly. 'If we stay we'll never get our bit of land in Spain.' I knew she was talking sense. We'd done our bit, we'd given Chris a hand while he found out about life running a holiday business in France. Now, it was time for us to hit the road again.

'We'll tell him in the morning,' we reluctantly agreed.

Despite the news of our departure seriously upsetting him, Chris took it in his stride.

'We'll combine your leaving party with the end of season party,' he informed us, rubbing his hands together and trotting off to plan his plans.

'Please don't make it a fancy dress party!' Jan shouted after his retreating back. We well knew, from bitter experience, what Chris was like when he got the bit between his teeth. There were times that once he'd made his mind up about something, he was impossible to move.

Over the following few weeks Chris plotted and planned away. He would occasionally grab Chantal and drag her off into the bushes for a quick update on what he had been up to. Rosy was continually around, eager to be in at the centre of all things. If there was a party happening she was going to help organise it and no mistake. Al sat around looking mean, moody and 'ard. He was far too mean, moody and 'ard to get involved in anything like this and, above all, anything that involved such childish behaviour. What would it do to his image and street cred?

Jan and I should have realised that something was slightly amiss when we walked past Rosy and Al having a rather heated argument.

'Well I don't know what to go as,' Rosy trilled in a wail of eardrum splitting distress at Al. Al had obviously had more than enough of whatever it was that was upsetting her.

'For God's sake,' he snapped at her, 'you're fat and you don't wear no clothes. Just shave your head and go as Humpty Dumpty. Nobody'll be able to tell the difference.'

''Ard. 'Ard but fair,' I thought. It took several hours for the penny to drop.

'Hang on,' Jan interrupted me from my reading, 'Al said Rosy could go as Humpty Dumpty.'

'Yeah. Pretty good description of her, if you ask me,' I laughed.

'Shut up, you chauvinist pillock,' she sniggered back at me. 'Al said she could "go as".' Jan stressed the last two words. 'You don't think Chris is playing silly B's behind our backs, do you?'

'He wouldn't. Would he?' She had me worried now. We looked at each other. Thinking about it, he had been very evasive when we asked him anything direct about his plans. All he would let on was roughly the number of people we were expected to cater for and that he had tracked down a band who said they would play. He also promised us faithfully that he had forbidden the members of the hunt from bringing either their weaponry or four-footed friends with them.

Short of packing our little red-and-white-spotted handkerchiefs and running away now, there didn't seem to be much we could do about things. We'd grit our teeth and get on with it. Looking on the bright side, there was no Gypo around to cause any malicious mayhem. On the other hand, though, we did have Rosy. We tried consoling ourselves with the thought that, actually, we had done several parties, dinner parties and get-togethers over the months we'd been at Moolong and, other than that little incident with Gypo, they had, by and large, gone off without any mishap. But I didn't trust Chris not to be up to something. He was scurrying around with an alarmingly sneaky, self-satisfied grin on his face.

As the time shortened from weeks to days so we started getting in all the extra booze and food we'd need for the party. Chris and I did a flying visit to Lesquerde to buy several more wine lakes. Usually we took barrels that, once full, were still manoeuvrable and could even be hoisted onto the lorry by one person if needs be. Today, because we were buying so much more than usual, we had brought some giant plastic barrels with us. This turned out to be yet another of those ideas, good in theory, totally useless in practice. Chris is about three inches taller than me so there was a slight inequity in our ability to reach the bed of the lorry easily. Add to this the gallons of liquid sloshing around in the barrel, making us stagger and lurch as we fought to keep our balance, trying desperately to maintain any sort of grasp on the smooth plastic of the barrel, and it was neither a happy nor comfortable half hour. We just knew the FUF was sitting on top of the lorry, watching us, laughing as we cussed and sweated and swore.

We came up with the cracking idea of asking Rosy to do the bottling for us. It was such a mindless, tedious job, filling bottle after bottle after bottle that, as she was so devoid of any grey matter, we knew she'd be more than happy to do it. All she had to do was to hold a bottle under the little tap at the bottom of the barrel, open said tap, fill bottle, turn tap off then place filled bottle on adjacent table to await corking. Chris explained this to Rosy. He even gave her a demonstration to make sure she understood. She seemed to grasp what was required of her. We left her to her bottling and went back to our own little jobsies that we had to do. A couple of hours later, Jan and I were in the kitchen when Chantal came crashing through the door, running in, giggling like an idiot,

"Ave you seen Rosy?' she asked us. 'She is,' she said, and then unable to finish her sentence through her tears of laughter just waved at us to follow her. The three of us hurried back to where Rosy was supposed to be working. The picture that greeted us as we reached the doorway almost made life worth living. Rosy in all her roly-poly, lycra-clad gorgeousness, was filling bottles, but swaying backwards and forwards as she took a swig from each one she filled before putting it, unsteadily, onto the table. She had filled several dozen. We watched incredulously. Had she been having a swig from each and every bottle? It certainly looked as though she had.

'Ugh,' she slurred in her drunken disgust, 'this one's corked.' Her face contorted in agony.

We relieved Rosy of her task. Jan and Chantal carried her back to Al, and we continued with our preparations.

Invitations had been sent and RSVP'd to; word was spread amongst chums and holidaymakers. The only person we hadn't been able to get hold of was Charlie, which was a shame, as it would have been fun to have had him here for our farewells.

Apart from still being convinced that Chris was up to something – though this may have been more to do with the normal feelings of suspicion and distrust I harbour towards my friends than any other more tangible reason – Jan and I were quietly looking forward to the day. We had also decided, in another of our slightly less sensible moments, to show off a bit and to put on as varied a spread as we could come up with. Tomorrow, there was going to be more than just ordinary burgers and 'babs at this barbie. We'd show these Johnnie Foreigners we knew a thing or two about burning food al fresco. The barbecue itself, a purpose built thing positioned close to the walnut tree of safety, was in about the best position to see all of the merriment that, we hoped, would be going on around us. A pair of fridges, each large enough to hold several trays of food, were resurrected from the back of a shed and set up close at hand so we wouldn't be spending all our time rushing backwards and forwards to the kitchen to fetch food as it was ordered. Two long trestle tables were set up alongside us to hold all the different salads, sauces, breads and other nibbles that we had prepared, as well as all the plates, napkins and cutlery.

The morning of the big day and we were all up early, bright eyed and bushy tailed. Jan was parking the van from which we had just unloaded tons of goodies various that we had bought in Quillan. I had my hands full of carrier bags as I staggered into the kitchen totally overladen. I flopped the bags onto the work surface and, thinking that I had them all safely positioned, let go. The carrier bag that was full of fresh sardines fell onto the floor, split open and spread its load all over the place. Cursing, I filled a bowl with water and flung the fish into it. That would do till I could get to them when I'd finished putting everything else away. I was walking into the washing-up room behind the kitchen to fetch the mop and bucket when Rosy bounced in. She saw the fish scales shining on the floor and squealed excitedly.

'Ooh,' she trilled. I winced. 'What silly Billy's been dropping sequins then?'

Eager troops of guests were gathering to see if they could help with anything, like putting up the bunting. Tables had paper tablecloths with matching paper napkins on them: everything was red, white and blue. How very patriotic it all was, whichever side of the sleeve you come from. The postman turned up with his delivery. He had a parcel for Rosy.

'Ooh,' she trilled. The postman winced. 'It's arrived.' Snatching the packet from the startled postman's hand, she scurried off to her lair.

I apologised for Rosy. I'd forgotten he'd not had the pleasure of meeting her before.

'*Ils sont fous, les Anglais*,' I told him, shrugging Gallicly. That ought to explain that. Then, making sure that he was still coming to the party this evening, I left him to continue his round with something new and exciting to tell people about the strange goings-on at Moolong.

Jan was in her garden, where she had been for most of the last couple of days, harvesting the salad stuff we would be wanting for today. She had an abundance. There were lettuces of different colour, shape and size; there were tomatoes of different colour, shape and size; there were different varieties of potatoes, beans and peppers; there were salad onions, radishes, cucumbers, lamb's lettuce and rocket. A veritable cornucopia of fruit and veg.

The kitchen was awash with the different sauces I had made, with trays holding strange-looking bits of dead animal marinading away, awaiting their turn to be threaded onto skewers. There were burgers to be made, dead chickens waiting to have their entrails removed and read. There were different pastas to be cooked and there were different rices to be cooked. It was just as well that we had decided not to open the restaurant today: if anybody got hungry before this evening it was hard luck, they'd have to make their own arrangements.

By mid-afternoon, all was as ready as it could be. We were prepped, cleaned down and raring to go. The only jobs left to do, other than actually cooking the food, were putting the salads together, which we were leaving till as late as possible as we didn't want them sitting around for hours going limp; and slicing up a mountain of baguettes, a job we didn't think we could delegate to Rosy. The thought of her with a knife in her hand was too terrifying to consider. There were trays of my special own-recipe burgers, there were kebabs, sardines, chops, foil packages of fish or meat with flavoured butters, marinaded chicken bits, kidneys, scallops, sausages various and giant prawns. Damn I was starting to feel hungry. When was this party supposed to start?

After a last check that everything was as it should be, Jan and I left the kitchen to have a quick shower and rest before the night's jollities began. As we made our way back to our apartment we could see that many of the holidaymakers were getting into the swing of it already: there were groups of drinking, laughing, playing people everywhere. The atmosphere, and it was still so early, was superb. This was going to be a night to remember.

All afternoon people had been arriving and by now there were quite a number of groovers all set to boogie the night away. We took our showers and were relaxing for a last, precious few minutes, drinking coffee on our terrace, when Chris wandered in holding a carrier bag, having managed briefly to escape from the bar. Chris, the swine, had, as we feared, been messing around. It was, he gleefully informed us, a fancy dress party after all.

'Oh, you should have told us, mate,' I told him, displaying my sorrow at being denied the chance to join in, almost convincingly. 'We could have got ourselves something organised then.'

'It's OK,' he grinned, passing Jan the carrier bag. 'I took the liberty of getting something for you.'

We promised Chris that we would change into them once we had done the cooking. He didn't look too happy about that.

'Think how much the things cost to hire.' I'd had a brainwave. 'You don't want to lose your deposit 'cos oil or something gets splashed all over them. Not to mention,' I was on a roll now, 'they're bound to be made of manmade fibres so they could go up in flames really, really easily and I don't think Jan or I overly fancy the idea of being flambé'd.' Jan winked her appreciation of my quick thinking.

'But you've not even looked at them,' Chris moaned at me.

'Sorry mush,' I told him, putting an end to the argument, 'I'm sure that they're very pretty cossies but I don't ever remember Jan and me having to offer ourselves up as candidates for immolation being written into our job descriptions. We'll change into them when we've finished work, honest injun.'

'Party poopers,' Chris told us, getting up to go. 'Well I'm going to put mine on now, so there.'

'See you later!' we shouted after him, laughing.

The band all arrived, in excellent time and together, laughing and joking. They had their equipment set up quickly, tuned their instruments and did a sound check. They certainly seemed professional enough. The sound of their instruments started people drifting over from the campsite. Before long the band started playing an innocuous combination of ditties that they probably played at weddings and bar mitzvahs. Kids would run up, asking for such and such a song to be played, and the band obliged. I think the only song they couldn't play was Mr Blobby's theme tune. Thankfully, the rest of the world seems to have escaped him. Unfortunately, they did know the bloody Smurfs song though.

The kids were dancing, grannies, granddads, aunts and uncles being dragged, reluctantly, from their seats where they were far more comfortable watching things going on rather than joining in. They hadn't drunk enough yet for their inhibitions to start to drop.

Jan and I were in the kitchen sorting out salads when Georges' car went past, honking its greeting to us. Georges and Sophie waved excitedly at us from the front. Chris, now dressed in full, glorious motley, bounded across to meet them, shouting and laughing hysterically, the bells on his bonnet jingling musically. When we saw what climbed out of the car, Jan's and my jaws dropped in stunned amazement. Chris leapt for joy. They had come dressed as Louis XVI and Marie-Antoinette.

'I really think we ought to transfer our account to his bank,' Jan giggled. 'I've never had a bank manager that I could swap stockings with before.'

Georges was wearing a very fetching pair of pink silk ones, by the look of it.

'Dear God,' I shook my head in wonderment at the sight, 'and to think, we've been worried about the thought of him seeing Rosy.'

I wandered outside to check how the barbie was coming along. All was looking good, and I reckoned we could start our feeding of the five thousand. Chantal, a comely serving wench today, was ferrying trays of drinks backwards and forwards as fast as her little legs could carry her.

The queue of people wanting something to eat was beginning to take my attention when I heard a familiar engine noise coming down the lane. Charlie's van trundled round the bend and into view. What an unexpected and jolly surprise. I waved gleefully as he drove past and into the car park: from the expression on Charlie's face I could tell he hadn't been expecting anything like this. It looked as though he had brought someone with him, too. Oh well, he would have to wait for the masses to be fed a bit before he could introduce me to his chum and fill me in on all the latest gossip.

It wasn't long before the first lot of food was ready and the tables were filling with hungry partygoers. This was turning into something more like a swarm of locusts than the feeding of the five thousand. Jan was having to dash back to the kitchen to fetch replenishment far quicker than we'd anticipated. You'd have thought this lot hadn't eaten for months. I hoped there was going to be enough left to feed us workers later, as I really didn't fancy a fried-egg sandwich after seeing all this lot go out. Charlie, who seems to expect people to drop whatever it is they're doing and talk to him when he wants, tried dragging me away from my cooking.

'Hewgs, I gotta talk to you,' he tugged on my sleeve.

'Charlie, it's lovely to see you but I am just a wee bit busy at the moment,' I pointed out to him, removing his hand from my arm. 'Just tell Chantal or Jan what you want to eat and I'll see you later.'

'Oh for Christ's sake, Hewgs, this is urgent.' He was almost crying.

'Not now, Charlie. I'm sorry.' I turned back to the food and flipped a couple of kebabs and chicken legs over. 'I am far too busy. Even you should be able to see that. Now don't be a nuisance and let me get on with this.'

'But what's going on?' he pleaded.

'Oh for God's sake, Charlie,' I snapped at him, 'what does it look like is going on? It's an end of season party. Now go away.'

'Oh Jesus Christ,' he suddenly squeaked in abject panic, 'what is she doing here?'

That reaction, I knew, could only mean one thing. Rosy. I squinted over my shoulder, following the line of Charlie's distraught, transfixed stare.

'Oh Jesus Christ,' I whispered, barely audibly, 'what is she wearing now?'

Rosy had decided to follow the patriotic theme to what I presume was, to her, its logical conclusion. Her latest lycra offering made her appear to be wearing a bikini of sorts which

I suppose was something of an improvement: at least she had dressed for the occasion. Her left breast proudly bore the *Tricolore*, her right the Union Jack; the bikini bottom, an area I had not felt the need to examine too closely before, now held a morbid fascination. I couldn't help myself: I peered down. Her mons Veneris was highlighted, far, far too graphically by glorious red, white and blue stripes. If that didn't put people off their food nothing would. As she got closer I could see that what I had mistaken for her bikini bottom was not a bikini bottom but a monster merkin on steroids. An overabundance of fake pubic hair, plaited into bands of red, white and blue. The band, having seen this paragon of beauty, struck up a raucous, electric version of the Marseillaise which snapped us out of our mesmerised states, Charlie disappearing into the crowd far faster than any French aristocrat had ever managed whilst trying to escape from Monsieur Sanson and his extreme hair-cutting service.

We hadn't had a chance to chat to any of our chums whilst we'd been cooking, but now that had been successfully completed we were at liberty to mingle. The band had begun their main, far rockier set and people were getting up to dance. Chris was far too caught up in the whole thing to notice that we hadn't changed into our cossies so, grabbing a glass of wine, Jan set off to chat to Nadine whilst I toddled off to find Georges, who had said he had something he wanted to tell me when I had a minute. Charlie appeared from the shadows, grabbing me by the arm.

'Hewgs,' he hissed, 'come on.' He dragged me towards the car park. 'I need to talk to you.'

When he told me, I couldn't believe what the idiot had done this time. There were times when I really did despair of my chums.

Charlie was making so much money out of this film and television supply work that he was trying to ingratiate himself with one of the major Mr Fixits of this world, trying to blag himself a regular contract supplying the rubbish he supplies so successfully. He had told this chappy that he co-owned Moolong and had invited him down for a quiet weekend, to be wined, dined and fawned over. Charlie, being Charlie, hadn't thought about bothering to check beforehand that we would either be prepared to play along with his charade or that we even had a room for a real guest, rather than someone who is quite happy to fall into a drunken sleep on a couch when there's nothing else available.

'Not a lot I can do to help you there, Charlie,' I said, almost sympathetic.

'But he's the best contact I've ever had, for anything,' he wailed.

I couldn't help laughing at my friend's plight. It was so comforting to see the FUF had decided to hit on someone else for a change. Telling Charlie to go back and look after his guest, I promised that I'd find him a sensible couple to come and chat to his friend: a bank manager and his wife. A French bank manager and his wife, to boot, and you can't get much more sensible than that. Mollified slightly, Charlie scuttled off to try to salvage his schmooze. I, not feeling Charlie's sense of urgency, set off in far less of a hurry to try to find Georges and Sophie.

'You've got to come and see this, Hewgs.' Jan had found me first. 'It's brilliant. I wish I'd remembered to buy some film for the camera.' She grabbed me by the hand and pulled me into the crowd. A cheering, clapping circle of people had gathered around what had become the main attraction: Georges and Rosy, now both uproariously drunk, indulging in some really rather dirty dancing and Chris, skipping round them, alternately hitting them with his rubber jester's pig's bladder or his toy cat-o'-nine-tails, his bonnet bells tinkling merrily.

'We have got to move our account to his branch,' Jan repeated, a huge grin covering her face. I told her, between laughing at the sight of Georges and heaving at the sight of Rosy, what Charlie had told me. It didn't look as though Georges was going to be in too much of a mind to sit and talk seriously to a stranger.

We fought our way back out of the throng so we could have a chat with any non-dancing, cheering friends that were here. We explained to several people that, as the season was pretty well over, we would be leaving within the next few weeks or so; but not to worry, as we'd see them before we left for a farewell drink and yes, of course we'd miss them and we'd remember them for ever and yes, of course we'd be back to visit whenever we could.

As we made our circuit we came, inevitably, to Charlie's table. His guest had turned his chair about, his back now facing the party, so he didn't have to witness the bacchanalian depravities going on behind him. Obviously, our quaint rural festivities weren't to his refined Parisian palate. I rolled my eyes at Jan. He looked as though he was going to be a barrel of laughs. At least we wouldn't have to bother pretending to be civil and polite to people we didn't like for much longer.

Charlie made the introductions and the man's name promptly went in one ear and out the other. He reluctantly extended an arm, proffering his perfectly manicured right hand to – gently, oh so gently, oh, if you must, touch, no, don't grasp – shake my grubby, work-stained paw. You could tell he wasn't used to mixing with or, even worse, touching nasty, smelly, sweaty, working-class oiks and peasants like us lot. The supercilious, snobbish sod had his nose turned so far up at the nasty smells around him that you could see his nasal hairs. I was tempted to ask him why he didn't pluck them. We made monosyllabic small talk for a couple of minutes and were just on the point of making our excuses when Georges stumbled up and flung his arms around my shoulders and Jan's. As he positioned himself more comfortably between us, his left leg did a little drunken wobble and he stumbled into me, making me spill half my glass of wine down my front. At least I had been justified in one of my excuses for not wearing fancy dress.

''Oogs,' he slurred at me, swaying between us. It always tickles me the way the French pronounce my name, it always comes out as ''Oogo', but to hear my more familiar name so drunkenly slurred made my evening.

"Oogs. *Chef. Mon frère. Cher ami.*' Oh goody, he's at the 'I love the entire world' stage of drunkenness. This ought to be good for a giggle. On hearing Georges' slurred but very obviously French French, Charlie's iceberg chum's eyebrow raised just a touch. Georges caught the movement so, recognising a fellow Froggie, he lurched straightaway into introducing himself. Iceberg was being coldly polite, answering and asking questions as though he really did give a damn. There was an interesting sparkle of disgust, dismay, disbelief and 'I wonder?' in his eyes when I heard Georges tell him that he was a bank manager.

Rosy's siren squeal rent the air as she spotted Georges and came hurtling towards him, spraying him with the contents of a bottle of champagne she'd found from somewhere. Georges flung himself from our support and, braying like a tumescent bull, rushed after her. After a chaotic race around the terrace, dodging around tables, chairs and various movers and groovers, he caught up with her, snatched the bottle from her hands and raised it aloft. With a triumphant howl he took a mighty swig from it. Rosy turned and stuck her ample backside in the air, waggling it at Georges' face. He poured the remains of the champagne over her back and then proceeded to dry hump her, to the beat of a song that I knew I recognised but couldn't put a name to. Iceberg pointed dumbly at the spectacle.

'Oh don't worry,' I told him, 'she's come as Charlotte Corday, she just didn't want to get her clothes wet.' It was as good an explanation as any he deserved or any other that he was likely to be given. As I was walking away from him

I twigged what the song was. No wonder I'd not been able to put my finger on it: I'd never heard it sung quite like this before. Now though, I had it sussed. Putting my arm around Jan's shoulders, we walked back to the bar, me singing along with the band, 'Hihon hihon, you're jus' anuzzer breek een ze woll.' Georges and Rosy were still humping rhythmically.

Despite the unearthly hour when we had all finally managed to get to bed, Chris, Jan and I were at our bench under the walnut tree by half past eight the next morning. Surprisingly, none of us was any the worse for wear after the night's excesses. Even Chantal came to join us for our early morning coffee. As I peered blankly around me, in the general direction of over there, I noticed that Charlie's van had gone. This was uncommonly early for him to be up and gone and we'd not had a chance to catch up. It was Chantal who supplied the answer, having overheard their little spat. Iceberg hadn't been impressed by Charlie's establishment and had demanded that Charlie return him to Paris, *tout de suite*. Charlie, not wanting to lose his contact, had reluctantly agreed. He went down in all our estimations when we heard that. As far as Chris was concerned, though, he had been given one piece of devastatingly unfortunate news last night. Georges, the undisputed star of the evening, had been given a promotion and would be moving to a much bigger branch on the other side of the country, in a month's time.

The unmistakable noise of Charlie's van grumbling down the road interrupted our sympathising with Chris over his tragic and untimely loss. He couldn't have got to Paris and back in that short length of time. Charlie bipped his horn and waved regally as he drove past us and into the car park. It appeared he had no passenger with him. He leapt from the cab and trotted across to us, grinning broadly.

'Where's your mate?' I shouted at him.

'Sod him,' Charlie said joining us. 'He's a prat.'

'Yes, we know that, but what have you done with him?' Jan laughed.

'Chucked him out at Toulouse. He was pissing me off so much I told him to fuck off and catch the bloody train.'

Charlie went straight back up in our estimations.

'Well hey, Charlie. You know what?' Chantal told him consolingly, patting him on the arm. 'Shit happens.'

Jan was right; her English really had come on.

WELCOME TO MY
NIGHTMARE

I was poddling about in the kitchen waiting for the evening's onslaught to begin when Jan came trotting in to tell me that my Old Man was on the phone. Wondering what the hell he wanted, I wiped my hands and strolled out to the reception desk to take the call. After waffling on about nothing for five minutes he eventually came to the point.

When Jan and I had been back in England shortly before Easter he had talked me into driving him up to London for a meeting at Conway Hall of the Saunière Society, a club dedicated to the Rennes mysteries. As I hadn't had a reasonable excuse handy I ended up having to take him. I hadn't enjoyed the experience one little bit. The esoteric isn't my bag at all and I had found some of the attendees to be more than a touch odd. I vowed I would never find myself in a similar situation again. At least here at Moolong, close as it was to Rennes, there was always some sort of escape as I had the kitchen I could retreat to.

It was at this Conway Hall meeting that I was introduced to John and Joy Millar, the founders of the Saunière Society. I've not met too many people their age like them. Joy was a short lady, a retired headmistress with a huge smile on her face, the sort of jolly auntie that anybody would want to have, and John, a ruddy-faced gentleman with shoulder-length white hair and a prosthetic hand. He apparently lost his hand whilst still a teenager, playing with wartime explosives. It seemed this had done nothing to diminish his fascination for armoury as he had shot for Lithuania's Olympic team, his father having emigrated to Scotland from Lithuania early in the last century. Both dressed in black. They were one cool couple.

From the various Rennies at that meeting and those I had met whilst living at Moolong, I was starting to appreciate the varying viewpoints people held on the subject of Rennes. For some, Rennes had been no more than a jumping-off point that had led them into digging deeper into some quite interesting historical highways and byways. There were, unfortunately, more than a few who were more interested in conspiracy theories and what the Vatican might or might not have been up to. I prefer to avoid people like this if at all possible. After all, it was quite difficult keeping a straight face on hearing someone state, in all seriousness, that it was the Vatican that ordered the BBC not to commission my father to make any more *Chronicle* films as they were so worried by whatever dark secrets he might uncover. I couldn't quite bring myself to enter these people's version of reality: mine is sufficiently strange already. By and large though, the Rennies seemed to be a decent enough bunch of folk who took the story at face value and that was more than enough for me.

Trouble was, as a complete atheist I have always found people's belief in a God of any sort quite mind-boggling and so I have never believed in any Son of any God. Neither have I ever been particularly convinced about the existence of secret societies of great historical import and longevity, nor have I subscribed to any conspiracy theories. So that, as far as I was concerned, just about wiped out any interest I might have in the entire Saunière story in one fell swoop. I hate to sound ungrateful but why couldn't my father have been David Attenborough or someone interesting like that?

The highlight of the Saunière Society's calendar was its annual pilgrimage to Rennes, led by the Old Man. It turned out he wanted me to accompany him on this next one. He went on about how useful it would be for me and Moolong's business as I would be able to do tours of my own whilst we were still living there. I tried pointing out that if that was something I wanted to do then I would already be doing it and anyway, we'd be moving on to Spain before too much longer. He persisted with his arguments. Fortunately, an order for supper came through to the kitchen so, telling him that I would think about it but not to hold his breath, I said goodbye and went back to work.

The following morning Jan, Chris and I were sitting under the walnut tree of safety having our breakfast when Jan asked me what the Old Man had wanted. I laughingly explained, fully expecting some sort of sympathy and backup for my reluctance to join the party. Jan and Chris, unfortunately, both thought it was a splendid idea and said they'd be able to cope more than adequately without me being around. We argued about it for a week or so with me digging my heels in and the other two constantly nagging me.

'That's that sorted, then,' Jan told me one evening as she walked back into the kitchen from having taken a phone call.

'What's sorted?' I asked, removing my hand from yet another expired poult.

'You, you're sorted. That was your father just called. I've told him you're going with them.'

I hit the roof. I raged and ranted but it did no good. Jan just gave me one of her *looks* and told me to grow up and to stop behaving like a spoilt brat throwing its toys out of its pram.

I pointed out that we had not long got rid of Bertrand and Chris II and that it was all right for her, she wasn't going to be the one stuck with a bunch of nutters who could only be as mad as they had been, probably even worse. All she did was laugh and go back to her vegetable preparation. I spent the rest of the service sulking. I'm sure my mood must have shown in my food that night. I was not a happy chef.

I had convinced myself that the only sort of people who would part with money to go on a trip like this would be those from the more colourful end of the Rennie spectrum. A week of being unable to escape from a bunch of people like that really didn't appeal. I also knew there would be no-one under retirement age for me to play with.

John Millar phoned to check that I was still joining them and tried to cheer me up by telling me that his rock star son would be coming along on the tour, to help keep the biddies and Templars in order. Being the old hippy, like what I is, I was mightily intrigued by this revelation. When he told me who his son was my immediate reaction was neat, neat, neat. It's not every day that a bunch of Rennies gets the pleasure of having a punk rock icon as their chaperone-guardian-minder. How they were going to react to being in the tender care of Rat Scabies, the drummer for The Damned, was something that ought to be worth seeing and give me a chuckle or two. Then again, knowing my luck, he'd turn out to be a total, complete and utter twat.

This year, the Old Man needed to be in the village a few days before the Society group was due to arrive, as an American film company wanted to interview him there. He had arranged to stay with a friend of his, Jean-Luc, who owned the bar-restaurant in Rennes and lived close to the bottom of the mountain, until he was due to hitch up with the group. I was to collect him from the airport, deliver him to Jean-Luc and then generally be on hand to drive him around to wherever he needed to be.

The day of reckoning arrived. Filled with foreboding I drove to the airport to collect him. We started to drive back towards Rennes, the Old Man giving me directions. I pointed out that I knew how to get to where we were going as I had lived around here for some time now and had had the dubious pleasure of driving along these very roads more than several times before.

He continued to give me directions. We crossed the narrow bridge at Couiza, where the Old Man indicated which turning I should take to reach Rennes. I gave him a *look*, turned and started along the roundwards and upwards road to the village. My heart sank as, nosing our way along the lane deeper into the village, I saw the size of the crowd of visitors here, still so many of them even at this late stage in the tourist season. Then, up that almost vertical last piece of road and into the car park and the one thing that will never change here: that view.

Breathtakingly, heartachingly, awesomely wonderful; it was, as far as I was concerned, the only possible reason to come up to Rennes. So few of the visitors bothered to stop, to look at it, to admire it properly. They were all in far too much of a hurry to get into Toytown.

The Old Man got out of the car and started to shuffle down the lane. I locked the car and followed, shaking my head as I remembered how deserted the village had been when I had first seen it back in 1975. There had been no need to take any automotive security measures back then. He turned and walked through a doorway in a wall. I followed, figuring I'd find out what was going on if I was patient for long enough. This was certainly a good enough start: he had walked into an al fresco bar and restaurant which I presumed was Jean-Luc's. He saw someone he knew and went off to have a quick chat. I found a table and sat myself down and was about to order a cooling bottle of beer when the Old Man came back. 'He' wasn't here, so we were going. I tried to protest. A few minutes to wash the dust from my throat was all I was asking for. No, and the Old Man started to shuffle off, we had to find 'him'. Muttering unkindly and non-filial mutterings, I followed.

We continued down the lane. He went into a building where one now has to buy one's entrance ticket to Saunière World. I followed. Everything here was so regimented, timetabled and controlled now. The mayor was obviously bleeding the tourists for every last euro he could squeeze out of them. Mind you, who could blame him?

The Old Man was greeted by a woman who obviously knew him well. She was a petite, attractive, blonde lady in her forties, nattily dressed in pink. He had a quick chat with her while I stood there, waiting for something to happen. Blonde lady and Old Man then walked past me, out and back up the lane. I was starting to get a bit fed up with this trudging up and down a lane so steep that you almost needed a funicular to drag you up it. They reached the car and stood beside it, waiting for me to catch up with them. The blonde lady introduced herself as Jenni Priestley, an English resident of these here parts, and told me what the hell it was that we were up to.

Jean-Luc, who was indeed the proprietor of the bar into which we had popped so fleetingly, was ill and had gone to see his doctor. He had told Jenni where he had hidden his spare front door key, so she could guide us down and let us in if we arrived before he got back. Dumping the Old Man off,

I took Jenni back up the mountain, turned round and drove back down again.

Jean-Luc had arrived back home whilst I'd been out performing my taxi service. He was sitting at his dining table, groaning and moaning quietly to himself, his head covered by a towel, inhaling vile smelling fumes emanating from the bowl he was sprawled over. He waved vaguely in my direction and spluttered some words of greeting. I uttered slightly more intelligible words of greeting and decided to leave him to his cauldron and went to unload the car of the Old Man's luggage.

By the time I had hauled all of the bags and assorted rubbish out of the car, Jean-Luc had finished his vapour-bath. He told us that there was a particularly virulent bug going around the area and that he had unfortunately caught it. There didn't seem to be anything the doctors could do about it other than say 'there, there' and prescribe vapour-baths, which, I guess, made a pleasant change from their more usual suppositories.

We spent the evening relaxing at Jean-Luc's. Considering his closeness to Rennes he turned out to be nothing like I had imagined. In fact he seemed perfectly normal, apart from his coughing and sweating. The Old Man and I chatted and sipped on glasses of a rare and aged Armagnac that Jean-Luc only brought out on very special occasions. Jean-Luc chatted, sipped and coughed. At midnight I made my excuses and toddled back to Moolong and my bed.

The following morning I was back at Jean-Luc's by half past nine to take the Old Man up the mountain so he could meet the film crew; left them to it and went to Jean-Luc's bar for a coffee. He came and joined me and we chatted, while he coughed and spluttered, about life, the universe and everything. He spoke extremely good English. Jean-Luc was not much older than me and had been the chef-proprietor of a Michelin-starred restaurant on Jersey. Even though I had never reached such lofty professional heights it gave us a starting point, something to talk about as we got to know each other better. He had, eventually, become fed up with the rat-race and decided to return, with his family, to the region of France where he had grown up, to lead a quieter, less stressful existence. He had come upon this place almost by accident, liked it, and so set up shop. When he opened, he had no more than the haziest of childhood memories of a story about a priest in the region that had found some sort of treasure. It amused him slightly to find that he had bought himself a business in this village with a treasure story attached to it

Once his staff arrived for work, Jean-Luc made his excuses and went back home to retire to his sick-bed. I mooched around for a bit then went and had a chat with Jenni, who seemed to like fairies as far as I could gather. I was running out of things to do. I had been into the bookshop and both of the gift shops, but then I remembered that there was another bar in the village, the Pomme Bleue. I'd noticed it as I'd driven past it but hadn't popped in there yet. I'd wander down and have a bottle of beer; that'd kill a bit more time while I waited for the Old Man to finish.

I had hoped that I would be just another mug punter when I walked into the bar, but unfortunately my fame had spread before me and I was greeted by a fairly large bloke who looked like a rather grubby, tatty old biker who had seen better days. He told me I was Henry Lincoln's son. It was pointless to lie as I was going to be around the place for a couple of weeks and the village was so small. He introduced himself as Tony and ushered me to a table in the garden, which he hurriedly cleared of the previous punters' rubbish, and asked me what I wanted to drink. He fetched me the beer that I asked for, then sat down at the table to join me.

He began to tell me his life history. He said he was something big in the Templars. I guess he expected, with my pedigree, for me to know all about things like that, but as I didn't give a fig about them, I neither knew nor cared what he was going on about. I drank my beer, then feeling bored and restless, went off in search of the Old Man and the Americans to find out how much longer they were going to be. They had no idea but it was probably going to take several hours yet. That cheered me up no end, so telling the Old Man to phone me on my mobile when he was ready to be collected, I scurried back to Moolong for a short respite of comparative sanity.

A couple of hours later my phone barked at me. It was the Old Man, having finished filming for the day and wanting to be brought back down the mountain so he could have a nap before dinner. Reluctantly, feeling as though I was just being used as some sort of servant, I drove back to Rennes to collect him.

The following morning I was feeling decidedly queasy. Brushing this discomfort to one side, I collected the Old Man and drove him back up to Rennes so he could finish being interviewed and filmed while I spent the morning sitting at Jean-Luc's, drinking coffee and feeling green about the gills. By lunchtime I really wasn't feeling right. I tried to convince myself it was a combination of tiredness and an overdose of coffee. Neither of which helped to explain the irritating, niggling cough that I was developing, though. I hoped I hadn't caught Jean-Luc's lurgy.

The Old Man and film crew came into the bar, the crew chatting noisily and happily now that they had finished the job. They were now out to have a bit of a knees-up, to celebrate before flying back to America the following morning. By the time the third of them had asked me if I was feeling all right, the world was starting to spin slightly, so I decided it might be a sensible idea to get us down the mountain while I still felt capable of doing it. I explained this to the Old Man and, as he too was happy to escape, we bade our farewells and scarpered.

I crawled back to Moolong and my bed. I was unconscious within seconds and stayed that way more or less continuously until the following morning, surfacing only to cough, splutter, wheeze and sweat and for the world to spin around me. Jan and Chris were not in the slightest bit sympathetic to my plight, Jan insisting it was no more than 'man flu' and once more telling me to pull myself together and to stop behaving like a spoilt brat throwing its toys out of its pram.

Jean-Luc and I were now both coughing, wheezing, spluttering and sweating. He would only make any necessary trips he had to, either up to his restaurant or to go to the cash and carry for supplies but otherwise he spent his time in bed, dead to the world. I wasn't feeling too happy: the Saunière Society mob were due to arrive this evening and I really didn't feel up to it. I was dreading it. I felt awful.

We were to join John, who had driven down from England in his car, and Joy, who was with the group travelling together from Stansted, at the restaurant where we would be dining this inaugural evening of the trip. Fortunately, I would no longer need to do any driving as we would be going everywhere together by hired bus. Even more fortunately, Jenni was joining the group for the meal tonight, so had volunteered to drive the Old Man and me to the restaurant. Jan drove me up to Rennes to join them, gave me a peck on the cheek and told me to behave myself whilst she wasn't there to keep an eye on me. She promised she really would remember to come and collect me at the end of the week then pushed me out of the bus and left me to my fate.

By the time we got to the restaurant I was feeling even worse. The sweat was pouring from me like Niagara Falls and the coughing was almost making me pass out as I fought to catch breath. I knew death was very, very close and the last place in the entire universe I wanted to be just then was with this bunch of Rennies. I wanted to be back home at Moolong, under my duvet, where I could cough, sweat and feel sorry for myself; not here, having to be polite to strangers and trying to remember their names. If there was to be any chance of me getting through this first evening with the group I knew I was going to have to sneak outside for a crafty smoke of one of the medicinal joints I'd rolled and stuck in my pocket before I'd left home.

I had just perched myself on the rim of a huge flower pot and lit up when a very tall, thin, Versace-besuited man of about my age wandered out from the restaurant and with an 'All right geezer, how's it going?' pulled what was very obviously also a spliff from his top pocket, then lit it and perched himself on the flower pot next to mine. I tried snorting contemptuously of life but totally ruined the effect by collapsing in a heap with another coughing fit.

'That good, eh?' he said and, slowly releasing the smoke from his lungs and grabbing me by the collar of my soaking wet shirt, pulled me upright again. Whoever this dude was, he had an interesting twinkle in his eye. Thank you God, there was going to be someone on the tour I could chum up with. Provided I lived that long.

Joy had introduced me to everyone as they had arrived but I was damned if I could remember this guy. Not that that proved anything. Thankfully, he made a mention of parents and the penny dropped. So, this was Rat Scabies then. As we smoked and chatted, and I coughed and sweated, we discovered our mutual interests in music, films and books – and a similar, questionable sense of humour. We discovered our dates of birth were less than six months apart and, much to our amused surprise, that we had a couple of mates in common too. Things were looking up. I was finding Mr Scabies a highly amusing chappy. He took a deep pull on his joint and turned to look at me, the twinkle in his eyes glinting behind the lens of his glasses.

'D'you wanna tell me why you were so bloody rude to me that last time we met?' he asked me.

'Do what?' My brow furrowed in stoned confusion. I just couldn't remember ever having met him before. I had never seen The Damned in concert so I couldn't have spat on him, causing him to harbour a grudge towards me for all these years. 'Conway Hall, 'bout five or six months back,' he reminded me, as though I was some sort of congenital moron. 'If you remember,' he explained patiently, 'I came over and introduced myself to you.'

'Did you?' I asked, totally flummoxed.

'Yeah.'

'I'm really sorry, mate,' I grovelled pathetically, 'I have absolutely zero memory of it.' It was his turn for the contemptuous snort now.

'You told me to fuck off,' he informed me. The shock of this statement caused my mouth to drop open and the burst of air from my lungs sent me crashing to the ground with yet another coughing fit. There have been many times in my life when I have wished that the ground could open up and swallow me, and this was yet another of those occasions. Through my coughing and spluttering I did my best to apologise and convince him it hadn't been meant. I'm hardly ever rude to people on first meeting them, and anyway, I quite liked some of his music. He kept me squirming for a bit longer.

'Nah, 's OK,' he finally relented. 'I'd seen you'd been collared by one of the mega-nutters. I was sorta tryin' to help you escape but under the circumstances guess I might have reacted the same sort of way.'

'I'm sorry. I didn't mean it. Honest.'

'Oh yeah?' He laughed.

'Yeah,' I told him as convincingly as the combination of laughter and coughing would allow.

We finished our smokes and floated beatifically back into the dining room to join the rest of the throng. From the raised voices and peals of laughter that were already ringing round the rafters of the restaurant it seemed that in the short time that Ratty and I had been outside, our party had been making some serious inroads into the wine. I had just sat myself down, raising a glass to my mouth, about to take my first mouthful of wine of the evening when John Millar marched up to me.

'Were you outside with my son?' he snapped at me. I looked up at him, blinking, not quite sure what to make of this strange question and his even more curious tone of voice.

'Are you warning me off, Mr Millar?'

'No,' he told me in a resigned, concerned sort of tone, 'just worried about birds of a feather.'

I coughed, spluttered and laughed.

'No probs there then, John,' I reassured him, raising my glass to toast him. He returned to his seat at the other end of the table and had a quick conflab with Joy and the Old Man.

I watched the worried glances they cast at Ratty and me. Let the fun begin, I thought, chuckling quietly to myself.

Courses were served and eaten, and wine was drunk by the vineyard. It's amazing just how much a little old lady can get stuck down her beak when she wants to. Conversations were flying backwards and forwards and the Rennies were having a whale of a time. Everybody was getting on famously. I smiled and nodded a lot as I couldn't make out what was being said at me through all the noise.

At the end of the evening, awash with food and wine, we piled aboard our tour bus for the drive back to Carcassonne and the hotel where we were to stay for the night. The buzz of happy, drunken conversation spun noisily around the coach. It looked as though the first evening could be termed a success.

Back at the hotel, we poured like excited schoolkids from the bus and swarmed into the reception area. Our bags were flung into a multi-coloured mountain of leather, plastic and synthetic fibres in the middle of the floor. People were reclaiming luggage and collecting their room keys, then dispersing for a few hours' much-needed kip to recharge their batteries in readiness for the full Rennes onslaught, beginning properly the following morning.

Ratty's chum Push, who used to be a rock music journalist but who now wrote proper books, had travelled down separately from us and arrived whilst we were still at the restaurant feeding our faces. He was another lanky chappy. Standing between Push and Ratty made me feel like Ronnie Corbett being flanked by John Cleese and Peter Cooke. They, it turned out, were writing a Rennie book of their own, to be catchily entitled *Rat Scabies and the Holy Grail*, so they were here to gather notes, do a bit of research and generally have a bit of fun. Things were looking up: it would seem that I might now have a rock star and a rock journalist to hang out with. Things weren't going to be that bad after all.

Having spent the day on trains and boat and trains, Push was asleep on his feet, so he crawled off to his temporary lair leaving Ratty and me to our own devices. We took the lift up to our floor to be greeted by the sight of several members of our party struggling to get into their rooms. The newfangled, modern, hi-tech door keys, the ones that look like bank cards, were proving yet again that modern technology wasn't all it was cracked up to be. Ratty, announcing his vast knowledge and experience of hotels and their doors, went to the rescue of Viviette, a short, grey-haired lady.

I coughed and slid my card key into the indicated slot and, not surprisingly, couldn't make it open my door. Cursing loudly, I tottered back downstairs to the reception desk, in the hope that I could find us some help. I was told by the charming lady receptionist that the keys most certainly did work. Between coughing fits, I tried explaining, as patiently and politely as I could, that as there were at least half a dozen of us that couldn't get into our rooms, maybe some vital piece of information in the instructions had somehow been lost in translation, so would it be possible for somebody to come up and show us how it ought to be done? Please? The keys worked, she replied, and there was nobody available to deal with such trivial matters, we'd just have to sort it out for ourselves.

Extending my heartfelt thanks for her so clear, precise and helpful advice, I stomped back up to see how Ratty was getting on. He had eventually succeeded in opening one of the doors. If the worst came to the worst, we could at least all bunk down on Viviette's floor. We finally worked out that the cards needed to be inserted into their cradle for exactly eight-and-a-half seconds, not a nanosecond more, not a nanosecond less, then ingress was permitted. Breathing sighs of relief the Rennies finally retired to their rooms leaving Ratty and me standing by my door.

'Fancy a night night spliff?' I asked him. He grinned at me, stuck his fingers into the breast pocket of his jacket and pulled out another one already rolled. Laughing, I put the plastic key in its lock, counted to eight-and-a-half then pushed open the door.

The hotel was situated overlooking the Canal du Midi and the view from the balcony was as magical and glorious as it ought to have been. We were looking up at the magnificently illuminated, fairytale old town of Carcassonne, with its turrets, towers and battlements standing clear and proud in the spotlit sky. On looking down, we could see all of this magnificence mirrored in the still, dark, Quink-blue ribbon of water below us. We leant on the balcony railing, gawping appreciatively at the sight. An elbow in the ribs roused me from my reverie.

''Ere, try this one,' Ratty croaked, holding in a toke and passing me his spliff.

'Cheers,' I replied, passing him my one in return. I had barely taken my first puff when – 'Oh shit,' Ratty howled. 'I don't fucking believe it.' I stared at him in astonishment, realising he had missed his mouth and dropped the bloody joint into the street below. This man was supposed to be a drummer, with superior coordination. There are some that said this man was one of the best rock drummers in the world, ever, so surely that must mean he had an even more highly-attuned control of his appendages? It was obviously true what they said about drummers. So much for me being impressed by meeting a rock star.

AND SO TO RENNES

The following morning I crawled, coughing and sweating, from my bed. Wrapping the dressing gown around me that the hotel had so thoughtfully provided, I pulled back the curtains and walked out onto the balcony. White cotton wool puffs of cloud hung still in the gentle, light-blue sky giving promise of the glorious day yet to come. Smiling contentedly I took in the view, as spectacular by day as by night. I lit a cigarette, coughed and leant on the balcony rail to watch the world go by. Joggers jogged in packs, pairs and singly along the canalside. A troop of soldiers marched past on the opposite bank, dogs were taken for their early morning drag, cars and bikes zipped about as people made their way to work. Just another ordinary day. It was certainly just another ordinary day for that poor sod down there in the torn jeans and what from this distance looked like carpet slippers on his feet. He was shuffling along the gutter, head down, I presumed looking for discarded cigarette ends. I watched him for a couple of minutes, on the verge of throwing him down a packet of mine when he stooped and snatched up his prize. As he turned and lit the thing, I saw who it was.

'What the bloody hell are you up to?' I yelled down at him. He spun round in surprise to see who had spotted him. Seeing no one, he spun the other way. I watched for a bit as he turned and gyrated in a wonderful display of confusion, looking as though he might be limbering up for an early-morning game of Twister. 'Up here, you plank!' I shouted.

He squinted up towards the noise, grinned in recognition and raised his hand in triumph, displaying his trophy.

'Found it,' Ratty, now dressed in what I discovered was his more normal, comfortable attire, shouted proudly back up at me, waving the joint he had dropped last night. I was impressed. I took back all the uncharitable things I had thought about him. This showed great dedication.

'Hang on a mo', I'll be right down!' I yelled back, dashing into my room and flinging my clothes on.

A pleasant morning was spent wandering around the old city, mooching about to get us in the mood for that which was yet to come. Ratty, Push and I visited a highly educational museum dedicated to the gentle art of torture through the ages. We sniggered at the useless plastic rubbish that souvenir shops sell, ogled any pretty lady tourists we saw and generally wasted time.

We met up with the rest of the party, as arranged, in the main square for lunch. In dribs and drabs they turned up, some clutching plastic carrier bags showing they had succumbed to the temptations of touristic consumerism, others not yet fallen for it, but all smiling broadly and looking totally happy and relaxed. The morning spent wandering around this real-life fairytale castle had, despite the huge numbers of other visitors crawling all over it, created the required subliminal effect. The waiter came to take our orders. I decided to treat myself to steak tartare. Apart from the fact that I love this dish it always amuses me when waiters patronisingly explain that the meat is raw. Our waiter had obviously had enough of ignorant tourists so just silently took my order, a small grin flittering across his face as he thought of what my reaction might be on seeing a pile of raw meat with an equally uncooked egg yolk nestling in its embrace. He looked quite upset when at the end of the meal he cleared our plates and found that mine was spotless.

Our little band of pilgrims tottered back from lunch, gathering together in the foyer of the hotel, outside which our coach was waiting patiently to collect us. Between the Rennies milling about and the mountain of our luggage there was precious little room for any of the other guests to manoeuvre. The hum of our group's excited conversation filled the reception area. This was it; we were finally on our way to Rennes. Rough as I felt, the Rennies' pleasure and excitement was contagious. Much to my surprise, I realised I was now actually quite looking forward to the week.

Ratty, Push and I, in true naughty schoolboy tradition, had already commandeered the rear bench seat of the tour bus. We sat sniggering and making sarcastic comments about the other members of the party as they, with varying degrees of agility, caused the bus to pitch and roll, clambering aboard and finding themselves somewhere to sit. They were a strange and disparate group, were the Rennies. There were a couple of faces I recognised from the Saunière Society meeting but otherwise they were twelve to fifteen new faces. Twelve to fifteen new characters for me to create my own version of their histories, to keep myself amused. As I had suspected, they were mainly of the more senior persuasion, though it was plainly obvious that whatever the number of years on their body clocks, it had done nothing to dampen their enthusiasm for life.

The bus dipped down alarmingly low on its suspension as Joe, one of the younger members of the party, being, I guess, only in his fifties and a giant of a man, hauled himself aboard. He was one of the people I had met before. This man-mountain flew over from Philadelphia for every single Saunière Society meeting and filmed every second of every meeting. He must have had the most complete record of all those weird, wonderful, eccentric and bizarre questions that had been asked over the years. It was a wonder he hadn't developed a nervous tic. Joe was giving us cause for great interest and speculation. Nobody seemed to know exactly what it was that he did for a living, although he sort of kept on sort of intimating that he might sort of be some sort of secret politico type bod. He certainly asked us some very pointed questions about our feelings towards President George Dubya and his cohorts. My answers to these questions would vary according to the sort of mood I was in at the time. As far as Ratty, Push and I were concerned, from hereon in he was to be known as Atomic Joe. We felt it rather dignified him, giving him an air of dangerous mystery.

With all the happy campers aboard the charabanc, we sallied forth. Carcassonne behind us, we headed now for Alet les Bains, a small town a few kilometres from Rennes and our base for the duration of this tour. The bubbling conversation rose in volume as we drove deeper into the region. For many of the Rennies, this was their first visit here and the thrill they were feeling was palpable. Push, Ratty and I grinned moronically at each other, though that probably had more to do with the effects of the crafty smoke we'd managed just before we had got on board the coach.

Cecile, a very pleasant, helpful and friendly young lady, our driver for the week and who, for her sins, was also having to stay with us for the duration, nosed the bus over the narrow, humped bridge and into the even narrower, winding lanes of Alet. Our vehicle wasn't the largest of beasts, with seating for only about two dozen passengers, but it still gave Cecile a few premature grey hairs as she tried to squeeze it through ancient streets designed for nothing wider than a portly horse, overshadowed by tall, steep, grey buildings. The locals stared at us in bemusement as we inched past. Had they never seen a bus before?

Cecile pulled to a halt when we came to a junction opposite the gateway to the hotel's grounds. The awfully oblique angle on its own looked as though it would cause her some problems but she then had to get the bus through the hotel gateway, set at an opposing but equally odd and oblique angle. It ended up taking her rather more attempts than she would probably have been allowed had she been taking her driving test. She acknowledged our cheers of congratulations as she drove the bus under the arched gateway and up to the front door of the hotel.

Monsieur and Madame Hotelkeep were waiting, ready to receive us, a long flat trolley standing by Monsieur's right hand in readiness for him to trundle our bags about. Whilst he was being organised by Madame, we parked ourselves around the wrought iron tables and chairs on the terrace and ordered drinks. Monsieur began to unload. We began to get loaded.

Once everything was satisfactorily under control as far as Madame was concerned, in that Monsieur was working and we were watered, she returned to the reception desk. A few members of the party, not so sure-footed as the rest of us, had asked for rooms on the ground floor. Having dealt with these special requests Madame, like a schoolmistress taking register, started to call names out, waited for a hand to be raised in acknowledgement, made a note on her list and then issued a key. It continued like this as she handed out the remaining keys to the remaining guests. When she came to the end of her supply of keys I knew the FUF was at it again. Keys had been handed out to all of the remaining guests, bar me. Joy patted me consolingly on the shoulder, telling me not to worry and assuring me that John had booked a place for me and that Madame had confirmed the reservation. This was no more than the merest of mere technical glitches.

Tobi and Gerda, a couple of extremely charming German Templars who lived in Rennes-le-Château and were friends of John, Joy and the Saunière Society, had only arrived back in France from Germany earlier that afternoon but, despite their tiredness, had promptly leapt into their car to drive down to join us for dinner. Hearing of my predicament, they very kindly offered me a bed for the night, so at least I wouldn't be sleeping under the stars.

It took about half an hour of cajoling, pestering and nagging by John and Joy before the mystery of the missing key was solved. The previous guest staying in my room had left without handing it back in, which Madame hadn't noticed. As far as she had been concerned, she had all the necessary room keys for our party, ergo, no keys left, no rooms left. A spare key was found and I tottered gratefully off to dump my bag. Our coven reconvened at about half past seven for pre-prandial noggins and natterings. I was collared by a large man, who I would have thought was in his mid-sixties, wearing baggy shorts, sandals, knee-length socks and a Paddington Bear type hat. He introduced himself as Harry and kept telling me that my cough was nothing more than a smoker's cough which would clear up instantly were I to give up the demon weed. I coughed, smiled and agreed with him. It was the easiest thing to do.

Madame appeared at the French windows and called us through to dine. Tables had been placed together to create one long refectory type table so we could all trough together, en masse, one happy family. Baskets of bread and bottles of wine aplenty had been placed in readiness for us along the length of the table. The Old Man, John and Joy were sitting at the furthest end of the table, the rest of the group grabbing chairs and places along either side, wherever they could. I positioned myself at the opposite end of the table, in front of the open doors so I had a cooling draught blowing onto my back and I could make a swift and easy escape if I felt that the sweating and coughing were becoming too bad.

As the meal progressed I could feel reality whirling in and out of focus. This was one mega-bug that Jean-Luc had decided to share with me. I stared blankly down the length of the table, diners' heads appearing randomly from either side, up and down the lines, as they leant forward to say something or to put some food or drink into their mouths. They reminded me of a toy I had been given when I was a kid. It looked like an over-sized table tennis bat that had several small wooden chickens on it. When a counterweight hanging below the bat was spun, the chickens appeared to be pecking at the ground. This was a version of this toy designed by Mervyn Peake. I made my excuses and went to bed.

The following morning, even as early as eight o'clock it was searingly hot. I crawled, wringing wet, from my bed to take a shower, trying desperately to make myself feel more human and ready to face the day's touristing.

Not surprisingly, our first stop of the day was to be Rennes-le-Château. This was the first time I had ever visited the place with the Old Man or as a member of a group led by the Old Man, a group that believed wholeheartedly in the infallibility of the Old Man and the mystery story of Rennes in one shape or form. On the one hand, the Old Man and the Saunière Society group; on the other hand, me who doesn't believe in one single, solitary part of the Saunière story with his hidden parchments and lost treasure for a moment. I wondered if I might feel brave enough to point out one or two of the things I thought didn't quite add up. I doubted it; I'd probably keep shtum and just snigger quietly to myself.

John and Joy herded us all onto the bus, Push, Ratty and I making straight for the back seats again. I plonked myself down beside the window, eager to see how Cecile would cope with getting us out of Alet. We were denied any fun: she had done her homework and found a nice easy route out of town which was more than wide enough for the bus. Spoilsport. Mind you, it did help to explain the expressions on the locals' faces as we'd driven past them the previous afternoon.

The road to Rennes twisted onwards, roundwards and upwards. This felt weird, sitting on a bona fide tourist bus that was by no means the only tourist bus crawling up the mountain this sunny morning. It was akin to Oxford Street in the rush hour. We laboured on, round and up, finally coming to a stop in the already half-full bus park a couple of bends in the road before the start of the village proper. There was no way that vehicles this size would be able to get through the narrow lanes of Rennes-le-Château.

Joy, in true headmistress fashion, gathered us together as we clambered from the bus and pointed us in the direction of the village – slightly unnecessarily, I thought, though probably a habit from all those years spent having to explain the obvious to children, in words of quarter syllables. There was, after all, only the one road up to the village. Ratty, Push and I, three middle-aged men already behaving like delinquent teenagers, dived, giggling, into the undergrowth, to take the more direct, vertical path.

Dishevelled, grazed and in my case coughing, wheezing and sweating, we made it to the top, scuttled past Tony the Templar's not-yet-open Blue Apple, and along the road to Jean-Luc's, passing an elderly gent dressed in the ubiquitous blue work suit taking his dog for a walk. The small, scruffy brown mongrel strained against the lead as it tried to pull its owner along the road – in spite of having half a breeze block tied to its collar. We figured it was in training for some sort of canine Olympics.

It was some small consolation to me to see how dreadful Jean-Luc looked. We sympathised with each other, in a manly, pathetic sort of way. He told us that he had never felt so ill in his life and that he was going home to bed, just as soon as the rest of his staff bothered to turn up. He checked his watch and coughed his dissatisfaction. They weren't due to start work for another half hour yet.

We had almost finished a bottle of beer each before the first of our party caught up with us. In ones and twos over the next quarter of an hour or so the others arrived, collapsing exhaustedly into chairs and ordering restorative drinks and coffees. Then, with John and Joy snapping at our heels like a couple of sheepdogs, we were corralled together and guided towards the church for the real start of this trip, the reason why we were all here: to hear the Old Man rabbitting on about Rennes-le-Château, *in situ*.

We funnelled down the lane, the Old Man leading the way, Harry, with Paddington Bear hat on head, elbowing his way to the head of the excited throng following hot on the Old Man's heels and into the cold, dark, dank, gloomy church. It was utterly lacking in atmosphere, apart from the dreadful taped muzak that they had playing.

With his audience around him, the Old Man started playing them like the old ham he was. He began with a pause so pregnant it would have made an elephant cross-eyed, then finally, he started his spiel. As other visitors to the church realised who the little old white-haired man was, they too gathered around. Ratty, Push and I were standing at the back of the group, indulging more in people-watching. A cough started to well up inside me. I did my best to suppress it: my eyes were bulging like the little red devil supporting the Holy Water stoup that I was standing beside, my face turning a complementary bright scarlet, my body contorting into a similar tortured pose. We looked like twins.

I lost the struggle. The pressure of the cough burst through. I had tried to bury my face in my hands to muffle the noise but all that seemed to do was amplify the horrendous racket. The fit racked my body, the barking coughs echoed around the church. People turned to stare. Grabbing me yet again by my sweat-soaked collar, Ratty pulled me upright and steered me out of the church. He propped me against a wall and stood back to await the end of this particular bout of hacking, looking worried. Ten minutes of coughing, wheezing and spluttering later and this attack finally abated. I needed to sit down somewhere quiet for a bit, to get my breath back, to recover. The *Pomme Bleue* being closer than Jean-Luc's and undoubtedly quieter, we would try there first, see if Tony had got round to opening up yet. He was just pushing open his front door as we got there. Ratty and I walked through the bar and out to the garden at the back, to give Tony a chance to sort himself out. Or not, as the case might be. We had no more settled ourselves down than he appeared, mug of tea in hand, pulled himself out a chair and sat down at our table to join us.

'All right boys?' he asked. Ratty and I looked at each other, whilst I coughed a conditional agreement. Tony instantly started to rabbit on about Rennes and its mystery, the last thing I was interested in just then. Ratty seemed quite happy so I just left them talking about it whilst I sat and suffered in slightly bored silence. Some twenty minutes later, Tony still hadn't grasped the concept that we may, just possibly, have wanted something to drink and that we'd not merely popped in for a chat, so Ratty and I left him to his tea and went off in search of the rest of our party.

They were spread all over the village, some still in the church with the Old Man, others poking in corners, looking under stones, peering over precipices or buying souvenirs and postcards. Tobi and Gerda, the village's resident Templars, had joined the party, as had Jenni, so Joy roped them in to helping herd us all together, to have an early lunch at Jean-Luc's before hitting the road for Rennes les Bains this afternoon. Here we were to be given a lesson about a previous incumbent of this parish who was the immediate boss and chum of Saunière, the Abbé Boudet. He was something of a local history buff and had supposedly even written a couple of books on the subject. From God knows where he had come by a sculpted stone head, which was supposed to represent the trepanned head of King Dagobert to whom, Saunière's mysterious parchment said, the 'treasure', which everybody was so keen to discover, had belonged.

I must admit I quite liked Rennes les Bains with its long, arrow-straight road running through it, framed by huge, pollarded poplars. It was a crying shame that it had been so devastated by the flood. Over the months, with a great deal of respect for the workmen, Jan and I had been watching the repair works being carried out. It really was quite incredible the speed they were getting the place back to normal.

POUSSIN'S HOLE

Cecile pulled the coach to the side of the road to let us disembark before going off to hide the bus in its appropriate, council-designated parking area. We trooped across the square towards the church for the next instalment of the history of Saunière and his cronies.

The door to the church of Rennes les Bains turned out to be locked, so I was volunteered to track down the holder of the key while the Old Man took the group for a tour of the cemetery. Coughing and spluttering I went off on my given errand. My initial idea was to ask at the bar in the town square, but the bar was closed. So much for that idea, then. I peered around me, pondering on this poser. Three of Methuselah's walnut-coloured, leathery-skinned brethren were sitting on a bench smoking their *Gitanes* but they didn't appear to be in the slightest bit friendly towards tourists judging by the way the were scowling at me. Otherwise the streets were deserted. Not a soul, not even a gendarme when you needed one.

Wondering what to do next and where to try, I was about to head towards the old thermal hotel – now fully restored from the battering it had been given by the flood in which a tree, being swept past, had completely smashed out one of its walls – when I was hailed in English by a man I didn't recognise. He turned out to be the owner of the bar who, having seen our arrival, was making his way back to open up in the hope we would pour money into his till. Assuring him we would be doing exactly that once we'd finished our little bit of touristing, I asked him if he knew where I might possibly be able to get hold of the church key.

'You'll be lucky,' he told me, "igh days and 'oly days, that's all it's ever open for nowadays. They don't seem to want to encourage too many tourists there.' If I was feeling brave, he suggested, I could try Madame someone-or-other who lived just around the corner. She was one of the church cleaners so maybe she would have a key.

Not entirely encouraged by this, I thanked him and, promising to see him later, weaved off to continue with this quest. As I turned the corner, I knew I had come to the correct place. Sitting on the stoep in front of this house were three ancient crones. Doubtless one of them was the holder of the key. Doffing my panama politely, I bade them good afternoon and croakily tried to explain the wee predicament my colleagues and I were finding ourselves in, vis-à-vis our inability to gain ingress to the town's place of worship. 'Hardly surprising,' the spokes-troll informed me sharply, 'because the church was locked.' I gritted my teeth and asked if there was

THE COOK, THE RAT & THE HERETIC

any chance of her telling me who had the key, so I might go and talk to them about it. She replied to the effect that she was said person and if I thought she was letting in any tourists so they could make a mess of her church and steal more things from it then I was very much mistaken. Her triplet sistren nodded their silent, unblinking agreement. Realising I didn't stand a snowball's hope in hell of winning this particular fight, I thanked them for their time, bade them an almost-civil farewell, coughed in their general direction hoping they would catch my germs and returned to the churchyard to break the news.

I must admit, to a certain extent, I could agree with the crones' point of view. Over the years, various mindless morons that should have their hands and other bits chopped off have stolen bits and pieces from key sites, including Abbé Boudet's head of Dagobert from the churchyard here, proving yet again how a lobotomised minority can ruin things for everybody else, residents and visitors alike.

The Rennies groaned their disappointment. They were placated slightly when the Old Man told them that this was no great handicap to either the trip or the storyline. We all had a rant about vandals and what we would like seen done to them then Harry, quite sensibly, asked what the contingency plan was. Tobi and Gerda announced that they would happily be 'plan B' and invited us all back to their place. We trooped back across the square, where the owner was standing by his bar door rubbing his hands in excited but futile expectation of pecuniary advancement. As we passed we waved amicably at him, making our way back to the bus then up to Rennes again. There Tobi and Gerda began to demonstrate their incredible generosity by pouring down our necks, from what seemed to be a bottomless well, copious amounts of a glorious sparkling wine whose velvety smoothness and subtleness of flavour fills your mouth so sensuously, Blanquette de Limoux. It is, I think, far superior to champagne, which it also supposedly predates.

The afternoon passed in a hazy blur, with the bug making everything seem unreal to me anyway then, as time wore on, exacerbated by the booze and the cheroots that Ratty and I were puffing on. Stomachs were starting to grumble and complain so we headed back down the mountain to the hotel for dinner.

We continued our imbibing sitting on the hotel's terrace. Harry came over to join us, sat himself down beside me, and quietly listened to what was being said around him. As he sat and listened he started to pick at the loose, greenish flecks of paint and rusty metal peeling from our table.

'You think they'd keep them better looked-after than this,' he grumbled. 'They're covered in rust.'

'Harry,' I told him, as though he really ought to know better, 'it's supposed to look like that. It's a very old and skilled technique that's been used here. Don't you watch *Antiques Roadshow*? It's known in the trade as verdigris burns.'

'Ah, right,' he acknowledged, looking quizzically at me, trying to work out if I was winding him up or not.

Day three was designated for an easy day's sightseeing as tonight the Old Man was giving a talk at Jean-Luc's. Everybody knew about this lecture and was looking forward to it. I'd disappeared early to bed the previous evening so hadn't heard anything about what was planned. Ratty and Push weren't particularly helpful when I quizzed them about it, either. They hadn't been paying any attention, being far too busy chatting to Richard, a French photographer chum of theirs who had turned up that afternoon. They introduced me to Richard at breakfast. Not being at my best so early in the day, even without any dreadful lurgy to contend with, I grunted my non-cordial greeting at him, he returned me a far more courteous greeting than any I deserved and the three of them left me to my coffee and croissant and my feeble attempts at re-entering the human race.

We were off to see the hole in the countryside where the tomb which Poussin supposedly used in his *Et in Arcadia Ego* masterpiece used to sit. It is the incredible similarity between the views of the countryside in the painting and in real life that really keeps this story trundling along. The 'Poussin experts' are quite emphatic that he never visited this region. Well, if he never did come here how did he manage to paint it so accurately? After all, he wouldn't have had the odd postcard or photograph of the place lying about to help him. Non-experts and Rennies hold that the evidence of their eyes rather says differently. Rennies are convinced that the existence of this tomb is proof of the truth of the Rennes legend.

It was while we were sitting on the coach that I thought that Richard looked vaguely familiar. I knew I'd never met him before, so put it down to him having 'one of those faces' and forgot about it and instead, never being able to pass up the opportunity of showing off and generally being a smart-arse, decided to impart a piece of useless information to my chums.

'Have any of you ever heard of the Whitechapel Club?' I asked. As they unsurprisingly hadn't, I explained. 'Well, back at the tail end of the nineteenth century a bunch of slightly iffy journalists in Chicago formed a little club and named it in honour of Jack the Ripper. The boss of the club was even titled The Ripper. Anyway, their bar was a coffin, they had loads of skulls to decorate their club-room, they had weapons that had actually been used in murders, a couple of blankets covered in blood that had been salvaged from the Indian Wars and various other gruesome and grisly artefacts. They even had a noose hanging from the ceiling. All in all they were a jolly bunch of perverts.'

The three of them looked at me. They couldn't work out why I was telling them this story.

'So,' I continued, 'do any of you want to guess what the club motto was?'

My question was met by three blank looks.

'Well, in that case it seems that I am forced to tell you,' I grinned. 'It was "*Et in arcadia ego*".' Their laughter echoed round the bus on hearing this. The Rennies turned to see what we naughty schoolkids were up to now but our arrival at the site soon put a stop to any curiosity they might have had.

We tumbled from the bus and huddled at the side of the road, gathering in a ragged circle around the Old Man. We looked across the narrow defile towards the hummock on top of which was the hole where the tomb had once stood. The Old Man started his shtick. He explained that Anthony Blunt, the renowned spy and colleague of Philby, Burgess and Maclean who, when not busy with working at that, was Surveyor of the Queen's Pictures and the world authority on Poussin, had pooh-poohed the premise that the painter had ever brought his palette to these parts; but we all know how reliable and trustworthy a person Blunt had turned out to be.

Suddenly, the angriest man in the world burst into the centre of our group like a blue overall-clad hurricane, demanding that we sod off and stop looking at his land. What right did we think we had to stand here on the road, looking at his land? He was sick of people like us, who did we think we were? On and on the little man went, the Old Man trying to get a word in edgewise. The rest of us watching this miniature tornado in either dumb amazement or amusement, Atomic Joe filming every second for the record (and in case it was ever to be called upon to be given in evidence). On and on the angry Frenchman ranted, the Old Man still trying to say his piece. I was pretty impressed by this furious fellow: I'd never seen anybody manage to keep talking over the Old Man quite so effectively and for quite so long before. Eventually, *Monsieur en Colère* stormed back to his house, no doubt, I guessed, to fetch either a shotgun or a chainsaw.

The Old Man explained, for those of us that hadn't been keeping up with the conversation, that the slightly-miffed gentleman that had been haranguing us was the owner of this land and had become so incensed by the continual flow of people tramping across his land to see the tomb, many trying to break into it, that he had finally taken a sledgehammer to it and destroyed it himself. The final straw was when, on coming home from the fields after a hard day's travail, he found that some hooligans had tried to blast their way into the tomb using explosives. He finished the job for them very efficiently, totally obliterated every trace that the tomb had ever existed. He probably planted land mines and caltraps around the place as further deterrent. All this proving yet again that various mindless morons should have their hands and other bits chopped off, then, come to think of it, be hanged, drawn and quartered too, for ruining things for everybody else.

Back on the coach, we knew at least that at the next site, we wouldn't get shouted at and be told to go away. We were off to visit a hermitage.

The idea of being a hermit had always appealed to me. I liked the idea of living in the middle of nowhere with no bothersome, upsetting neighbours to contend with. I suspect that was what this poor bloke thought when he started to chisel himself his bijou two-up two-down residence out of the mountainside. God knows what he'd make of the numbers of coaches in the car park and the volume of trippers hiking along his narrow, almost non-existent path and up to his front door.

This troglodytic eremite had been a busy little brother. He had excavated a chamber to serve as his chapel that was considerably bigger than many an ordinary parish church. I did wonder about the authenticity of the tearooms. Mind you, I guess he would have worked up a bit of a thirst chiselling away. Who knows?

Deciding that once you've seen one hermitage you've seen 'em all, I began to make my way back to the bus to discover that a couple of the older Rennies were only just setting out. Doreen was one of the oldest on the trip and still, at over eighty, an active animal rights campaigner who had proudly told us that she had been arrested for knocking a policeman's helmet off his head. Vi, accompanying her, was a flamboyant lady a couple of years her junior, who had been something to do with the setting up of the Young Vic theatre company. They really were a rum bunch, were the Rennies. I recommended the tearoom to them; they looked as though they could do with a cuppa. I was going back to the coach to catch a quick nap in an attempt to make myself feel more up to attending the jollities at Jean-Luc's later. A smug grin crossed my face: I'd got it. I'd just realised who it was that Richard reminded me of. There could be a bit of mildly malicious amusement to be got out of this later.

THE WRATH OF RENNES

By the time Ratty, Push, Richard and I had finished our evening amble about Rennes and turned up at Jean-Luc's, there was already a fair-sized crowd. Jean-Luc had somehow dragged himself from his sickbed: the poor man looked as dreadful as I felt. A good couple of hundred punters were scattered around the garden, eating, drinking and chatting before the start of the evening's fun: some rowdy groups of locals up from Couiza and Esperaza; the Rennies; Tony the Templar in leather waistcoat and headband looking like a roadie for a Showaddywaddy tribute band; and, dotted around the place, ordinary folks on their hols, who were chuffed to bits to find out that they would actually be able to hear the Old Man lecturing here in Rennes-le-Château.

Push spotted a vacant table at the very back of the garden, on the edge of the audience. He and I forced our way through the crowd leaving Ratty and Richard to buy the drinks. As we sat waiting for them, our eardrums were rudely, terribly and viciously assaulted by the banshee screams of feedback. Jean-Luc had placed speakers at strategic points and in trees around the garden. He had set up a small stage at the front where the Old Man would be strutting his stuff, just as soon as Jean-Luc had sussed out how the microphone was supposed to work.

Like a pair of nervous tortoises Push and I brought our heads back up, our necks re-emerging from our shoulders.

'Pair of wimps,' Ratty sneered, looking at us disgustedly as he plonked a bottle of wine and three glasses onto the table in front of us. Richard had decided to stay hanging around the bar; he had spotted a couple of rather attractive young ladies and fancied his chances at chatting them up. 'Call that feedback?'

Before we had a chance to get into any idiotic, good-natured bickering about decibels, pain level and Richard's laughable libidinous optimism, Jean-Luc managed to press the correct button on the mike and introduced the Old Man and the start of the evening's hooley. The evening, it transpired, was a giant questions-and-answers session. When Jean-Luc asked for the first question almost everybody shot a hand into the air, desperate to be chosen. Groaning inwardly at the thought of what weird, wonderful and idiotic questions would be asked, I turned to the other two.

'I think it may be time for us to go do our early martyr impersonations,' I told them.

'Wha'?' they chorused gormlessly.

'Go get stoned,' I explained.

'Up the Tour Magdala?' suggested Ratty.

'Now you're talking,' agreed Push. The idea of getting mellowed standing on top of the Tour, perched as it was on the very edge of the mountain, seemed perfectly reasonable to us and ought to give us some damn good views to admire too.

Grabbing the bottle of wine and clutching our glasses, the three of us crept in the shadows along the wall of the garden and out of the side gate, leaving Richard to his lechery. Giggling like naughty schoolgirls, we trotted down the lane, the noise of the symposium fading behind us. We would have to go via the cemetery and over its back wall to reach the tower as the gates to its grounds were firmly locked at night. The mayor didn't want people getting in to see things in his village without paying for the privilege first.

'Sod it,' Ratty muttered angrily.

'Wha'?' Push and I chorused gormlessly in reply.

'Not thought 'bout that. Bloody cemetery gates are locked.' He kicked the grey metal doors and rattled the handle again in the vain hope they might suddenly and magically open for us.

'What's the problem?' I asked, passing my wine glass to Push, shinning up the wall and perching myself atop it. 'Here, pass the stuff up.' We passed wine bottle, glasses and ourselves up, over and down the wall in relays. We scurried through the moonlit graveyard towards the steps Saunière had so cleverly and thoughtfully built into its back wall by leaving several stones jutting out from it, thus creating this very useful *escalier*. As Push hurled himself up the second wall and rolled commando-style over it, I saw the sheer lunacy of what we were up to and keeled over with helpless, stomach-cramping howls of laughter. What the hell did three middle-aged men think they were doing, skulking in a graveyard in southern France, in the middle of the night? Giggling inanely I picked myself up and followed him over. We scrunched along the path, discovering the pleasing noise a hundred years or more of holm-oak acorn cups make when crunched under feet tramping along a gravel path.

'Sod it,' I heard Ratty mutter angrily again.

'Wha'?'

'Not thought 'bout that. Bloody tower door's locked as well.'

We stood staring blankly at the door and each other. This was messing up the plans and no mistake. We peered upwards, calculating the possibility of scaling the wall but dismissing that fairly rapidly. None of us overly fancied the idea of tumbling squillions of feet to our doom, our bodies coming to rest, smashed and broken beyond all recognition and repair, on the rocks below. Where would be the fun in that?

What little sense there was lurking in our collective noodles eventually managed to kick in and we worked out we could just as easily smoke and drink standing beside the *Tour Magdala* as we could standing on top of the thing. There was, after all, hardly going to be a great deal of difference between the views in the pitch black of a country night. This Nobel Prize-winning realisation meant that within seconds we were toasting each other with our wine and puffing happily on our exotic cheroots.

THE WRATH OF RENNES

We smoked and drank and chatted. We laughed at the story of Rene Descadeillas, the curator of the museum at Carcassonne, and what happened to him here in this garden. He was adamant Saunière had discovered nothing, he told anyone who asked him, as there was nothing to discover. He was later proved to be a teller of porkies when, on indulging in a bit of illicit excavating himself close to where we were now standing, he had dug up three bodies and had no option but to inform the authorities — ~~who promptly wanted to know what he had been up to in~~ Saunière's garden. The bodies turned out to be something to do with the wartime Resistance so he couldn't be given the blame for them, but it certainly put paid to his reputation. We discussed the curiousness of some of the Rennies we'd met over the years and why people insisted in believing the whole questionable story. Ratty and Push seemed to expect me to be able to give them some sort of coherent reasoning as to why I didn't believe in it. I thought about it for a second.

'It's 'cos people need fantastical religious dreams and notions to hang on to. It helps them to cope with their insecurities and make their lives more bearable,' I offered. 'Rennes is just the most popular of these lunacies at the moment, that's all. And anyway,' I continued, 'we Soskins have the Fuck-up Fairy as our family herald. We don't get to rewrite history: we're far too busy ducking out of the way of all the cowpats that life keeps lobbing at us to have the time to be able to discover anything new and amazing. Not to mention,' I added, 'if something looks too good to be true then that is undoubtedly what it is.'

'You're gonna have to do better than that if you want to win any goldfish, Hewgs,' said Rat. I merely raised a cynical eyebrow at him.

The lights of the towns, villages and farms twinkled up at us as we stood on top of the world, arguing over which blob of light was what.

'That's Couiza.'

'How can it be? That's Esperaza.'

'Oh no it's not, it's far too big to be either of them.'

What the hell, we didn't care. We were perfectly happy here, in the peace of this garden, for a few minutes of escape from the 'mysteries' of Rennes.

Our wine now drunk and our smokes smoked, we were fully mellowed and ready to return to the symposium to see what excitement had been going on and if Richard had had any luck with his lechery. We gathered our debris together and crunched back along the path, through the garden, towards the railings which ran up to the bottom of the Tour Magdala and over which we hoped to make good our escape. Push and Ratty walked on ahead of me as I ducked modestly behind a bush to relieve myself. Zipping myself back up, I trotted out to find my compadres. The garden was deserted. Ratty and Push were nowhere to be seen. It was blatantly obvious that they were going to play an incredibly childish prank and that they were hiding behind a bush, intending to leap out from behind it, to try to scare the blistered blue barnacles out of me.

'Oy you swines, where're you to?' I hissed. Answer came there none. I peered through the shadows, trying to make out where they were hiding. 'Stop messing about. Where are you?'

My voice, rising in volume, was answered by a severe 'Ssshhhh'. It seemed to be coming from a bush a few yards in front of me. There, squatting behind it, were the other two. Grinning, I crunched across to them. As soon as I was in range Ratty grabbed me by the arm and yanked me down into the bush beside them.

'What the fuck?' I yelped in surprise.

'Shut the fuck up,' they hissed in my ears. I didn't need to be told twice.

Beams of light from two torches were playing across the garden, searching out whatever irregularity it was suspected lurked herein. The deep bass 'rrrhumpf' of a dog's voice cut threateningly through the silence. Bloody buggering hell, we were busted. No doubt about it. Oh thank you FUF. This one could prove to be a tad embarrassing. Why were the sons of Henry Lincoln and the heads of the Saunière Society and chum lurking in the garden when it was locked closed, when everybody else in Rennes-le-bloody-Château was fully occupied listening to the Old Man lecturing?

Who the hell was looking for us anyway? Was it the *gendarmes*? If it was, I hoped bloody Descadeillas hadn't left any other bodies lying about. Christ, the mayor was an ex-paratrooper: what if it was his lot chasing us? We knew he didn't take kindly to people taking liberties in his village. Dear

God almighty, what if it was true and the Vatican really did have spies planted here as people kept telling us? It could be a pair of mad, murderous albino monks on the other side of the railings after our blood. Whoever they were, you could bet your arse they wouldn't believe the truth of what we'd been up to. They'd just know we had been up to some sort of illegal excavations or grave robbing when all we had done was smoke a wee spliff by the Tour Magdala. Cursing and swearing under my breath it occurred to me that I hadn't done any hiding from the police since the Easter of 1975, just a few months before I had very first come to visit this place.

My chum, Dave Green, and I had decided to go on a little camping trip to the New Forest to look at birds and flowers and stuff. All our mates had laughed at us and said we'd never do it, so we didn't really have any option. Go camping or lose face. We went camping. By the time we reached the Forest, the snow was falling so heavily that visibility was almost zero. Undeterred, Dave blindly turned the car off the road and on to a featureless white blanket. We struck camp, drank a couple of bottles of rough cider, smoked a few joints and then decided that baying at the moon would be a clever thing to do. The police, their idea of cleverness being slightly different to ours, hadn't agreed with us.

'Jee-jee-jerhee-ssuuusss.' The cough hurtled from my body and shot into the still Rennes air. I tried frantically to hold my breath, to suppress the coughing, but that just made my ears bulge and my eyes pop. The torchlight swung round, cutting through the shadows as it made its way towards us, following the line of the low box hedging that ran along the side of the path. The light edged closer to us as we shrank deeper into the undergrowth.

'Shut up,' Rat hissed, almost sitting on me. Pressed up beside me I could feel Push's body convulsing as though he too was fighting against a coughing fit. The sibilant, saliva-filled spray of wind that crossed my face proved me entirely incorrect. He was giggling like a teenage girlie that had just been goosed for the first time. Lights flashed above our heads, the beam separating into two then coming back together as the possibly pontifical police tried to pinpoint where the noise had come from. Odd snippets of their muttered conversation drifted across, too far away to make out what they were actually saying.

The sound of footsteps told us they were moving down the lane, towards the garden gate. The panting of the dog, straining against its leash, carried across to us all too clearly. If they got hold of the key to the gate we would be well and truly stuffed. Push, pulling himself together, made a dash across the garden, towards the railings and freedom. He was up, over and hidden in the shadows of the car park before you could blink. Thank God, it looked like escape was going to be easy.

Oh no it wasn't. The sound of Push's Olympic sprint over the acorn husks and gravel had been heard and heavy-booted feet came dashing back in our direction, the dog snarling and howling rabidly. Ratty and I stared at each other, wondering what the hell to do now. The torchlight search was slower, more thorough this second time. Trying to use this to our advantage, Ratty and I began to wriggle our way alongside the hedge and inch ourselves closer to the railings and escape.

'Ahur-ahur-ahur.' Was there nothing I could do to control this dreadful cough? The dog howled excitedly, smelling blood. Thank God they hadn't managed to get into the *Tour*'s grounds yet. If they did we'd be well and truly stuffed. The torchlight whipped round in our direction as whoever it was tried again to find the source of the noise. Dear God but they were persistent. Ratty hurriedly rolled himself deeper into the shadows on his right, I went to my left a split-second before the beams came together, picking out the spot where we had just been lying. The beams criss-crossed the air above us. We were in a nightmare, surrealistic *son et lumière*. This situation was ridiculous and getting ridiculouser by the second.

The posse continued, inexorably, ever closer. I couldn't have pressed myself tighter into the ground if I'd tried and I was most decidedly losing all feelings of goodwill that I had ever harboured towards things canine. This one's barking was awesomely ferocious: it made the Hound of the Baskervilles sound like a little, fluffy Yorkshire terrier. Having scanned the garden to its edge at the bottom of the Tour Magdala, the *gendarmes*, paratroopers, papal army, albino monks or whoever the hell they were went back down the lane. Ratty and I slowly lifted ourselves up and started creeping towards the railings. The sudden hacking cough that exploded from me couldn't have advertised our position to our hunters more clearly. The lights spun around and there, as if picked out by a sniper, perfectly positioned in the crosshairs of his telescopic sight, gloriously illuminated by the torchlight, was their prey.

We stood there, frozen, Ratty with his hand clamped firmly over my mouth. The *gendarmes* yelled, the dog howled, we squealed. Ratty pushed me away. He ran one way, I ran the other. There were headless chickens charging about everywhere. The police were dashing one way then the other, tripping over the dog in their frenzy to arrest us; Ratty and I trying desperately to escape them. Doubling back on myself I made a mad scamper for the deeper shadows of the garden, under the walls at the back, as far away from the torches as possible. The next second I was flailing through the blackness, frantically trying to hang onto my spectacles as I fell, crashing into the path.

'You fucking clumsy bastard,' Ratty groaned painfully, rubbing the kidney I had just accidentally booted him in.

'Well I didn't see you lying there,' I hissed back at him. We lay there panting, trying to get our breath back, watching the *gendarmes* move back towards the gate. I was sure they would have located the key by now. The second they were out of sight, we scurried the last couple of yards to the railings. Push popped up from behind a car where he had been hiding, watching the spectacle in horror, and waved urgently at us to get the hell out of the garden, pronto.

Ratty hopped up onto the crossbar of the railings, hoiking his legs over the spikes in readiness to jump down into the car park. Unfortunately, as he released his hold and had passed the point of no return, the back pocket of his jeans snagged on the spearhead spike of the railings. Wriggling like a fish on a line, he was caught. I tried hauling the material from the spike but Ratty's weight hanging unsupported was too much. Whatever strength Levi's have, this was way beyond their intended tolerance levels. With a reluctant, painful 'rrriiippppp' his jeans tore and the railings released Mr Scabies from their hold. He fell, stumbling into the car park, boxer shorts-clad buttock winking in the moonlight.

The pocket of his jeans was left hanging limply from the spike, like a sad and droopy blue pennant. I snatched the material from the railing and flung it down to Ratty in readiness to take my turn at the high jump. I grabbed hold of the railings and froze. I could now see why Ratty had had that little problem getting over them. The crossbar, on which I needed to get my feet so I could haul myself over the railings, was at roughly my eye level. Cursing my parents for not having put enough Baby-Bio in my socks when I was a kid, mewling and whimpering pathetically to myself, I hopped and bobbed up and down trying desperately to gain some height. Somehow, miraculously, I managed to get a toehold and, using every ounce of strength I could muster, hauled myself up. Hands pushing down onto the crossbar, arms ramrod straight, elbows firmly locked, I tentatively removed a foot from the bar in preparation to lift myself over the spikes and onto the other side of this lethal hurdle, and to freedom.

Sweat was pouring from me, drenching my clothes. My palms were soaking wet, making it difficult for me to keep a firm hold on my support. My glasses started to slide slowly down my nose. I was having to keep my head tilted back to stop them from slipping off. Slowly and carefully I edged my left leg upwards and forwards, my nose ending up resting on my knee. I managed it: leg number one was over, my heel now wedged in the narrow gap between two of the spikes. Arms still rigid, I took a deep breath. I was almost there. One last push would have me almost free. Hup, I flicked my right leg over the spikes. I tried to wedge my right heel between the railings so I could steady myself before flinging myself into the car park but the awkwardness of this position was making it difficult for me to keep my balance. My heel slipped from its perch, my leg falling through space. Making contact with nothing but thin air, the impetus of this movement caused my weight to shift and, in struggling to maintain my balance, my left elbow unlocked and my other heel slipped from under me. I could feel the railing spike beginning to stick into my leg. The point was forcing its way through my jeans, into the soft, fleshy part of my upper inner thigh, very close to some bits that I really preferred not to be skewered. The more I struggled to regain control, my back arching as I tried raising myself up off the spike, the further I slipped down. I was having a hell of a time trying to keep myself supported.

'Rat! Rat!' I howled. I couldn't see a soul. Tears of pain and panic were streaming down my face, mixing with the perspiration. Oh Jesus, that spike was going to be right through my leg and out the other side any second now. My elbows were wobbling and there was no way I had sufficient strength left to hold myself. Seeing the danger I was in, Ratty and Push sprang from the shadows, one of them getting their hands stirruped under my foot so I could heave myself off the spike and hurl myself, sobbing gratefully, back into free France, safe at last. Grabbing an arm each, Ratty and Push hauled me back onto my feet then supported me as I hopped, barely able to put any weight on my injured leg, quickly back to the safety of Jean-Luc's garden.

We were almost in sight of the entranceway when a grey figure loomed out of the shadows towards us. I yelped in alarm, convinced that this would be our hunters who had been waiting for us to pass so they could grab us, and then relaxed slightly as the shape became recognisable. The Paddington Bear hat gave it away. Ratty let go of my arm and walked across to Harry who had been watching the whole sad, sorry and ridiculous episode from where he had been lurking in the shadows. Giving him a meaningful look, Ratty conspiratorially tapped the side of his nose with his forefinger, then, with just a hint of menace in his voice: 'Best say nothing about this, Harry. Eh?' he warned him. 'Best say nothing.'

We carried on towards the symposium, leaving Harry staring after us in open-mouthed shock. Who knew what he thought we'd been up to whilst we were actually in the garden? Come to that, what had *he* been up to? Why hadn't he been with everyone else like he should have been?

Ratty and Push went back to the gathering but I desperately wanted to have a look at my leg to see what damage had been done to it, so I continued hobbling back to the tour bus where, hopefully, I'd be able to drop my trousers without an audience. As I had anticipated, the bus was indeed empty, and I made my way painfully towards my seat at the back and collapsed onto the cushioned bench, my head in my hands. Why had the FUF decided to pull this particular little prank? I was too old for all this idiocy. A stabbing, electric smash of pain shooting from my thigh to my groin brought me crashing back from my bout of self-pity to reality. I stood, undid the buckle of my belt and dropped my trousers then, steeling myself, peered nervously down towards the injured muscle. I couldn't see a thing; it was far too dark. I hopped around for a bit trying to find enough light to see by, then discovered that by standing with the foot of my damaged leg on my seat and gently grabbing hold of my thigh and turning it I was just managing to get sufficient moonlight falling onto it to illuminate the wound.

Ratty came trotting down the lane, the bus dipping as he clambered aboard. He had decided to beat a strategic retreat from Jean-Luc's garden as the gendarmes were now prowling around, clutching the strip of denim ripped from his jeans which, in all the chaos and confusion, he hadn't picked up when I'd flung it at him. He did a double-take as he realised I was standing there with trousers at half mast and my right hand firmly clutching my crotch.

'What the hell are you doing?' he asked me suspiciously.

'What does it look as though I'm doing?' I snapped back, indignantly. 'I'm trying to see how deep the bloody hole in my leg is.'

Ratty extended his neck slightly and he squinted, reluctantly and with revulsion in the general direction of my genitals.

'Jesus, that looks horrible.' His nose shot upwards in surprise and disgust at the sight.

'Cheers. I love you too,' I retorted.

His hand went to his trouser pocket and he brought out his cigarette lighter in order to use it to get a clearer look at my injury. When I saw the mess my leg was in, I felt my stomach turn. My entire inner thigh was now a mass of deep royal purple, blue and black bruising. In the centre of this discolouration, quite clearly pressed into my muscle, was the nausea-green-tinged spearhead shape of the railing and, at its very tip, showing stark, porcelain, corpse white we could see the point where my skin had been stretched, almost to its limit, so close to being torn open and letting the spike rip right through my thigh, impaling me. I felt sick, collapsing heavily back onto the seat behind me, my trousers fallen round my ankles.

'Jesus,' Ratty repeated in awe, 'that looks horrible.'

MEETING THE MOLE
AND THE MASTER

The following morning I was dead with a capital 'D'. The bug was raging, sweat cascaded from me and the hacking, relentless cough left me feeling utterly, utterly drained. That, combined with the throbbing, burning pain from my leg, meant I was going nowhere today. A day in bed asleep should enable me to recover sufficiently to join in with things again the following day.

Forty-eight hours of delirious, sweaty sleep later and I felt no better. In fact, I was feeling worse each time I regained consciousness. Despite feeling so awful, I decided that enough was enough and that I would try to get out with the group. I figured a day of laughter and silliness with Ratty and Push might just work as some sort of medicine.

Harry patted me consolingly on the back as I hauled myself aboard the bus.

'Give up smoking, Hugo. I've told you.'

I wheezed and spluttered my thanks to him for his advice and reeled up the aisle of the coach to my seat in the back corner. I settled down comfortably and tilted my panama to cover my eyes in readiness to snooze the drive away.

'Where we going today?' I mumbled at Ratty, sitting beside me. 'Anywhere interesting?'

'Puislaurens,' he told me. This was one of the many Cathar strongholds of this region, that perches in its ruined glory high atop an almost vertical mountain. One theory has it, if I've been paying attention and have got things right, it was the Cathar's treasure that Saunière had found and which the Rennies were so keen to rediscover.

I groaned. If I'd known that, I'd have stayed in bed.

I knew it was quite a serious hike to get to that château. Jan and I had climbed up there a couple of times, to dangle our feet over the edge of the mountain. We'd let them hang in space as we admired the huge, panoramic landscape all around us; the sort that this region does so spectacularly well. That the Cathars sited their castles at the top of such steep mountains says a lot for the strength and stamina of the poor bloody labourers that had to haul all their tools, equipment and kit and kaboodle to the top of mountain before they could even start to think about doing any building work. It also says a lot for the severity with which the Church then suppressed heresies. This was the age when 'should I renounce my eccentric beliefs, accept the truth of what the Catholic Church tells me and return to its fold?' really was a burning question. Oh well, it was out of the question me being able to cope with that trek today. I'd just spread myself along the seat and go to sleep whilst the others went hiking. That would be OK; it was nice to be out breathing some fresh air again.

I was awoken by Ratty, who having been up to the top of the mountain and back again, was looking slightly flushed of face and sweaty.

'Wha'?' I groaned gormlessly, as I crawled back into consciousness.

'Have you been lying there all day?' he asked me.

Oh terrific, I'd lost the entire day, sleeping on a coach. I might just as well have stayed in bed at the hotel. As I prised my eyelids apart and got the world more or less back into focus I realised that Ratty wasn't looking quite his normal self.

'You feeling all right?' I asked with a touch of concern in my voice.

'Dunno,' he said, 'I feel a bit odd.'

'Oh mate,' I said, doing my best not to sound too much like Jonah, 'hope you've not got this bug thing starting up, too.'

He groaned self-pityingly.

'I'm supposed to be playing at Tony's tonight,' he moaned at me. I stared at him. I really couldn't have heard that last sentence correctly.

I had.

Jenni knew a couple of young gospel and blues singers who played the clubs and bars around the area and had talked Tony the Templar into booking them for a show. When she discovered that Ratty was going to be along on the Rennie tour and that the tour dates coincided with this couple's planned performances *chez* Tony, she decided that they ought to combine talents. She scrounged around and managed to borrow a drum kit, then indulged in a bit of immoral blackmail all round and the deal was done. Only in Rennes-le-Château could you have a punk legend drumming with a couple of semi-pro gospel singers.

When we got back to Alet, Ratty, who by now was looking decidedly green about the gills, was the first person off the bus. He sprinted to the front, leapt off and disappeared into the hotel. Push and I gave each other knowing looks. It looked as though Scabies probably did have it too.

Jenni had arranged to drive down to the hotel at half past eight to pick up any of us that wanted to go up to Rennes to hear this great gig in the sky. She arrived in plenty of time but Ratty hadn't reappeared yet. We explained to her that he too seemed to have caught this awful lurgy thing that was going around. Just then Scabies, now a more unnatural shade of green than any he would have been seen wearing even when punk was at its most sartorially outré, reeled out of the hotel and lurched over towards us. He had been kneeling, with his head down the toilet bowl, throwing up ever since we had got back from Puislaurens. That at least meant he probably didn't have the same dreaded bug. That cheered Jenni up no end: she refused to accept Ratty's protestations, told him he'd feel better when he started playing and dragged him to her car. Richard, Push and I followed.

The Pomme Bleue was heaving when we arrived; there must have been almost two dozen people hanging about. Even our Ratty had to laugh when he saw the chalkboard outside the place advertising the evening's attraction: '*Nadia et Sergio aussi Rat Scabies.*'

As he noted, 'You really know you've made it when you see your name written up in chalk.'

Tobi and Gerda had, in true national stereotypical manner, commandeered the best-situated table to watch our chum's performance. Sergio took his place at his keyboard, Nadia picked up her microphone, a very sick-looking Scabies picked up his sticks and sat at his borrowed drum kit. Sergio tinkled, Nadia warbled, Ratty paradiddled. The audience applauded appreciatively. A couple of songs into the set and the musicians, who hadn't met before tonight, were starting to get a feel for each other and to produce a really quite passable noise.

A small Englishman appeared in his dressing gown, obviously not in a good mood. What is it about this region and small angry men? It must be something in the water.

Tony's neighbour, for it was he, was complaining about the noise emanating from our *soirée*. Some people had to get up in the morning, he ranted. Unless it was turned off this very minute he would call the police and lodge a complaint against Tony's licence.

I had never had the privilege of meeting this man before but I had heard all about him: he was known as the Mole. Over the many, many years that he had lived in Rennes, he had been secretly excavating a warren of tunnels under the village in his search for the supposed source of Saunière's wealth. Underneath Rennes it was like one giant Swiss cheese, thanks to him and treasure-hunters like him. It was a wonder the village hadn't collapsed in on itself.

Doing the one thing that I hate more than anything else, I decided now might be the time to try a bit of the old, 'I say, my good man, d'you know who I am?' routine and attempt to make this idiotic, selfish man see some common sense. It was, after all, barely nine thirty, a time when most people around here were starting to think about eating, not going to bed. Like all the small angry men before him he didn't give a hoot about being unreasonable, nor that he was depriving not only Tony, Sergio and Nadia of earning their living but also a couple of dozen people of a night's not exactly raucous and rowdy entertainment. Unless the music ceased, this killjoy repeated, he would call the police. Tony, knowing that this little weasel would go out of his way to cause him trouble if he didn't comply with his demands and, not wanting any bother with the licensing authorities, reluctantly told us the show was over.

Ratty, who had been sitting at his drums looking immensely relieved at the goings on, without warning spun on his stool and threw up into a collection of Tony's nicely-planted flower pots. He apologised profusely but Tony, it seemed, thought that it had been a special punk finale. To puke on demand, a rare talent indeed.

Breakfast saw Ratty fully recovered. We figured he must have eaten something that had disagreed with him and that he had succeeded in leaving whatever it was behind in one of Tony's flowerpots. I was glad he was feeling better. I wished I was.

Today we were to visit another church: an ancient, small, square, grey building, imposing in its stark simplicity, standing in a minute hamlet miles from anywhere, reached by a long, winding green lane. Walking up this lane I had been stopping to admire the scenery when Ratty came up beside me, and I remembered I had something to tell him.

'Here, your mate Richard?' I started.

'Yeah, what about him?'

'Well, have you ever noticed how he bears a striking resemblance to someone intimately connected to this story?' I asked him with a smug grin on my face.

'Soskin, you don't half talk some garbage at times. What are you going on about now?'

I ignored his derogatory comment.

'Think about the Priory of Sion.'

'For God's sake,' Ratty howled impatiently, 'get on with it. What about the Priory of bloody Sion?'

'One of its grand masters?' I really didn't think I could make this any clearer for him.

'Who?' He looked as though he may have been contemplating hitting me by this point so deciding that discretion was the better part of pain avoidance, I yielded and supplied him with the answer.

'Pierre Plantard. The last and not-quite-so-recently-deceased holder of the post.'

Ratty looked at me with a questioning grin on his face as he thought about what I was saying.

'You know that photo of him, in one of my Old Man's books, the one of him sitting there, dandling his son on his knees? Richard looks just like a young version of Plantard. He could be his son.'

The grin that spread across Scabies' face almost cut it in two.

'Man,' he laughed, 'we gotta do something with that.'

We caught up with Push, who was taking photographs of anything and everything, and told him. Richard was trying to chat up Cecile, which was good, because it meant he didn't have to know what we were up to.

Making sure we were standing within earshot of Tobi and Gerda, the three of us got into a huddle and started to talk in a guarded and mysterious way about Richard and how glad we were that, seeing as he was who he was, he had been able to join us on this trip. When their curiosity got the better of them, they interrupted us, apologising that they had overheard but what was this we were saying about Richard? Binding them to their sacred Templar oath of secrecy we told them that he was Plantard's eldest son. Even though he would neither confirm nor deny it, our research suggested that he had probably inherited the mantle of Grand Master of the Priory of Sion from his father on his death. Their eyes lit up and they scurried off to make themselves known to him.

Tobi and Gerda had never been inside this church before: whenever they had come up here it had been locked and they had been unable to find anyone to let them in. That today it was open for us they added to their list of 'mysteries' connected to Rennes-le-Château. Had they asked, they would have been told that it was down to the mysterious powers of the telephone and the key holder, who, having been forewarned of our visit, had left the place ready for us.

The church of St Salvayre looked as though it had stood on this spot since the dawn of time, its interior as primitive and simple as its exterior. The stone-flag, groove-worn aisle had been polished smooth over the centuries by the feet of the village's inhabitants coming here to pray, to lay their troubles at the feet of their Lord and to share their joys with him. Low, narrow, wooden pews on either side of the furrowed aisle faced east towards the altar; a strangely imposing, brooding presence in the gloom of this unlit, sparsely-windowed, ancient place of worship.

The Old Man explained how some people feel a power emanating from the altar. The Rennies queued to lay their hands on it, to see if they could feel the force. One by one they tried; one by one they felt nothing. A pained squawk came from behind me. Ratty had whipped his hand from the altar as though he had been scalded. The Rennies turned, alarmed at the outburst of noise to see Ratty, nursing his hand. The punk had the power. Funnily enough, nobody else did.

As we were readying ourselves to leave, Richard trotted over to tell us that Tobi wanted to ask him for some photographic advice, so he was going back to Rennes with them now and would see us later at the hotel for supper. Ratty, Push and I grinned mischievously at each other. Oh what naughty little malchicks we were.

We gathered for our early evening aperitifs on the terrace. People lounged about in groups, talking quietly to each other. I was perfectly happy watching the hotel's resident chickens scratting about. It had been a good season for these dickie-birdies, and lots of fluffy yellow baby chicks were rushing about all over the place, darting in and out between our feet and being as cute and adorable as only baby chicks can be. Doreen, our animal rights campaigner, sitting at the table behind us, was in paroxysms of ecstasy over their adorable cuteness. As we sat and sipped our drinks, knowing full well that Doreen was within earshot, I steered the subject round to local gastronomic specialities. Ratty, Push and I waxed lyrical about the various pieces of dead animal that we had eaten throughout our lives and journeys and some of the more disgusting things that we had tried. I asked if either of them had ever had the pleasure of trying the local delicacy, 'chick kebab', one of the main dishes for which this region had become so famous. As they were ignorant of this, I filled their culinary lacuna for them. I explained that the recipe called for three live, one-day-old chicks per kebab. The essential part of the preparation is to give the chicks a quick tap on the head to render them only unconscious: no more, or it would totally ruin the flavour. Then thread the concussed chicks lengthwise, without any further ado, straight onto the skewer, feathers, innards 'n all, and instantly onto the flames of your barbecue.

'One of the greatest dishes I have ever eaten,' I told them, smacking my lips with appreciation. Doreen stormed off in disgust. Ratty and Push both looked shocked and disgusted at the thought of this dish.

'You are one sick puppy,' Push told me. 'You eat that?'

I shrugged and smiled. I thought they ought to have got to know me a bit better by now. Tobi's bright red convertible roared into the hotel grounds and he parked alongside our bus. A hugely cheery Tobi and Gerda got out of the vehicle, and a very confused Richard climbed out after them. The excited Tobi and Gerda went to join the Old Man, John and Joy; the confused Richard came and joined us.

'Do you know,' he told us in amazed disbelief, 'they didn't want to talk about photography at all? They think I'm Plantard's son and running the Priory of Sion.' He turned to me. 'They wanted to take photos of me holding your father's book open at a photo of Plantard. What on earth makes them think I'm related to him?'

Ratty, Push and I sympathised with him. We had no idea how these Rennies could come up with such preposterous notions.

Forty-eight hours later the tour was over. The Rennies had been, seen and bought themselves the T-shirts. They had had a superb holiday, and had thoroughly enjoyed themselves. I dragged myself from my pit, dressed, then threw the rest of my clothes into my suitcase. Who gave a toss about trying to pack neatly? I went to the car park to bid farewell to the

Rennies as they were put onboard the bus to take them back to Carcassonne, the airport and the flight back to England.

I was relieved the tour was over and everybody safely on their way back home. But I had, despite everything, pretty much enjoyed it and much to my surprise had enjoyed the company of the Rennies. I was actually quite disappointed that the bug had made me miss so much of the goings-on. I knew that Ratty, Push and I would be staying in contact with each other, but now all I really wanted was to get back to Moolong, my bed and a chance to be able to die in peace.

As arranged, Jan turned up to collect me. I crawled weakly into the van. The look she gave me when she saw the state I was in was mildly gratifying. At least I might get a bit of sympathy.

'Dear God, Hewgs,' she said worriedly, pecking me on the cheek, 'you look dreadful.'

'Thank you darling,' I moaned. 'It's nice to see you again, too.'

'How did it go?'

'I'll tell you later,' I promised her, groaning and closing my eyes, 'but please, can you just take me home now?'

THE EMPEROR'S
GOT NO CLOTHES

Our last week in France passed in a blur. As we ought to have expected, things didn't go smoothly from the off. Over the months we had, of course, bought and been given odds and sods along the way so, with what we had brought with us from England, we could now furnish a château with the amount of stuff we had. Using the tried and tested tactic of underestimation, evasion and downright lies we managed to con Chris into agreeing to store our rubbish until we could get back to collect it.

Our last night at Moolong was to be a quiet affair. Chris was going to prepare a meal for us. There were the three of us plus Chantal and Charlie, who was leaving the day after us. We would have a few drinks and nibbles, chuckle over the season just gone and wallow in a bit of good, honest, nauseastalgia.

'Oh, there's just one stipulation,' Chris told us as the five of us sat under the walnut tree of safety having our morning coffee, croissants, and cigarettes. Giving Jan a carrier bag that looked awfully familiar, Chris gave us one of his highly shifty grins. 'Seeing as you two didn't wear them to the party, I took the liberty of recovering them from your apartment and you can damn well wear them tonight.' He gave us another one of his shifty grins and disappeared inside, then returned carrying a tray on which were five glasses and a jug of tomato juice.

'Bloody Marys are OK for breakfast,' he assured us. 'The tomato juice counts as food and there's a couple of sticks of celery in it if anybody gets really peckish.'

By lunchtime we were all legless and everything in the entire world was hysterical.

'Let's get changed into our cossies,' Chris giggled and slurred.

'Yeah!' we all cheered.

It took Jan and me a few minutes to work out which small black piece of clothing went with which but after a couple of minutes juggling we had it worked out. It was almost tempting to swap them over. It didn't matter who wore what: we were both going to look like prize idiots. With tears of laughter streaming down our faces, barely able to stand, we managed eventually to get ourselves dressed. I think this was the first time in all the years I'd known her that I was sorry Jan didn't wear make-up because just then I had a real need to borrow some.

We tottered back to the others. Chris in motley, Chantal as serving wench and Charlie as gendarme, in the one uniform he had saved as a souvenir of his first haul. But to huge rounds of applause, the winners were Jan and Hugo as a *Cabaret* chorus girl and Frank-N-Furter. I rather thought the stockings and suspenders suited me.

I wish I could remember something of the rest of the day but the last thing I do remember was Chris changing the jugs from Bloody Marys to Bucks Fizz. It's probably just as well I was suffering from alcoholic amnesia.

So there it was. Several days later, our hangovers had subsided sufficiently that we finally felt capable of getting our act together and heading over the border into Spain to begin the next part of our adventure. Chris decided that we would have one more last supper together, promising that this time he wouldn't let us get totally hammered and we really would be capable of leaving tomorrow morning.

Jan, Chris and I sat and munched our last meal together. We drank our wine sitting on the terrace opposite the llamas' field, burbling happily to each other. I stretched back and belched contentedly. Chris brought out the post-prandial coffees while I rolled myself a spliff. We grinned comfortably at each other. I lit my joint and took a deep pull on it then, out of the blue, he gave me a slantendicular look and flung at me, 'You've never really told me your take on it all.'

'On what?' I squeaked, holding in a lungful of smoke. Chris waited politely for me to finish coughing.

'Rennes,' he said, simply.

'Oh Christ, Chris,' I whined, 'you know what I think about it all.'

'All the time you've been here, all I've ever heard you say is that it's a load of rubbish and that there's never even been a treasure.'

'Which the locals are always remarkably quick at shutting me up about,' I butted in.

'And that constitutes proof, does it? You're going to have to do a great deal better than that this time, Hewgs.' Chris could be boringly persistent when he put his mind to it. 'I've read *The Da Vinci Code*, I've read several supposedly serious books on the subject, I've even flicked through some of your Old Man's stuff. You say there's no story and I'm fed up with hearing it, so come on, start explaining yourself. This time you can bloody well prove it's all a load of rubbish.'

Jan sniggered at my discomfort as I screwed my face up in pain.

'Oh come on man, give me a break.'

'Hugo.' He *looked* at me.

'Oh God,' I sighed in resignation. 'Well let me open a bottle of wine first.' Prevarication comes naturally to me.

'Just make do with your coffee,' he told me. 'I'll get us another bottle in a bit.'

I was beaten. I shuffled about in my chair and tidied my cigarette packet and lighter; Jan smacked my hand away from them. Chris gave a quiet warning, clearing-of-the-throat type noise.

'And you'd better make it good,' he threatened, 'or I'll give you a bill for your board and lodging while you've been staying here.'

'Look,' I tried explaining, 'it's more a collection of thoughts about the whole thing rather than a complete concrete put down of it all.'

'But you said it's all rubbish,' he repeated.

'I did. It is.' I picked up my coffee, trying to gather my thoughts. I'd never actually attempted putting it all together into one logical, rational, coherent argument. I wasn't even sure if I could. It quite happily festered away in my mind in a soupy collection of nebulous images, feelings, suspicions, whatever. The underlying fact was that I just didn't give a damn about Rennes-le-Château or its story, and that was why I had never tried working it all out. I really wasn't sure I could even be bothered to. With my elbows on the table and my head resting in my hands, I started, slowly, to try to make sense of my thoughts.

'OK, well there's a couple of things first,' I began. 'I guess the most obvious thing is the blind acceptance that there is actually a mystery of some sort to be solved. The answer to a problem is usually awfully simple. Life may be a pain but it ain't that convoluted, it's just that humans like making something out of nothing. If you can't see the answer straight away then start looking behind doors and under pillows. Reds under the bed, all that sort of thing.

'Second, we look at things through our twenty-first-century eyes, not the eyes of the people that were living when whatever was happening happened. Our lives have changed, some would even say progressed. A century ago life was a continual fight to survive. Even when we three were born in the middle of the last century it wasn't really that much different. The war hadn't long been over, there was still the tail-end of rationing, national service still going, television was in its infancy, a motorcar a luxury. It's the birth of the leisure and money-rich era of the nineteen-sixties which meant that the struggle just to survive was gone. We now had spare time, money and energy to indulge in other things. We'd "never had it so good". Our fantasies had a chance to develop unhindered.

'Third, we're dealing with over two thousand years of history covering the whole of Europe and the Holy Land. With a timescale and playing field as large as that you're bound to be able to make stories tie together somehow. I would think that even Inspector Clouseau could successfully prosecute a case with that little lot to play with. A timescale like that and I'd guess that we could all weave our family tree back to prove we're related to Jesus.'

I sat back, I had their full attention. My thoughts were starting to coalesce.

'Then, you see, it isn't one story at all, it's a bit more complicated than that. It's rather like someone having unravelled a couple of jumpers and then somebody else coming along and knitting one jumper out of all that same wool. You'd be able to see the component parts of those original jumpers but have no way of telling how they'd fitted together previously let alone that they had ever existed separately.

That's what's happened here, a couple of unconnected stories have been knitted together using nothing more than hearsay, speculation and wishful thinking.

'First there's Saunière and how, why and where he got his dosh from. Second is how and why the mystery was created. Third, the turning of that local 'mystery' into a full-blown and very ambitious con and then, on to number four, the end result so far, the full horror that is the Rennes story of today.'

Chris nodded his encouragement at me.

'So, number one then,' I continued, 'how Saunière got his dosh.' I took a slurp of my coffee and rubbed my balding bonce with my hand. 'He was an extreme pro-royalist. He was always getting himself into trouble with his bosses for spouting off about it in the pulpit. His chum Boudet, the Rev down the road at Rennes les Bains, was of the same political persuasion and figured Saunière might be a bit of use to him for their cause.'

'What cause?' Chris interrupted indignantly.

'Eh? Oh sorry, restoration of the monarchy. Didn't I say?'

'No, you didn't and that's just as idiotic as...'

'No, no, no, no, no,' I stopped him, grinning like a maniac. 'That's it. You're looking at it with twenty-first-century eyes. Towards the end of the nineteenth century it was very far from being a ludicrous idea. Think what the political state of Europe was like then. Half of the countries were at war with the other half. Anarchists were popping up all over the place murdering, assassinating and blowing people up, socialist parties were being created left, right and centre, and there was massive unemployment. France was no different; she had all these problems too. President Carnot was assassinated in Lyons in 1892, the wine industry had almost been destroyed by phylloxera, and there had been huge banking scandals. France was in total political and economic turmoil. The national unrest was so great that in elections around the country the pro-royalty movement was actually making pretty good ground. The Duc d'Orléans was lurking in readiness at the Belgian border, waiting for things to kick off properly so he could rush over and stake his claim to the throne.

'Now, here's an interesting little coincidence. 1891 was a pretty bad year for France: there had been a pile of trouble with workers going on strikes all over the place, but at Fourmies things turned really nasty when troops opened fire on some striking miners, killing nine of them, and it just happens to be the year 1891 that Saunière had engraved on a pillar at his church, supposedly in honour of finding the parchments and starting his building works. A backwater like Rennes is a perfect spot for some serious political shenanigans like that to kick off and don't forget, the Blanchefort family, seriously part of the top drawer of Frog Society, has ruled this area since time immemorial. What really made Saunière interesting to Boudet and his buddies, though, was where he lived. He had a mountain top village all of his very own to play in which, as there's only the one road up to it so nobody can get in or out of the place without being seen, meant complete secrecy and security for people to gather together to plot and scheme.

'Saunière is really immaterial, it could have been any old compliant priest up there, it's the village's position that's the important thing. It is totally, completely and utterly secure. We know that some minor Hapsburg used to toddle up there for a visit and I can't really see him going to all that effort just for a quick genuflect. Can you? Minor or not, he was a toff and so were others that used to turn up there. Now then, it goes without saying that if you're plotting the restoration of the monarchy you're going to be knocking around with people that are used to slightly more salubrious surroundings than a tatty old presbytery in a tatty little village stuck up the top of a mountain that you can only reach by a tatty old goat track. Not a problem. Have a comfortable house, the Villa Bethania, built so the toffs've got somewhere to shit, shower and shave and a nice new road laid so they can get up and down the mountain easily for their meetings, which they could then hold in the totally secure Tour Magdala which they had specially built perched on the very edge of the mountainside, thereby making it impossible to eavesdrop on. Trouble is, with Saunière fronting the building works it was going to be only a matter of time before he got his collar felt by his bosses. When the time came he'd need a bloody good excuse to stop his gaffers forcing him to spill the beans 'bout where all this money was coming from. He had his ecclesiastical 'get out of jail free' card at the ready, though, thoughtfully supplied by the Church itself. The official secrets act of the confessional. You can just imagine him, can't you? "Sorry your popeship, I'd love to tell you where all me dosh's come from but, the confessional, you know how it is, it's just more than me job's worth."'

Jan sniggered at my impression of Saunière the spiv.

'So,' I continued, 'Saunière gets this all sorted for his playmates and in return he gets to enjoy the benefits of their wealth.'

'Ha,' Jan leapt in, 'gotcha. Even if they were royals that's still a ridiculous amount of money they'd have had to have given him to get all that done.'

'Twenty-first-century eyes again,' I said, tapping a lens of my glasses with a thumbnail. 'It wasn't loadsa loot at all. This was the golden age of the huge country estates, when you'd have a servant whose only job was to push your pooch around on a sunbed so it didn't wear its little self out. The wealthy then make most of our current crop of millionaires look like paupers. Giving Saunière a few million francs in cash to tart the place up and keep it victualled, with no nasty bank and paper trail to be followed, was probably cheaper, easier, more convenient and certainly more secure than trying to find a suitable gaff where the conspirators could gather. Not to mention that the small army of staff needed to maintain such a place would, of course, be a huge security risk. But then the first world war came along and screwed everything up anyway.'

'What?' Chris' face crumpled in confusion as he tried to make the connection.

'Well,' I explained, 'not only did the war wipe out that huge wealth the toffs had, not to mention most of the toffs that had the dosh, but it changed the whole political face of Europe. Now it would be a totally pointless exercise trying to restore the royal family to the throne. Nobody cared, they all had far more important things to worry about. The movement was dead. Then again, so was Saunière. He'd popped his clogs in 1917, so that's him done and dusted, thank you very much.' I downed the rest of my coffee. 'While we're on the subject of his death,' I continued, 'here's a little illustration of how wishful thinking helps move this story along. On the morning of Saunière's funeral, Marie Denarnaud, his faithful housekeeper, sat him on a chair in his garden in his full, Sunday-best fig. The villagers supposedly trooped past, each plucking a tassel from the hem of his surplice. This, according to my father, must hold some deep, hidden significance.'

'Twenty-first-century eyes?' Chris asked with a slight grin on his face.

'Absolutely,' I told him. 'Attitudes towards death and the Church were totally different a hundred years ago. We all know about the great Mediterranean wedding tradition of cutting up the groom's tie and keeping a piece of it as a souvenir of the occasion. Well, in an early-twentieth-century, small, isolated rural village the priest would have been one of the most important people in the place and his parishioners would have wanted to pay him their last respects, so sitting Saunière in a chair so the villagers could collect their *mementos mori* would have made this collection far simpler than if he had been lying in his coffin. Think how undignified it would have been otherwise, having to stick your hand into the coffin, grope around under your dead priest's bum then tug on his clothing to try to yank your tassel off. See, sit him in a chair and it's all perfectly dignified, no unwelcome groping of buttocks, just file past, dip your knee and remove the tassel, next parishioner please. Easy peasy. Why does the incident have to be anything more than that?'

'Hang on there just a minute, Sherlock,' Jan stopped me.

'Wossat, my dear?' I asked, sucking coffee drops from my moustache.

'What about the church then?' she insisted. 'All that stuff in there?'

'Stop looking for mysteries,' I pleaded. 'The most obvious explanation is more than likely going to be the right one.'

'You're in danger of sounding like your father,' she laughed at me.

'And you're in danger of getting a kick in the kneecaps,' I assured her. 'The church is just a piece of gaudy, tasteless, kitsch, *fin de siècle* decorating. Saunière could hardly expect the visiting nobility to worship in a church with a leaking roof and plaster falling off the walls. All that happened was that, feeling a bit flush, he employed the Laurence Llewelyn-Bowen of the day to give his church a makeover. They hot-footed it down to the ecclesiastical B&Q at Carcassonne or wherever and said "We want one o' them, one o' them, a dozen o' them, a set o' them and one o' them in black." I've seen that same set of stations of the cross all over France and in different sizes, too. It's only the actual decoration of each piece that is individual. You bought a plain plaster statue jobby and then had it coloured in how you wanted it. Saunière was just rather lacking in the taste department.'

'What about the bloody parchments, then?' Chris squeaked indignantly.

'He had nothing to do with any parchments. Ignore them, they don't exist yet,' I squeaked back, equally indignantly. 'All Saunière was, was the man who fronted some building works and paid the bills. That is it.'

'But...' Chris wailed in exasperation.

'But me no buts sirrah,' I told him. 'I told you this was more than one story and Saunière's is just the first of them. So,' I continued, 'have patience and all will become clear. The years since his death had given a certain mystery to the story and tales were created and woven into the local folklore of the priest and his prodigious spending. Don't forget that this is still a very rural area. Look what the hunt are like when they get together, with all their tall tales of derring-do and accidentally shooting the odd beater. Their stories get woven into the folklore then passed on by word of mouth, when and wherever people gather together, getting embroidered on as they go along. New stories need to be added and old ones embellished to keep the storybook full and interesting. After a quarter of a century or so and two world wars most of the people that were around in Saunière's time and knew him were dead and with it any first-hand accounts and memories of what really went on. Now no obvious explanation of how he came by his money can be seen, ergo, as Toyah so aptly put it, 'it's a mystery' and, as we all know, there's nothing people like more than a good mystery, especially when there's money and the Church involved in it.

'Anyway, in 1946, the French Government changed the franc as a way to get round wartime profiteering, and everybody had to declare how they came by their cash before they could have it converted into the new currency. Village legend has it that Marie, Saunière's old housekeeper and confidante, was seen in the garden of the Villa Bethania burning sheaves of francs to get out of doing this, thus leaving herself penniless. So, in 1946 poor old Marie is seventy-eight years old and totally potless. All she's got is Saunière's legacy to her, a house that she can neither afford to run nor maintain. It's starting to look horribly as though poor old Marie's going to be spending her final days on the streets, sleeping rough, a bag lady. Unless of course she can find some way of turning her one and only asset from being a house worth half a dollar into a house worth half a million dollars.

'Her canny old peasant brain starts ticking away. Jean, Jacques, Pierre or whoever the labourer had been when there was the restoration work going on in the church all those years ago, had been heard saying he'd seen Saunière find something under the altar. Just the sort of thing for somebody to say in the bar one evening, to make themselves a little bit more interesting for the night and for something different to talk about. After all, it makes a pleasant change from discussing Marcel and his curious predilection for quadrupeds, yet again. The whole village knew it was just that, nothing more than barroom ramblings. The village may know it but nobody else knows it. This story of her priest and his bottomless purse had already got round and about a bit, so what if she said he really had found something and that something was, say, a parchment? Not an unreasonable thing to find in a church as old as the one at Rennes, after all, and it was that parchment that had led him to the treasure, and that he had bequeathed her that very parchment.'

'Dear God, Hewgs,' Chris laughed at me, 'you are one devious-minded bastard. I'm glad I don't have to do business with you.'

'I am deeply hurt and offended that you should think me so base a fellow,' I told him, trying to sound as pained as I possibly could. 'Cut to the very quick I am.' I pressed the back of my hand to my anguished brow. 'I knew a couple once,' I continued, 'that bought a pub 'cos the locals had told them it was haunted. They wanted to believe it badly enough that they actually thought they did see a ghost, so they bought the place. The locals never let on.' I laughed. 'Anyway, back to the story. 1946, Marie's skint, then up rolls one Noel Corbu. When Corbu turned up at the village Marie could see *'pigeon'* tattooed right across his forehead. Already obviously greedy, Corbu was ripe for plucking and Marie had no trouble convincing him the villagers were 'walking on gold'. She told him how Saunière had found a parchment in the church which, he had told her, had a hidden message in it and that after finding the parchment they had wealth beyond their wildest dreams. You can imagine the little old lady looking pathetically up at Corbu, her gnarled, arthritic, liver-spotted hand clawing at his shirtsleeve.'

I contorted my body in imitation of the ancient Marie. 'Monsieur,' I croaked, 'ah 'ave zis parchment, 'e left it to me when 'e died. Unfortunately, ah am just a little old peasant lady who cannot read so ah cannot understand it. I do not need much, if you look after me and let me stay here for ze rest of my life I will make you a rich man. I will leave you ze parchment and pass on all of my priest's secrets to you.'

Chris clicked his fingers to snap me out of my characterisation.

'The pleading doe eyes staring up at him combined with his greed and bingo, job done, Corbu was plucked. He agreed to her terms, bought the Villa Bethania from her and let her stay on. Well, it didn't seem likely that she'd last much longer. Seven long years later, in 1953, she had a stroke which deprived her of the power of speech and left her unable to pass her "secrets" on to Noel, then she finally pegged it. This left poor old Monsieur Corbu well and truly stuffed and up the creek without a frying pan. Marie's story of the parchment had worked; she'd managed to keep her roof over her head. All she had wanted was to remain for the rest of her days in the house that she had lived in, that had been her home for so many years. She achieved that, but with her death it meant that Corbu was now the sole repository for all there was of the legend of Rennes-le-Château.

'So this leaves Noel with a wee problem. He's stuck with this ramshackle building he's bought from Marie. She'd told him about the parchment with the hidden message in it and used that as the lever to make him keep her for the rest of her life. He was only to get it when she's dead but whoops, she had her stroke and Bob's your uncle, no parchment for poor old Noel. This, in the words of the prophet, "is a bit of a pisser". Being an avaricious bugger, Corbu wasn't about to let this stop him. There was treasure out there, Jim lad. He ripped the place to pieces looking for the parchment but couldn't find a thing. He dug a warren of tunnels under the village, looking for his treasure, a regular little mole he was, but still he came up with not a Merovingian *merguez*. After a few years of back-breaking and totally pointless digging he must've realised he'd been had so the best thing he could do would be to flog the place on and get the hell out of Rennes.

'He had the same problem that Marie had, only worse now. The house was in an even more dilapidated condition than it had been when he'd first arrived. There was no way anybody would consider buying it in the state it was in. Oh look, a treasure story on the doorstep. That should do something for the value of the property. Good old Corbu opened a restaurant there and regaled his customers with the story of the priest, his mysterious but now unfortunately lost parchment and his treasure. He managed to get an article about it into a local newspaper, and it was even picked up by national television. That ought to raise a bit of interest, make the house worth a bob or two. Finally it worked. In 1964 along came Henri Buthion who bought the place, as hungry for the treasure as Noel had once been. And that's it for Corbu and his contribution to the story. He came, he saw, he was conned but it was he who created then released into the outside world the fabulous story of Berenger Saunière and his parchment bearing a hidden message.'

I stretched and scratched my stomach thoughtfully. Chris trotted off to fetch us another wine vat. Unless I was very much mistaken, my gibberish was sounding as though it was making sense. Well, it did to me.

Chris came back and refilled our glasses.

'How's it sounding so far?' I asked him.

'Not bad. Come on, I want to hear more of your theory,' he told me. 'Keep on chundering, Hewgs. I'm not letting you off the hook that easily.'

'All right then. Don't say you didn't ask for it. This is where things start to get interesting. So, story the next part. Pierre Plantard and his partner in crime de Chérisey and their creation of the parchments and the Priory of Sion. These two were a couple of high-class con merchants who maybe dined at Corbu's restaurant, maybe saw the newspaper article or the television programme. However they found out about the story doesn't matter but it sure as hell made them jump for joy. These two had a serious scam in the construction stage, and this was just the sort of thing they were on the lookout for.

'The woman who was claiming to be Anastasia was taking legal action to try to prove who she was, so she could inherit the Romanov pile, and she wasn't being laughed out of court. Plantard and de Chérisey had worked out there must be lashings of loads of francs hanging around in limbo in banks around the world that would belong to various descendants of the French aristocracy if they could prove their pedigree. All these two have got to do is create a family tree that proves one of them is a legitimate claimant and they'll split the proceeds. If it was good enough for a questionable Anastasia to have a go why shouldn't they have a bash at it as well?

'They'd been beavering away for years, creating their little genealogy and now there's this story come to light. They couldn't believe their luck. Now they knew about the parchment and its hidden message this gave them a cracker of an idea. If they could create their spurious pedigree based on a lost parchment found in an ancient church, weave King Dagobert, who is France's version of King Arthur, and a treasure into it, tie themselves into that, well that could really let them hit the jackpot. Big time.

'They had already worked out that they needed shadowy historical figures and curious, unexplained events woven into their story to cover any of the holes in it that they couldn't legitimately tie together, and they had already gathered plenty of them. What better than creating a secret society and have that working away behind the scenes, manipulating events over the centuries? Secret societies aren't in the habit of leaving the minutes of their last meeting lying around for any old Tom, Dick or Harry to pick up. Wouldn't exactly be too secret a society then, would it? So they cobbled together their version of a parchment with a hidden message in it, linked it to the Priory of Sion by inference then added a few odd squiggles, swirls and curlicues to give that extra authentic air of mystery to the whole thing. Having managed to create a parchment with a glaringly obvious "secret message" they then went on to create a second parchment. That too would have a "secret message" but this time hidden by using the most ball-breakingly, fiendishly complex code. And that's why Plantard and de Chérisey created what has since become the cornerstone of the whole "mystery".

'The secret society and the forged documents are both safely gathered together so now Plantard and de Chérisey are ready to set phase two of the operation into action. They knew that this was something they wouldn't get two tries at. It had to be right first public outing or they'd be scuppered. They needed bits and pieces of the story out in the public domain already, to give them some semblance of credibility. Using the same tried and tested method as Corbu they decided they too would get something published about Rennes and its gold. They went one better than Corbu though: they weren't interested in an article in a little local newspaper, they wanted a much bigger audience. They found themselves a hack called de Sède and through careful filtering of what they wanted public knowledge, they supplied him with enough information for the first book on the subject to be written, but cleverly they made no mention of any hidden codes and their decipherment. They especially made no comment about anything to do with Dagobert and treasure. Then they sat back and waited to see what'd happen next.'

'Which was?' Chris asked, taking a glug from his wine glass.

'Which was along came my Old Man,' I replied, taking a sip of my wine. 'The fact that he wrote television fiction for a living and wanted to make a film about the Rennes story must have seemed like manna from heaven to the conspirators.' Chris sprayed his wine all over the place as he burst out laughing.

'So there we are, it's 1969 and the Soskin family's on holiday in France with French chums of the Pee and Emm and their offspring, staying on a goat farm in the Gard region. This is where those of a certain disposition, who like to read meanings into things, may like to take note. The name of the farm we were staying on was, tun-tun-tah,' I fanfared dramatically, 'Le Tomple, the temple. Spooky eh? Anyway, we were out being grockles one day when the Old Man picked up a copy of de Sède's book, expecting a jolly good yarn that wouldn't tax his then not-too-good French. Just as Plantard and de Chérisey had hoped, he spotted the raised letters in the parchment. He scanned the illustration in de Sède's book, picking out the letters one by one, the letters the author of this book had failed to see. Can you imagine how he must've felt? Destiny was lying in his hands in the shape of a rather cheap paperback book he bought as a holiday read. See, that's what the message needed to do, hook you straight away. No time to even think about it. Right between the eyes. Thank you very much. Gotcha. That's why the message wasn't published: a member of the public had to find it and to start investigating the story for themselves. That's what gets Plantard and de Chérisey's ball rolling.

'Unfortunately for our chums, this is where the FUF stuck his nose into their carefully laid plans because it was a writer of *Dr Who* that found the message, not a writer of *Dr Qui*. If a Frenchman had cracked the code it would have been a totally different story. A Frenchman would have run with the Dagobert clue, as Plantard and de Chérisey wanted, but Dagobert isn't of any particular interest to an Englishman. It'd be like a Frenchman discovering King Alfred's cake recipe: he'd think of it as nothing more than an historical curiosity, shrug his shoulders and say "*bof*". It's because the Knights Templar were hinted at and they are of interest to an Englishman that the emphasis of the story moves away from France and over to the Holy Land and that's what starts to steer the story away from Plantard and de Chérisey's aims and towards the global stage and lunacy.'

'You are a rotten sod at times,' Jan informed me, with good-humoured prescience.

'Thank you, dear.' I raised my glass to her, acknowledging her perspicacity.

'You're welcome,' she grinned, chinking her glass against mine.

'Look, it's getting late. Let me get on or we'll be here all night. OK, we're now early seventies, everybody's into the hippy-dippy new age stuff, the Age of Aquarius and all that rubbish so, intimating that there may be proof that there was a Templar treasure waiting to be discovered, that Jesus may really have lived, were just the sort of things people wanted to hear then and if the Old Man was the man to prove that…?' I let the question mark hang. 'Because he believed what he was reading it became a reality, his television programme and the resulting attention it attracted proved he was right.

'Now, don't forget that these films were shown on the BBC and back then the Beeb was taken very seriously indeed.

Even better is that they were shown on BBC2 and that was mega-serious, there could be no doubting the veracity of the programme's content. If there had been any doubts the Beeb just wouldn't have made it. People were writing to the Old Man with their ideas and offers of help. The more Plantard and de Chérisey fed him, the more he was taken in. They could have mentioned Kublai Khan, Chiang Kai-Shek or Stig of the Dump and he'd have rushed off researching away, he was completely taken in by it all. It was like a bloody great historical tombola stand; the Old Man would stick his hand in, see what he pulled out and then try to weave it into the story. However tenuous the link, it was enough to send him off down new avenues of historical detective work. This story was going to mean the total rewriting of European history. This was going to mean major, major fame. The trouble is the Old Man's existence quite literally depended on the story's existence. He had killed off Henry Soskin and recreated himself in the form of Henry Lincoln and it was Henry Lincoln who had given the world Rennes-le-Château. Without Rennes-le-Château, Henry Lincoln wouldn't exist. There was no way he would or could have even considered the teeniest of possibilities that maybe it was a con. Absolutely impossible, which is why in *The Holy Place* he actually writes that it doesn't matter if the clues are genuine or fake. Well, I may be wrong but I would have thought that that would be a pretty good indicator of whether there's likely to be any truth in any of the whole of the story. If they're genuine then all well and good but if they're fakes then doesn't that rather beg the question of who dunnit and why?' I shrugged my shoulders and left it to Chris and Jan to work that one out.

'Now it's the start of the electronics revolution. Videos are about so you can watch what you want, when you want, as often as you want, but when the Internet in all its glory came along, well that's when the whole thing really kicked off and started to go ballistically mega-crazy. It doesn't matter how off the wall an idea is, there's somebody out there who'll agree with it or vociferously disagree with it. This is how the Rennes story has evolved into the industry it is nowadays. Not through any history mystery but through the individual requirements of each of the participants in the story and the power of television and the Internet.'

I counted out the list on my fingers. 'Marie wanted to keep her roof over her head. Corbu lusted after the treasure he'd been promised. Plantard and de Chérisey were chasing wealth and title. My father wants to be remembered as the man that showed how history was wrong and needed rewriting, and as for the world, well they never change, people will always need something, anything, to believe in.

'The area is quite happy to play along and to keep on taking the tourist dollar, yen or euro, so they aren't going to rattle any cages. It's gonna stay being a holiday visiting spot for some time yet. All self-perpetuating.'

I rubbed my eyes. It was two o'clock already. How had that happened? Chris sat back in his chair, quietly mulling over what I'd said.

'That still doesn't explain the churches round here all being in straight lines and all the same distance apart,' he said.

'Stop it!' I wailed. 'You're still at it. You're still looking at it wrong. Think about how villages came into being.'

His eyebrows shot up as he tried to follow this next sideways jump in my thought process.

'No, don't look at me like that, it'll make sense. Each Stone Age settlement had enough land and food to supply so many people. Once that number had been reached the overflow had to depart to pastures new, to find themselves a new gaff. They wouldn't have wanted to walk for more than say, I dunno, half a day. They had to be far enough apart that both communities had sufficient room to grow food and hunt so they could survive yet close enough that they could band together in times of danger.

'As these settlements became permanent they started to build places of worship. Now villages grow and change shape but the church, maybe rebuilt a few times, will be left, more or less, where it's always been, so of course they're more or less the same distance apart. It was based on the "half day's march" measure and the topography of the Aude region pretty well dictates where you can build and how far your settlements can spread. The population level and village size round here really won't have changed that much at all over the millennia, it still looks pretty much how it will always have looked. As to making complex geometric patterns, well, d'you remember those toys we had when we were kids, the thing with cogged wheels and discs that had holes in them for sticking different coloured biros through and drawing pretty patterns? I think they were called Spirographs. Well that's exactly what this is. The topography of the region around Rennes gives you the perimeter of the area to play in and the churches work as the pen-holes in the inner disc. Put your pencil on a church, join it to any of the others within the framework and hey presto, a pretty pattern appears, or as the Rennies like to look at it, "sacred geometry". Wonder of wonders, as if corroboration of this miracle were needed, it is found that Bornholm has this "sacred geometry" too. And what do Bornholm and the Rennes area have in common?' I asked them.

Chris shrugged, shaking his head in reply.

'They're both islands,' I answered myself. 'One literally. Bornholm is an island off the Danish coast and the Rennes region is an island of foothills surrounded by mountains on one side and flatter, more forgiving terrain on the other. On Bornholm, you can't extend your boundaries because of the sea. Around Rennes you can't extend your boundaries because you either have unusable mountains to contend with or flat, workable, useable land in front of you and where there is an abundance of such open land then the option of where to settle and how far your settlement can spread is almost limitless. That's why the "sacred geometry" peters out as you move away from the foothills. Everything is too widely spaced to be able to make pretty patterns any more. Villages became towns, so now instead of lots of little churches scattered about there were fewer but bigger churches built instead, positioned more by the ease at which they could be defended than by nature's dictation.

'People want to believe in something, that's the long and the short of it. This story was right mix, right place, right time. Even if it could be proven beyond all reasonable doubt to be complete and utter hokum there'd still be people who'd believe it.'

Chris sat there quietly for a couple of minutes digesting what I'd been saying.

'OK,' he asked uncertainly, 'what about the parchments then? What about all the stuff in them. Surely...?'

I sighed heavily, interrupting him again.

'Stop looking for mysteries. The bloody parchments then. The parchments that nobody has ever seen. All religions, tin pot or mainstream, demand a leap of faith and the parchments are Rennes' leap of faith. Without the parchments the story couldn't exist, therefore they have to exist.

'And exist they do, making their debut in de Sède's book, just a couple of line drawings, not even photos. Doing it that way, Plantard and de Chérisey didn't have to go to the time, bother and expense of actually faking any parchments so there's no way of gleaning any information about their age, no way of checking anything about them, the perfect "fakes". Then their secret messages are of different difficulty because of their requirements. The first one was a very subtle piece of hoodwinkery. It had to be simple 'cos the message had to be easily seen, which it was. The sprat to catch the mackerel. Parchment two, however, was a totally different kettle of chicanery. This one had to be a real humdinger. Plantard and de Chérisey weren't trying to flog a pile of old bricks remember, they were after title. This one had to be a real work of art. I mean, that parchment two is so humongously complicated that you could never really be sure that the person you're trying to get your message to had managed to decipher it correctly. There are just far too many parts to it. Using this code would have given even poor old Einstein a bad hair day trying to work it all out. First find a key word, then juggle its letters about, then move a letter here, move another one there, move that one over there to where the first letter had been, then go round a chessboard with the knight. Oy vey, you got a migraine before you even started. So, far, far too complicated to use for real but just the sort of thing that would give credence to what our lads were thinking about. It's the complexity of the code that convinces you that the information hidden by it must be seriously important. The only way the code was 'cracked' was because the Old Man was given the solution by the people that had created it.

'As for any other added details on the parchments, well, it's just that, added colour to give more interest. It's hardly Plantard and de Chérisey's fault that people chose to read strange things into them. They didn't create the connections, they merely created some pointers, signs and clues to try to send people in a particular direction. It was the over-active imaginations of the Rennes researchers that created the historical links they now all take to be gospel, and that's what's taken them to all the new, unintended areas of investigation. I doubt Plantard and de Chérisey would've thought in their wildest dreams that it would turn out the way it did. It's almost as if they were too successful at it and it became too big to be of any use to them any more. Sort of shot themselves in the feet. All that hard work for sweet FA. The story had taken on a life of its own. All eyes were certainly on the parchments but, as far as Plantard and de Chérisey were concerned, for none of the right reasons. Remember,' I waggled my eyebrows, mimed rolling a cigar between my fingers and put on my best Groucho Marx voice, 'a scam can only work because somebody wants to believe in it. Unfortunately nobody wanted to believe in their intended version of the scam, it just wasn't big enough or magical enough any more.

'By the middle of the Eighties there were millions of people who wanted to "believe", who'd laugh or think you were insulting their intelligence if you asked them if they believed in Father Christmas or the Tooth Fairy but were perfectly happy to believe in God and that a secret society has been guarding the descendants of the son of God for the last thousand years or so and that that secret society is still going strong, performing that self-same task today though I do wonder who was guarding God's family for the thousand years before the Priory of Sion came along. Not to mention,' I added, 'two thousand years makes for something like one hundred generations and that makes for one very, very diluted bloodline, and that's ignoring the generations that didn't breed for whatever reason or were wiped out by plague, pestilence or war. Born of a virgin, walked on water, rose from the dead and his great-great-great-God–knows-how-many-times-great-grandson is hanging around, waiting to be revealed in all his esoteric glory. Yup, sounds pretty convincing to me.'

Chris sat there for a minute considering what I'd come up with so far.

'Well what about the Poussin tomb then?' he persisted.

'I do wish you hadn't read anything about this,' I groaned. 'I did see it in all its glory before that idiot farmer smashed it to smithereens' I told him, 'and it certainly looked pretty convincing to me. The experts said Poussin had never been to this part of France but how can they categorically and definitively know all of the places he visited or passed through? I mean, can either of you remember all the places you've ever been to? There don't seem to be any records of the tomb's existence before the early twentieth century when apparently an American bought the land and had a couple of his female relatives buried there. Maybe it was this American that had the tomb built because it's in such a tranquil setting. It would be wonderful if it had been there all those years and Poussin really did paint it 'cos it's always nice to see an expert get egg on his face, but then again I rather hope he didn't because of what mad Rennies drove that farmer to do. I think this is just a wonderful, serendipitous bit of happenstance that was far, far too good an opportunity for Plantard and De Chérisey to let slip through their fingers. Yet another piece of meaningless, totally unrelated gibberish that this region with its turbulent history keeps dropping so kindly into their laps, that looks good to lob into the melting pot to add to the confusion. I s'pect they had a bottle of bubbly to celebrate it too,' I laughed.

'It is pretty important to the legend, though,' I continued, ''cos it's about the only thing in the whole story apart from the churches that people can touch and see. Even if the tomb itself isn't there any more, the site is still there for comparisons. It's this wonderful bit of serendipity that really helps push the story that little bit further, that and something else the Old Man goes on about, a letter that Poussin was supposed to have sent to a mate of his saying that he'd met someone that had a secret that "kings would have pains to drag from him". As far as the Old Man is concerned this proves Poussin was involved in some sort of conspiracy. Well why couldn't the expression have just been a colloquialism of the day, rather like our "wild horses wouldn't drag it from him"? It doesn't prove anything. Maybe he was just talking about somebody having an affair with somebody else's wife? It's one of the great syllogisms of Rennes. If it's true that Poussin painted the tomb from life and we "know", because of that letter, that it's true he was involved in some sort of conspiracy, then it follows the entire Rennes-Saunière thing has to be true. Why couldn't Poussin have just been trotting down the road on his horse one sunny morning, seen the tomb and thought "that's a pretty tomb, I think I'll paint it"? Then again, who's to say it's not the other way round and that when the American gent bought the land he thought "hey, if I have a tomb built on that lump of ground there it'll look just like it's from that Poussin painting"?'

'I s'pect you're right,' Chris yawned and rubbed his face. 'Hmmm,' he pondered quietly for a moment. I could feel another question coming.

'You see,' I continued before he got a chance to speak again, 'with each generation worldview changes, people get greedier, things become bigger and better, we demand more and more from life and so the story has evolved alongside, growing grander and grander in concept. Think what the world was like for each of our players. Think of the expectations of each generation and look how the requirements of the story have grown with that expectation. The dramatis personae: Saunière, Marie, Corbu, Plantard and de Chérisey and Lincoln. The first is unimportant, the second wants a house, the third a treasure, the fourth a title and the last wants historical immortality.

'These are entirely separate pieces of flimflammery. The Rennes legend and confusion has grown through the Rennies trying to tie these totally separate stories together into the one that they want it to be. So there, my friends, that is why there is not, nor has there ever been, any treasure of Rennes-le-Château.' I thumped the table decisively with my fist. My argument was concluded. My case was rested.

'I still think there's too many coincidences there,' Chris said cautiously.

'What bloody coincidences?' My voice rose an octave or two in amazed indignation. 'The only things needed to happen were somebody reading a newspaper article and somebody else reading a book. They're the only coincidences, hardly the sort of thing that'd get Arthur Koestler spinning in his grave in excitement. All the rest is pure fabrication, the result of the over-active and fevered imaginations of the followers of Rennes which is why you are forever hearing Rennies wailing that the story only raises more questions, it never gives any answers. The trouble is everybody starts working from the assumption that de Sède's book is to be believed but if it isn't, because of its different motives and gameplan, then trying to plait fact into its fiction, to achieve your own end, is only going to raise more questions.

'I sure as hell ain't saying that all the research has been a waste of time and effort. There has to have been some worthwhile stuff to have come out of the hours of work all the Rennies have put in over the years and I most certainly have met some incredible and amazing peeps as a result of it, plus made a couple of seriously good friends, too. After all,' I pointed out, 'we'd have never met had it not been for Rennes.

'I'm not knocking anybody's religion or belief. Everybody's entitled to their own thing and the Rennes industry gives a lot of people employment, belief and happiness so who has any right to knock it? The whole Rennes story is a wonderful ripping yarn which has the grip it does because of the power and spread of the Internet. Rennes is the ultimate *deus ex machina*.

'Look on the Rennies as twenty-first-century heretics that, if they'd been around a few hundred years ago, would have been burnt at the stake for their non-conformist ideas. I've just had a thought.' I laughed. 'Perhaps I should write the Old Man's biography? I could call it *My Father the Heretic*.'

'A catchy title,' Chris agreed, as Jan laughed at the idea.

'I'm glad you like it,' I grinned at him. 'I'll start writing it tomorrow. Now can we please talk about something else?'

'Yeah, OK my little iconoclast, I think you've got me convinced. I'll let you off your bill.'

'Thank you,' I bowed to Chris in acknowledgement of his largesse. 'Right, I'm going for a pee,' I told him. 'Pour me a drink and I'll be back in two shakes.' I stood up to go to the loo. Pushing my chair back, I hadn't quite unravelled my leg from around the chair so ended up a flailing windmill of arms and legs yet again as I tripped over my own feet. My glasses flew off into the shrubbery and I fell, grazing my elbows on the gravel. Jan and Chris laughed; I lay there and moaned. Jan reached down and patted me comfortingly on the head.

'Never mind, dear,' she giggled. 'Don't worry about it. It was just your little chum the FUF reminding you not to rock any boats.'

The following morning, after a last wander around the place, a last goodbye to the llamas and then tearfully hugging and kissing Chantal and especially Chris goodbye, we clambered aboard the bus to set off to look for our piece of land in Spain.

We climbed the mountain for the last time, stopping at the final bend in the road that gave us our farewell glimpse of Moolong, empty now of almost all the tents and vans that had littered the place throughout the summer. A last mournful honk on our horn, a last wave at the two of them still standing in front of Moolong, watching us, they raised their arms in farewell. We drove on in silence, eyes stinging from the tears trying to flow, each of us lost in our own thoughts, none of which included Rennes-le-Château. We were going to miss Moolong and Chris and the llamas, the chums we had made along the way, and our countryside wanderings. It would have been so easy to stay but we knew if we didn't get going we would in all probability have stayed until we were finally evicted or died.

We hit the pass through the Col de Saint-Louis, the road spiralling, corkscrewing round on itself. Stirling Soskin put the bus into neutral to freewheel down this most serious of downhill combi racing tracks, my attention fully focused on the enormity of the task ahead when – 'You remember that first meal we had at Moolong?' Jan interrupted. 'Did you ever pay Chris for it?'

A Chateau Of One's Own

Restoration Misadventures In France

SAM JUNEAU

A Chateau of One's Own

Restoration Misadventures in France
Sam Juneau
£7.99

978-1-84024-553-0

Sam and Bud were ordinary first-time homebuyers in their early thirties. Their intention in moving to France was to create a simple life and spend more time with their children. The home they actually bought was an impressive seventeenth-century chateau in the Loire valley with over thirty rooms, 156 windows and 40 acres of land.

With only modest savings, the couple launched the challenging project of restoring this crumbling monster of a building to its former glory and opening a bed and breakfast in the process. This is the hilarious story of behind the scenes at a B&B that required constant disaster relief: think *Fawlty Towers* in an extraordinary setting.

A Chateau of One's Own will appeal to those like Sam and Bud who want to escape from the rat race, who work hard and have hardly enough time to play. It's the perfect read for anyone considering a grandiose home makeover project and for all of us who dream of a life in France.

Sam Juneau was born in New Orleans and is a television producer and writer in the UK and the US. He and his wife live in France with their children and 22 cats.

'Hilarious... Engaging tale... A refreshing warts-and-all account of what follows that impulsive buy'   SCOTTISH SUNDAY EXPRESS

'Their story will appeal to those who... want to escape from the rat race... It's the perfect read for anyone considering a grandiose home makeover project and for all of us who dream in a life in France'   BRITMAG

Richard Wiles
Bon Courage!

A French renovation in rural Limousin

Bon Courage!

A French Renovation in Rural Limousin
Richard Wiles
£7.99

978-1-84024-360-4

A dilapidated, rat-infested stone barn set amidst thirteen acres of unkempt pasture and overgrown woodland might not be many people's vision of a potential dream home. But for Englishman Richard and his wife Al, the cavernous, oak-beamed building in a sleepy hamlet in the Limousin region of France is perfect.

Tussles with French bureaucracy allied with fierce storms that wreak havoc on the property do little to dampen their resolve as they immerse themselves in the *calme* of this quiet corner of France, dreaming of taking trips in Richard's hot-air balloon and starting their very own llama farm. The couple's colourful, often eccentric neighbours watch their progress with curiosity: the jovial ex-gendarme and his wife, who seems able to foretell the weather; the lonely widow who offers copious amounts of *gâteau* in exchange for convivial chat; and the brawny cattleman with suspicious motives for cleaning up the couple's land.

Told by a well-intentioned if often hapless do-it-yourselfer, Richard's hilarious and heartwarming tale of a new life in France resounds to the Gallic refrain, '*Bon courage!*'

'This book will trigger dreams...'   COUNTRY HOUSE AND HOME

www.summersdale.com